A Man's Mischief

Trevor Sharp

Colophon

Editor: Tiffany Avery
Author: Trevor Sharp
Publishing Company: Mischief Publishing
Book Design: Arina van Londen

Copyright © 2024 by Trevor Sharp
All rights reserved.

No part of this book may be reproduced, distributed, or transmitted on any form or by any means, including photocopying, recording, or other electronic or mechanical methods, without the prior written permission of the author, except in the case of brief quotations embodied in critical reviews and certain other noncommercial uses permitted by copyright law.

ISBN Paperback: 979-8-9912752-2-4

Fonts

Hitch Hike, Roboto Black, Apple Chancery and Times New Roman

Email
trevorsharp4u@gmail.com

trevorsharp4u2

Trevor Sharp

Acknowledgments

A special thanks to Colleen Finn whose extensive knowledge and critique inspired me to develop this memoir into a work of art.

Table of Contents

A Man's Mischief

Introduction	6
Foreword	10
Chapter 1: Don't Call Home	11
Chapter 2: Honesty in Relationships	35
Chapter 3: Brothers and Sisters	42
Chapter 4: Kristy and Katy	56
Chapter 5: Stranded	59
Chapter 6: Porsche vs. Motorcycle	68
Chapter 7: Dinner Conversation—Lena	76
Chapter 8: One Good Roundhouse	78
Chapter 9: Birds and Panties	89
Chapter 10: Disappointment	102
Chapter 11: Girlfriends and Jealousy	106
Chapter 12: A Conflict Between the Heart and Mind	116
Chapter 13: Bikers and Body Shots	141
Chapter 14: A Hot Mess	151
Chapter 15: Did You Meet the Representative?	158
Chapter 16: Rationalizing the Irrational	173
Chapter 17: Dinner Conversation—Amy	190
Chapter 18: The Psychology of it All	192
Chapter 19: The Hideout	207
Conclusion	222

Introduction

One of Trevor's earliest childhood memories was when he was five years old, and his brother Greg was seven. As they were walking, Greg and his friend Don, who were walking side by side, were leading the way. Trevor and Don's sister, Kay, were following behind. Don and Greg were the same age and two years older than Trevor and Kay, who were also the same age. Greg kicked a rock and sent it bouncing down the road. It came to a stop a few paces ahead and directly in line with Don's line of travel. Everyone in the group knew that when Don got to the rock, he would again send it bouncing down the road.

Trevor looked at Greg and Don walking in front, then glanced at Kay walking beside him. Trevor felt fortunate that Kay was his best friend and buddy. He thought his brother had been cheated, since he was stuck with Don.

Don, Kay, Trevor, and Greg all lived in the same neighborhood. Kay had blue eyes and long blonde hair that wasn't usually well-kept. She had a face with delicate features similar to that of a porcelain doll. When she was younger, she couldn't say Trevor's name correctly, so she called him Key. She would walk to Trevor's house, knock on the door, and ask if Key could come out and play. So, it was Kay and Key going out to play. Sometimes, Trevor would go to Kay's house and ask if she could come out to play. Kay's mother would always be sitting in front of the television, watching soap operas. Trevor was amazed that anyone could be as unproductive as Kay's mother. It was quite a contrast to Trevor's family. His father was either working on a deal or closing one. His family rarely watched television and if they did, it was a family affair.

Kay and Trevor spent a lot of time together building forts, playing with sticks, and participating in childhood games. They were as close as two neighborhood kids could be. Trevor couldn't remember the two of them having discord; if they did, it had faded from memory.

One day Kay and Trevor were playing when Kay wet her pants and had to go home to change. As she was walking away, Trevor noticed her pants were only wet in back and not in front. He knew little girls had a different anatomy, but he couldn't figure out how her pants could be wet in back and not in front. He was curious about the differences between the anatomy of a girl and that of a boy. He knew he shouldn't bring up the subject and surmised that Kay must be curious about his anatomy also. Even at five years old, Trevor knew better than to ask Kay to show him hers. It wouldn't go over well, so he didn't broach the subject. Somehow, he knew, if she was the one to instigate the disclosure, things would go much better.

Another day the two buddies were playing inside the fort they had built when Kay's curiosity got the best of her. She asked Trevor what his private parts looked like.

Trevor said, "I will show you, if you show me." As they sat on the ground inside their fort, each of them pulled their pants down and showed the other what they looked like underneath. There wasn't any touching. It was just two little kids satisfying their curiosity.

Kay said, "Mine looks better than yours."

Trevor agreed. They both pulled up their pants and that was the last time either of them mentioned their anatomy. They found out what each other looked like and that was behind them. Neither of them would intentionally do anything to hurt the other. They were unconditionally the best of friends.

Even at this age, Trevor realized that girls and boys were not just different physically, but they were different emotionally. He couldn't help but wonder about the various differences between boys and girls.

When Trevor was seven, his family moved away, and he had to say goodbye to his childhood buddy. Although he knew he would miss Kay, he thought it was best they didn't grow up together. He knew if she became attached to someone else it would break his heart.

Trevor and his brother Greg were very close and did almost everything together. For the most part, they had a wholesome upbringing. If their parents argued or had discord, it wasn't in front of them. The children were taught to be well spoken and mannerly. Adults often commented that the two brothers went from diapers to manhood. In this regard they were unusual. They were little men.

From the time of Trevor's earliest recollection, adults consistently tried to give Trevor and his brother gifts. Their father, Howard, trained them well. As a rule of thumb, if someone offered to give them something, they were not to accept it. If they were offered a second time, they were still not to accept. It was only upon the third insistence that they were allowed to accept a gift.

As early as Trevor could remember, his father would use him and his brother as a sounding board when trying to solve a business problem or come up with an idea. Howard often took his sons with him when he was doing business and by doing so, it set the stage for him to be perceived as an honest, trustworthy man. A father with two good looking, well-mannered little men.

Howard was an unusually brilliant man. He only had a sixth-grade education but could do math in his head faster than the average person could reach for a calculator. Everyone who knew him realized he had a way with people and consequently, he had a constant flow of visitors. Another unusual thing about Trevor's father was that he didn't like to be alone. He kept Trevor at his side so much that Trevor became annoyed at being his father's shadow.

Howard would often meet people he hadn't seen for a long time and wouldn't remember their names. Proper etiquette dictates that during an introduction, the older or more important person is introduced first. For example, if Howard was introducing someone to his son, he would say the older person's name first and his son's name last. This was how introductions occurred when Howard remembered the name of the person being introduced. During introductions, Trevor would pay attention to who was introduced first. If the introduction was started by his father using the other person's name first, he knew his father remembered the other person's name. If he introduced Trevor first, he knew his father didn't remember the other person's name. This was Trevor's cue to immediately ask the other person what his or her name was. This saved Howard the embarrassment of not remembering someone's name.

Howard's sons became very useful to him and in return his sons received an education in business at a very young age.

In many ways, Howard was not the norm. He didn't fit a pattern. His method of raising children was to work them so hard, they wouldn't have time to get into trouble. From this, Trevor developed an extremely strong work ethic. In Howard's way of thinking, parents had children to serve the family, a huge contrast from today's parents who serve their children.

Howard also didn't brainwash his sons with religion. He let them figure it out for themselves. He must have had the same views towards offering advice about women. Trevor had to figure it out for himself.

This adventure begins when Trevor and his second wife, Lea, had been separated for long periods of time, only to come back together to try to salvage the relationship. Trevor's work ethic had paid off and he and his wife decided to do what they wanted to do instead of what they had to do. This was fine, except for the fact that they didn't want to do the same things or do them together. Menopause had arrived several years earlier for Lea, and life together had become a challenge.

The couple attended relationship counseling, which seemed to bring up more questions than answers. Do counselors really have the answers? Are men and women really different? Is there such a thing as love, or is it nature's illusion, designed to propagate the species? Do men cheat more than women? Are all women the same? Are humans a monogamous species? What is the difference between the average person and those who achieve extraordinary accomplishments?

Trevor, seeking to answer these questions, set out on an epic adventure to satisfy his curiosity while riding motorcycle, playing golf, and carousing.

Foreword

All of the events in this account are true, although the names have been changed to protect the guilty. The places mentioned actually exist, however the names may or may not have been changed. Although some of the events may be out of sequence, the conversations are as near verbatim as possible. Even though the author came to certain conclusions, the fact that these accounts are true allows each reader to form their personal, unique, individual, conclusions based on their experiences and perceptions.

Chapter 1

Don't Call Home

British Columbia is a very large province. In comparison, it is larger than the states of Washington, Oregon, and California combined. It is also a beautiful province, mostly covered by pine trees, mountains, and lakes. Beautiful glaciers and large rivers are also part of the scenery. At certain times of the year, the wildflowers have a fragrance that would make someone very wealthy if they could capture and sell it.

The ride through British Columbia was a group adventure consisting of four riders. Each rider owned their own business and looked forward to the feeling of the open road and the adventure of a motorcycle ride. Jim was a hippy when he was younger, so now that he is successful, he is a yuppie and rides a BMW. Mike is a successful businessman and also rides a BMW. Actually, both have BMW motorcycles and BMW automobiles. They had recently attended an advanced motorcycle riding course, where they met Jeff. Jeff fit right in since he had just purchased a new BMW motorcycle. This was Jeff's first ride with the group.

The BMW motorcycles were each different models and Jeff's new bike was an adventure type BMW. GPS on motorcycles was just being implemented at this time, and Jeff was the only rider with GPS. Trevor was riding a Japanese made cruiser that looked similar to a Harley Davidson. So, he looked more like a bad guy.

This adventure began on a nice sunny day, four men on the open road headed through BC, Canada. The plan was for everyone to meet for breakfast in a designated town south of the Canadian border. What more could a person want than a motorcycle ride through BC with your buddies?

Each rider came from a different area. The BMW riders had to ride sixty to eighty miles to get to the rendezvous. Trevor was a different story. His ride was about 300 miles. Oddly enough, no one arrived at the designated time of arrival, but all four riders pulled into the parking lot at precisely the same time. This is kind of an unusual phenomenon that had occurred many times throughout Trevor's riding history. Riders leave from different places and distances with an approximate meeting time and end up exactly in synch upon arrival.

Breakfast was great—four men enjoying a meal, laughs, more laughs, teasing, and motorcycle talk. Jim, Trevor, and Mike had not seen each other for several months, so it was a meeting of camaraderie and a special kind of friendship that only people who ride together can share. The gist of the conversation went something like this: since Trevor is the only one who isn't riding a Beemer and he has loud pipes, he will surely get searched at the border.

After a short ride through the lush summer terrain on a nice two-lane road, the four men arrived at the Canadian border. Jeff, the new member of the group, was in the lead. Trevor was second, and Jim and Mike followed up in the rear. There was a long line of cars when they pulled into the border crossing, so they knew they were in for a wait.

After sitting for a while, Trevor noticed Jeff pull out a small syringe and inject himself in the leg. Trevor was going to keep this in the back of his head so if something happened, the group would know how to deal with his condition, whatever it may be. The riders needed to look out for each other. Something like a diabetic reaction while riding a motorcycle could be a real problem.

Well, Jeff made it across the border, no muss no fuss. Trevor's crossing wasn't a problem, nor a question. Now it was Jim's turn. He pulled up and the border patrol asked him a few questions, one of which was "Have you ever been in handcuffs?" He figured it was better not to lie, so he said he had. The next thing he knew, the border patrol was looking up his records. While this was taking place, Mike got across the border with no fuss. The other three men, Jeff, Trevor, and Mike, were now on the Canadian side of the border. They watched as border patrol took Jim's bike into the inspection area. They unloaded and searched his luggage, took the seat off, and did the most thorough search Trevor had ever seen. They searched the cracks, crevices, and cavities of the motorcycle, all of which took a couple of hours.

In the meantime, the other three riders went on to the restaurant to wait for him. The search turned up that Jim had been arrested for marijuana possession when he was seventeen years old. He was now fifty-nine and the oldest rider in the group by ten years or more. He looked the part of a typical yuppie with a nice head of black hair trimmed with a $200 haircut. Three hours after entering the border crossing, they were back on the road. The joke was on Jim. Trevor had easily made it across the border with his cruiser, loud pipes, and bad boy looking motorcycle.

That afternoon, the adventurers pulled into Penticton. It was a pretty little town at this time of year with nice hotels and restaurants lined up along the lake. Although they hadn't done their usual distance of travel that day, it would be difficult to find a nicer place to settle for the night. Everyone except Mike liked eating when hungry, getting a place to stay when tired, and being at the next town when you get there. Mike liked a schedule and wanted to know where he was going to be and when. Even Mike liked the idea of staying in Penticton. They were able to find a nice hotel with a large suite, two queen beds, and two roll-away beds. The room was also furnished with a couch and a couple of comfortable chairs.

Soon, everyone had their bikes unloaded and were deciding where to go for a bite to eat. During the conversation, Trevor asked Jeff about injecting himself prior to crossing the Canadian border.

Jeff replied that he indeed had diabetes and was only expected to live a couple more years. This probably had some bearing on him buying a new motorcycle and going on a motorcycle adventure.

No one was very familiar with the town, so they walked along the lake until they found a suitable restaurant. A pretty waitress about college age attended their table and took their order for drinks. She seemed like a shy, reserved type of person who was just out of mom and dad's house trying to make a few dollars. She looked like the kind of girl who may be a little insecure and not very worldly.

She appeared to be the type of young lady who could have her self-esteem easily crushed by the crude comments of men.

While she was retrieving drinks, one of the riders made a comment that she was pretty.

Jeff replied, "I wonder what her panties look like."

She had on a nice sundress without panty lines.

Someone else said, "Maybe she doesn't have any."

Jeff took it from there. He was going to find out about her panties. He said he would ask her about them when she returned with drinks. Even before he had drinks, he was exhibiting bad behavior. He started making comments about her until the guys told him he was going to be in a boat load of trouble if he gave her a difficult time. He soon realized he was going to be very unpopular if he pursued his inquisition about her underwear.

When she came back, Trevor was closely scrutinizing him and was ready to jump into the conversation should he be less than a gentleman. Dinner went fine from then on.

Since they had time to spare, they decided to go out to play pool. Jim was a good pool player and Trevor was good when he was on. Mike began learning about pool when he started riding with Jim and Trevor. It would be the first time any of them had played pool with Jeff.

They played a few games and all was going well until Jeff started to get surly. He made a comment here and there and finally he said, "I didn't realize I was riding with a bunch of pussies."

From there things didn't get better. That is not a good comment on a bike ride with the guys. Someone asked him why he would say that. He came out with a comment about how they had just traveled a short distance that day and were already staying the night. He definitely had not considered the fact that Trevor had ridden 300 miles just to get to the border.

The guys started wondering if he was having a diabetic reaction. He didn't seem to exhibit the usual characteristics of a diabetic running low on blood sugar. He simply became surlier and more disagreeable as the evening progressed. Usually, if a person has low blood sugar, their speech gets slow and people listening feel like they want to finish their sentences for them. For those of you who are familiar with a cassette player running low on battery power, that is how a person with low blood sugar usually reacts. He had no sign of slow speech, didn't appear as if he had too much to drink, and no one knew what was wrong with him. The only solution they could find was to take him back to the room and see if they could get him to eat. Eating would solve the problem if he had low blood sugar.

Back at the hotel, they discovered that Jeff had MREs (military rations), which stands for meals ready-to-eat. He had all these nice little convenient packages of food ready to eat in case he had a diabetic reaction. By this time, he was acting as if his batteries were starting to run down. He sat down on the couch and the guys helped him open the neat little packages. Trevor was sitting on a chair next to the couch. After Jeff started to eat, he seemed to improve, but his batteries were still weak and his speech was slow.

Trevor had been watching television and noticing the neat little packages of food. Out of curiosity, Trevor began to wonder how the food tasted. Military people must eat these all the time. How do these neat little packages of food taste? He looked over and Jeff, who had a cracker in his hand that looked something like a graham cracker. He asked Jeff if he could try one. Jeff handed him the cracker and Trevor stuck it in his mouth. As he started to chew, he looked over as Jeff was flicking his finger and hand, unsuccessfully trying to dislodge a big, long, slimy booger from his fingers. The same fingers he had just used to hand Trevor the cracker. His motion resembled that of someone trying to do 'around the world' with a yoyo. The yoyo was tenaciously remaining in play as the slimy booger extended and retracted from his fingers.

Morning came early and everyone slept well. Jeff was back in the saddle—his batteries had recharged.

The first thing he said was, "Trevor has a woody."

Trevor was a little groggy and replied, "That happens to me every morning." A few seconds later his brain fired and he asked Jeff why he would notice. Everyone laughed, and another day of fun and camaraderie began.

There is a story about a snake slithering down a hillside. As it was going down the hill, the tail became jealous of the head. The tail was jealous because the head was always in the lead. The tail began arguing with the head. The disagreement continued until the tail adamantly refused to follow. The head was smart enough to realize they would need to move in order to survive. Finally, the head relinquished its position of leadership to the tail. Of course, the tail of the snake didn't have eyes, ears, or a tongue to enable it to lead successfully. As the story goes, the snake traveled for a short distance, slithered off a cliff, then died. Like the snake, some riders make good leaders and others make good followers. In most motorcycle groups, some want to lead, some want to follow, and others don't care. Motorcycle clubs generally have a leader who takes the lead and some sort of hierarchy on down the line as to who follows whom.

Each day, Mike, Jim, Trevor, and Jeff took turns being the leader. They didn't have communication systems, so the lead biker would glance back every so often to make sure all riders were present. Riding in a group takes some organization, otherwise people will stop all the time. Someone needs to stop for gas, a coat change, restroom, or food. One rider may like to go fast, another will be inclined to go slow. Some riders are more suited to lead. However, rotating the position of leadership kept everyone feeling equal.

There is a stretch of road in Canada that consists of towns named 70 Mile House, 93 Mile House, 100 Mile House, and 150 Mile House. Since Canada uses kilometers instead of miles, the riders had no idea why they didn't name the towns in kilometers instead of miles. These towns were named in succession according to the distances between them. Lillooet, BC, was considered the starting point (0).

The group was traveling along this stretch of road with Trevor in the lead, Jim was second, Jeff next, and Mike brought up the rear. It was a beautiful stretch of road with tall pine trees on each side of the road. A few turns every now and then kept the ride interesting. They traveled a good distance that day and just kind of fell into the groove. Each person had their favorite tunes playing through their helmet speakers, and life was good. With the tall trees and the winding of the road, it was difficult to see the last two riders. The person in the lead sometimes depended on the rider behind him to make sure the next rider was still following. After you have ridden for a long distance, it is easy to get into a state of euphoria and forget to look back for a while.

All was going well when Trevor noticed Jim coming up fast behind him. Jim passed Trevor and pulled over to the right-hand side of the road. Jim hadn't noticed the other two riders in his mirror for a while. At this point, they could sit and wait or they could go back and look for the other riders. Since there were two of them, they figured if one had difficulties, the other could help. Maybe someone had to take a nature break.

Trevor and Jim conversed for a while, trying to figure out what was best. Should they go back and find the other guys, or should they wait?

Shortly, they noticed a sign advertising a restaurant ahead. They decided it would be best to go the additional quarter of a mile and wait at the restaurant. Surely Mike and Jeff weren't far behind.

Jim and Trevor pulled into the restaurant, leaving their motorcycles close to the road so the other riders would notice them as they traveled by. They waited for about an hour before Mike and Jeff finally arrived. Of course, Jim and Trevor had been guessing and wondering all this time what could have possibly happened to them. An hour is a long time to be behind.

Mike's explanation went like this: Jeff had taken the end cap off his muffler and stuffed the muffler with pot when he left home. As they were traveling down the road at sixty-five to seventy miles per hour, the end cap came off of his muffler and pot blew out all across the road. That would have been quite the photo opportunity: two guys out on the road, trying to salvage the remnants of pot scattered everywhere. It must have been very expensive, or he thought he really needed it badly. Otherwise, they certainly would not have spent an hour trying to collect his stash.

Jeff didn't mention one word about the incident at this time or any other time during the remainder of the trip. The border crossing could have turned out quite differently had they chosen to search Jeff's motorcycle instead of Jim's.

It was getting later in the evening so the riders decided to look for a campground. The largest expense of traveling by motorcycle is usually hotel rooms. When traveling across areas like British Columbia, it can be quite a distance between towns. Everyone except Trevor enjoyed camping.

At the restaurant, they inquired about a campground. The owner of the restaurant told them they would find a nice one if they backtracked a couple of miles. Derrick, the owner of the restaurant, was very nice and invited the riders to his home on the lake. He had a beautiful home and a well-polished Harley Davidson. He gave everyone a beer and visited until his girlfriend arrived.

The riders back tracked a couple of miles to the campground Derrick had suggested. It was not what they had expected: no showers, no fire pit, and shabby restrooms that were a long way from the campsite. It was not a good setup. They bitched and moaned about the camp but survived the night.

The next morning, they traveled for a couple of miles and passed the restaurant they had eaten at the night before. About a half mile past the restaurant, they noticed a beautiful campground with showers, nice restrooms, and all the amenities one would expect or want in a campground.

That morning when the riders had left the campground, the attendant had asked them how they found out about the campground. When they explained that Derrick had recommended it to them, he told them that Derrick recommends their campground and they recommend his restaurant. In fact, Derrick is part owner of the campground. That explained why Derrick had recommended the campground they stayed at instead of the nicer one. This is how the term "Derrick Effect" came into being. The Derrick Effect is when you ask someone for a recommendation, and they have an interest in recommending a particular person, place, or thing.

From that day forward, if the group asked for recommendations, they would always follow up to ensure that they did not become a victim of the Derrick Effect. They made sure the person giving recommendations did not have a direct benefit for giving the recommendation.

***

BMW motorcycles are a well-engineered piece of machinery. The one Jim rode and the one Mike rode were not really sport bikes and not really touring motorcycles. They were a touring and sport bike combination. The adventure BMW Jeff rode was a combination highway bike and off-road bike. All BMW motorcycles fill up with gas every 200 miles. Trevor was riding a Cruiser, which is best suited for bar hopping. It sounded great and looked pretty parked outside a bar. It guzzled a lot of gas, so he had to fill it up about twice as often as the other motorcycles.

The adventurers like to take side roads and hit curves rather than taking main roads that are straight and uneventful. It can be a long way between gas stations in Canada, particularly if you stick to the back roads.

It was a new day and the riders had planned their adventure over breakfast. They found a really nice back road that looked very fun. It was Jeff's turn to lead the way. Trevor would take up the rear. Trevor calculated the distance and amount of gas it would take to make it from town to town and discussed the fact that he would need to stop for gas in the next town. Jeff had a GPS and would be in the lead, so he would set it for the next town. Everything should have worked perfectly.

As it turned out, Jeff took a cut across road that bypassed the town. Maybe he smoked too much weed. Possibly he hadn't learned how to use his GPS correctly. It probably was the latter because navigation errors were a reoccurring situation when Jeff was in the lead.

The next thing Trevor knew he was looking at a road sign that read 238 kilometers to the next town. At first, he had heart palpitations because he was thinking in terms of miles instead of kilometers. When he realized the sign was in kilometers instead of miles, his mind was somewhat eased. As he was riding along, he began calculating the mileage in his head. He soon realized they must have passed the town he had in mind, and he did not have enough gas to get to the next one. He may not have enough to make it back to the town they had bypassed, either.

Trevor seemed to be the only one who noticed that they had missed the town. Everyone else seemed to have forgotten he needed to stop for gas. Oh well, either way, he knew he was going to run out of gas. They might as well keep moving forward. He passed the time by contemplating what he was going to do when he ran out of gas. One of the riders would have to go to the next town, buy gas, bring it back, and fill up the motorcycle.

Every so often, they would pass a road construction crew. Trevor began thinking that he may be able to buy gas from the crew. Maybe they have some sort of small engines that require gas. Down the road they went. The inevitable was going to take place in some way, shape, or form.

Along about midafternoon, the cruiser was headed up a steep incline when it suddenly sputtered to a stop. Trevor pulled over to the right side of the road. On the left side of the road there were a couple of road workers in a pickup truck. They were the only road workers for as far as the eye could see. Trevor walked across the road and asked the workers if they happened to have gas. One of them reached in the back of a pickup, grabbed a can of gas, walked across the road, and poured the contents into the motorcycle. The problem was solved in minutes.

Trevor emphatically insisted that the road workers accept some money for gas, but they were insistent and wouldn't take a dime. That was typical Canadian hospitality.

When the riders reached the top of the incline, there was a town about a mile ahead. It was all downhill, so Trevor could have coasted into town had he not procured gas from the road crew. Well, on the positive side, they now knew the cruiser runs completely out of gas at exactly 157 miles. This was not the last time a need to fill up became a problem.

A few days later, they were on the road again. Their next destination was Prince George. With a population of 75,000 people, they decided it would be the perfect place to stay. Prince George is located approximately in the middle of British Columbia and the surrounding area is relatively flat.

They were lucky and it was another beautiful day to travel. Everyone stopped at Williams Lake for a restroom stop. Trevor was hyper vigilant now about keeping his gas tank topped off. He decided better safe than sorry and filled his motorcycle with gas at the station across the street. The other guys were waiting so he was in a hurry. When you are in a hurry, it seems like there is always an inevitable delay. Today, it was the card readers. They were out of order. Trevor had to go inside to pay. Everyone was waiting on him, so he hurriedly filled his motorcycle and quickly returned to the other riders. He felt secure because he wouldn't need to get gas before the other riders needed gas.

The wildflowers were in bloom and there was a plethora of unique smells in the air. The riders relished in the indescribable combination of aromas from a variety of plants and flowers as they continued down the road.

Trevor began thinking about his stop at the gas station. He remembered going into the gas station and giving the clerk his credit card but didn't remember going back to retrieve it. Knowing the other riders would follow suit and pull over, Trevor passed the other riders and pulled over to the side of the road. Everyone waited while he searched his wallet for his credit card. It was gone.

Luckily there was cell service, so Trevor was able to locate the name and number for the gas station. The gas station clerk told him his credit card was at the station, but they wouldn't mail it. They would only hold it. The only way to retrieve his credit card was to go back and show them his ID.

The other alternative was to cancel the card and use a different card or apply for a new one. He didn't have a backup card and it would take too long to apply for another one. Even though he was fifty or sixty miles north of Williams Lake, his best bet was to go back and get his card. This would add another 100 to 120 miles to his trip.

The other riders could go ahead and locate a place to stay, maybe relax a little and enjoy a nice quiet evening. It meant Trevor would be two hours or so behind them. Trevor went back and retrieved his card while the others went ahead and located suitable accommodations.

When Trevor pulled into Prince George, he was pleased that the other riders had already located a hotel. It had been a long day of riding for him, considering the fact that he had doubled back to Williams Lake.

Trevor and Jim were staying in one room and Mike and Jeff in another. The rooms were great and the other three had already eaten. Trevor unpacked his luggage and settled in. It was a wonderful evening with perfect temperatures, clean smelling air, and a beautiful sunset.

As the riders were walking downtown, they came across a cigar shop. Jim mentioned that each rider should smoke a cigar in celebration of the occasion. Jim and Mike seemed to be knowledgeable about different manufacturers, varieties, and types of cigars. Jeff didn't seem to have any knowledge of cigars, but he was probably willing to smoke a cigar just to fit in.

On second thought, he appeared to be a person who would smoke anything. Trevor, on the other hand, didn't care for smoking. He also didn't care about following along just to fit in. Trevor watched and listened as each person selected a cigar. As they were walking down the street, each of the smokers lit up in celebration of the occasion. When they walked past a bar called the Pink Cadillac, Trevor asked everyone if they would like to have a drink in celebration of the occasion. Everyone else was content walking down the street smoking a cigar. Trevor went into the bar and everyone else continued down the sidewalk. He would have a drink in celebration of the occasion.

The Pink Cadillac resembled the Roadhouse bar in the Patrick Swayze movie *Roadhouse*. It was smaller, and of course there wasn't a cage in front of the band stand. It had a rectangular configuration with the entrance in front and restrooms in the back. There was a long bar that ran full length of the room to the right of the entrance. It extended all the way from the entrance to the restrooms.

Trevor walked in and found a bar stool at the far end of the bar. The best locations for meeting people in a bar are at a table or bar stool that is en route to the restrooms or where people order drinks at the bar. This was a good location because people will walk through the area to get to the restroom. If a lady is interested in a guy, she will make sure to parade by several times to get his attention. Trevor was not interested in hooking up but was pleased to sit and have a drink. It had been a long day and people watching is always interesting.

When traveling, it is interesting how you can walk into a restaurant or bar and people look at you like you are an alien. It seemed everyone in this bar had purchased their clothes at the same outlet store. Trevor didn't really feel like an alien, but everyone seemed to know each other, and it was definitely a local crowd. For the most part, he seemed invisible. He didn't mind and was happy to people watch. He sat there watching everyone, had two or three drinks, and listened to the band. A couple of hours passed. He talked to no one and no one talked to him. The law of averages implies that things will unfold in time.

Trevor does not lack for attention from the ladies and they often tell him he is a handsome man. An American Indian lady noticed him sitting at the bar and came over to begin a conversation with him. She looked like she was in her early forties, was a little on the plump side, and seemed like she spent a lot of time in bars. Actually, she looked like an American Indian barfly. She had consumed her fair share of alcohol that evening, and Trevor was guessing she was an alcoholic.

As she approached, Trevor expected her to hit him up for drinks. The conversation went like this.

The Barfly said, "I noticed you sitting here all alone."

Trevor replied, "I am from out of town and just enjoying a little down time."

She then proceeded to ask him if he liked her.

He replied, "You seem like a very nice person."

She said, "I didn't ask you if I was nice." She muttered, "You can have me."

Now Trevor thought she wanted money for drinks or sex. He didn't want to buy her drinks or have sex with her. She looked like she was a high-risk health hazard. He was on the spot. It is very difficult for him to be rude to a female when she offers herself up. For a man to get refused for sex is one thing, but for a woman, it is another.

Trevor thought for a moment before he replied. "I am on a long trip and on a shoestring budget." He figured this would be a polite way to say he wasn't going to pay for sex, and he thought it wouldn't damage her ego. Also, this would open the conversation as to whether she was looking for money or sex.

She responded with, "You can still have me. You can do whatever you like."

Now he was on the spot. How should he reply to this one? This was not expected. He thought quickly and explained that she was very attractive and he should have told her earlier that he was married.

She explained that his wife was not there, and she would never know.

He said, "I would know, and I wouldn't want to feel bad about it."

The anger and frustration on her face was evident as she stomped across the floor and out the door, like a toddler throwing a temper tantrum.

On this matter, women do not easily take no for an answer.

As Trevor was sitting there, he reflected on how hurtful it can be for a woman to offer herself up and be refused. When he was in his late twenties, he had developed a professional relationship with a woman who was older than him. She (Danielle) was the first woman Trevor enjoyed mentally and spiritually. She was also very attractive and men where envious of his association with her. She and Trevor had developed an emotional bond but kept their relationship professional.

Before long, Danielle got married, and eventually, Trevor married also. When Trevor got married, she told him she would have married him. Trevor always cherished her honesty and the fact that she freely told him how she felt. Her admission meant the world to him!

They were both married and a few years had gone by when they had the perfect opportunity to consummate their attraction. Danielle had arranged the perfect scenario and all was set. Trevor realized that there was no way this would have a positive ending. He would not marry her because she was older than him, and it would also cause dissention in their present marriages.

His conscience got the best of him and he didn't meet her at the designated time and place. He tried to contact her several times throughout the years. Many years passed. He even tried to contact her through mutual friends to no avail. They say, "Hell hath no fury like a woman scorned."

Men get rejected all the time but to a woman, it is a different story. Women don't often get rejected for sex, but if they do, they can take it very personal. It is interesting . . . when a person doesn't interact with others, how people are not inclined to associate with them.

Trevor wasn't invisible now, he was interactive. Soon a very attractive, wholesome-looking blonde came by on her way to the restroom. She was about five foot four, she had nicely shaped and well-muscled legs, a pretty face, and perfectly shaped, natural voluptuous breasts. She looked wholesome. As she came back from the restroom, she smiled at Trevor. Trevor was off and running.

As she walked by, he touched her on the arm and asked her why he hadn't danced with her. Since he hadn't danced with anyone, he expected some kind of wise crack comeback. She said she didn't want to dance, but it opened a conversation. Her name was Jill, and she stood and talked for a while before she ended up sitting at the bar and having drinks with Trevor.

She got down to business finding out about this guy traveling across the country on a motorcycle. Again, Trevor tried to get her to dance, but she was not interested. Trevor had always considered dancing to be foreplay, in preparation for more foreplay. He was surprised she didn't want to dance.

Evidently, she worked for the Canadian Postal Service, which explained why she had such nice, shapely, athletic legs. She was also an avid camper and camping was her passion. She didn't drive to the bar that day because she was having a camper installed on her pickup. She informed Trevor that she was looking for a rich man who likes to camp. If she had a rich man, she could afford to camp more often.

Trevor realized that people like to talk about themselves and they love being listened to. It is a large part of the bonding process between two people. That is why people who talk all the time are such a bore to others. *People don't bond by talking, they bond by being listened to.* The most offensive people are the ones who just want to talk about themselves. If you are going to seduce a woman, let them talk, act interested, and ask questions. They will usually ask about you, in time. They want the short version. *Their questions will cue you into what they are thinking.* They might say, "Tell me about you." The best response to this is, "What would you like to know?" If you answer their question with an inquiry, you will learn a lot.

Jill and Trevor had great chemistry and obviously liked each other a lot. Jill offered to show Trevor her cabin and have him stay the night with her.

Hmm, thought Trevor. *Stay the night with a beautiful woman in a cabin in the woods or at the hotel with Jim?* This was a no brainer. Tonight he would be staying in Jill's cabin.

Trevor tried to call Jim on his cell phone to let him know he would not be staying at the hotel that night. The phone rang but there wasn't an answer. He tried several times but still no answer. Trevor explained to Jill that he would need to stop by the hotel to let Jim know he was going to stay at her house and not at the hotel.

Jill had come to the bar with a girlfriend. Jill, Trevor, and her girlfriend piled into a cab and went to the hotel. It was late at night and the ladies sat in the lobby while Trevor went up to the room. As he headed up the stairs, Trevor teased the ladies about the possibility of them being gone when he came back from the room. The thought did cross Trevor's mind that the ladies could be gone when he returned.

When Trevor opened the door to the room Jim was sound asleep. He tried to wake him. "Hey Jim, Jim," he said. "Hey Jim!" There was no response. Trevor grabbed him by the shoulder and rolled him back and forth until he woke up. "Hey Jim, are you awake?" he exclaimed.

With a startled look in his eyes, Jim replied "Yeah, yeah, what's up?"

Trevor explained that he had met a hot chick and that she and her friend were waiting for him in the lobby. He told Jim that he was going to stay at her place tonight and that he would call when he got up in the morning. Trevor explained that the riders could be late getting started tomorrow because he didn't know how far away she lived.

When Trevor got back to the lobby, the gals were still sitting there with smiles on their faces. They were both very attractive with bubbly personalities. Trevor really liked both of them! There are a lot of pretty women in Canada—at least they are the type of women Trevor is attracted to. Many are blonde with blue eyes and of Scandinavian or Irish descent.

Much to Trevor's relief, the cab was still waiting outside. They left for Jill's cabin in the woods and dropped her friend off along the way. Jill's place was nice and comfortable. It had a good homey feel. The cabin was rustic and without frills. It could be most accurately described as a little log cabin in the woods, something out of a Robert Kincaid painting.

As soon as they were through the door, the foreplay began. In an instant, their clothes were on the floor and they were on the couch. Soon they were hand in hand and headed to bed. This was definitely better than sleeping with Jim at the hotel. Trevor enjoyed her beauty, touch, personality, wholesomeness, sensitivity, and charm. He even liked her smell better than that of the wildflowers he had smelled while riding through the mountains. Trevor liked everything about Jill except the fact that she was a camper. He had lived in the mountains without the conveniences of running water and electricity when he was younger. Now he liked a good bed, a hot shower, and the conveniences of modern life. Still, he did like Jill and her place. It was the perfect interlude for a motorcycle trip.

Experts say that men go to sleep right away after sex because their brain releases a cocktail of chemicals. In Trevor's experience, women almost always go to sleep instantly after sex. It doesn't matter if it is the first time you have sex with them or if it is the hundredth. Jill went to sleep instantly.

In contrast, Trevor was wide awake for what seemed to be an eternity. When he finally fell asleep, he was lying in bed thinking it was going to be daylight soon.

The next thing he knew, his phone was ringing. He found his pants and located his phone. Jim was on the phone and he was in a panic. Excitedly,

Jim exclaimed "Where are you? I called everyone looking for you and nobody knows where you are."

Trevor responded, "I talked to you last night and told you I was staying with the gal I met at the bar."

Jim didn't remember Trevor waking him up and telling him he was staying overnight with Jill. He totally drew a blank and did not remember.

Trevor had never smoked pot but began putting two and two together. He surmised that the smokers had gotten totally blasted last night and Jim had no recollection whatsoever of their conversation. Jim was pretty wound up and Trevor was telling him to calm down, all is cool. He told Jim he would get a taxi and be at the hotel shortly. Trevor thought Jim was upset because he would be late and everyone would have to wait on him. Jim explained that it was a bigger problem than that.

Jim said, "We have a real problem! This morning when I noticed you hadn't been here all night, I called your phone. I meant to call your cell phone but confused the numbers and left a message on your home phone. Your wife is going to be really pissed!"

Trevor inquired, "So what did you say?"

Jim said he left a message asking where Trevor was and that no one had seen him since they left him at the Pink Cadillac last night. Jim also explained that he said, "Where are you? It's eight in the morning!" on the answering machine.

Trevor realized this was a huge problem. He told Jim he would meet him at the hotel as soon as he could get there. There is nothing nice about getting out the door like your ass is on fire the morning after. Trevor was in a big fat hurry, and Jill didn't have transportation because she was getting a camper put on her pickup

Like a trooper, Jill called for a taxi. When he arrived, the taxi driver insisted on twenty dollars up front. Trevor had spent all of his cash the night before and the taxi driver wouldn't accept a credit card. This was embarrassing! Jill came forward with a twenty and paid the cab driver. She smiled the whole time as if she didn't mind paying for Trevor's ride. It seemed a little ironic for a woman to pay for a guy to leave the morning after. Trevor felt ashamed that she had to pay for his ride.

Jeff had a sudden emergency and left for home early that morning. He was long gone by the time Trevor got to the hotel. Jeff's return trip home was about 700 miles, and he did the entire trip in one day. That was the last time Trevor or Jim heard from Jeff. The following year, Mike planned a trip with Jeff. He asked Jim and Trevor to join, and their response was thanks but no thanks. Mike and Jeff left on the trip together and again, Jeff left for home soon into the trip. When Trevor asked Mike what happened and how the trip went, he refused to comment. All he would say was that it was a disaster.

Breakfast at the hotel was a meeting of the minds. How were they going to solve the problem of the message on the answering machine? Trevor could check and listen to the messages remotely with a couple of codes. When he finally figured out how to do it, they listened to the message. The message went like this: "Hey man; where the f*^#k are you at? No one has seen you since we left you last night at the Pink Cadillac. I called everyone and no one knows where the f*^#k you are. What the hell happened to you?"

They all knew this was going to go over like a lead balloon when Trevor's wife listened to the message. Certainly, she would check the phone messages as soon as she got home. They had to solve this problem right away.

Lucky enough, Trevor's wife was in Boston and would not be home until morning. They knew the messages could be checked remotely, which lead them to believe they could be erased remotely. You have to go through a menu and series of codes to do this, but nobody knew how to do it. Trevor didn't even remember which company manufactured the phone. What if Trevor's wife decided to check the messages remotely?

They eventually arrived at a possible solution. They would locate an electronics store that sells the same type of phone and that phone should have directions on how to erase messages remotely. Since the phone wasn't new and the model could be out of date, it seemed like a long shot to find an electronics store in Canada that sells the same type of phone.

After breakfast they located a Best Buy store. In the phone department, there were several makes and models, so Trevor began studying the pictures on the boxes to determine which one they needed. When he finally found a phone that looked similar, he purchased it and took it to a nearby coffee shop. He studied the directions for erasing messages remotely, called his home phone, and within a few minutes had erased all of the messages.

There were other important messages that got erased and it was a couple of years before the effects of the deletion subsided.

Prince George was now in the rearview mirror, and their next destination was Prince Rupert. They were hoping for nice weather, although Prince Rupert only has 955 hours of sunshine per year. That translates to 39.7 days of sunshine per year. The average high temperature in the summer is 59.9 degrees Fahrenheit. The annual rainfall is 100.5 inches of rain. To put that in perspective, Seattle, which is well known for a rainy climate, has an annual rainfall of 34.1 inches.

It was another beautiful day on the road. All was in sync when they got to Kitwanga, British Columbia. There, they noticed a sign that read "219 Kilometers to Hyder, Alaska," which translates to 136.08 miles. In less than three hours they could be in Alaska. That sounded like a good idea. They could say they had been to Alaska.

It was a great road but it was uneventful. There wasn't much traffic, just a lot of straight stretches without curves. Mike had a relatively new motorcycle with a top speed of 150 miles per hour. He began to cut the monotony by winding it up to top speed and passing Trevor and Jim. When you are about half asleep and don't know a motorcycle is coming by you at 150 miles per hour, it can spook the hell out of you. It is like the sound of a hornet amplified many, many times streaking past. Mike entertained himself by spooking the shit out of Jim and Trevor. Each time he jetted by at 150 miles per hour, Jim and Trevor became more vigilant about looking in the rearview mirror before changing lanes.

The population of Hyder Alaska was eighty-seven people. There was an old yellow school bus that had been converted into a crab stand. The crab was cooked and prepared inside the bus and people would sit outdoors to eat. There was also a bar that capitalizes on the fact that people go to Hyder just to say they have been to Alaska. The popular thing to do in Hyder is getting "Hyderised." This consisted of buying a shot of whisky, doing a salute or toast, then putting it down the hatch. Many people do this several times. Jim and Mike officially got Hyderised.

The next day the riders headed south and continued their journey to Prince Rupert. Once again, Mike entertained himself by buzzing past his fellow bikers at 150 miles per hour. Although Hyder, Alaska was their longest distance from home, Prince Rupert was their main destination.

To make traveling costs more efficient, the travelers would commonly book a room with two queen beds and get a rollaway bed for the third person. After a while of being close and doing everything together, this can cause people to get on one another's nerves. Being tired can also add to the friction. Mike grew up in a caste society, liked to have his way, and seemed very competitive. For some reason, Mike and Jim could only travel for about five days before a conflict began. They had gotten along great until they arrived at the hotel in Prince Rupert.

They started unpacking and Jim sat his helmet on one of the beds. It must have been the bed Mike wanted and he thought Jim was claiming it. Jim explained he had to put his helmet somewhere. The tensions rose and the argument began. Mike got upset and decided he would get his own room. Every ride, Mike and Jim would eventually get on each other's nerves over some little thing. Even though they would have a spat, the next day all would be fine. It just seemed to be the straw that breaks the camel's back. It turned out fine for Trevor since he now had more space with just him and Jim to share the room.

The next morning was very nice with plenty of sunshine. Mike and Jim were back in good graces again. They all headed downtown to eat breakfast. Prince Rupert is a fishing town and there were bald eagles sitting in the trees as you would imagine seagulls or starlings in another town. This was because there are a lot of fish being caught and processed in the area. The eagles seemed to make an easy living off the excess fish parts that are discarded by the fishermen.

As they crossed the street in the center of town, there was a huge fish head about the size of a football lying in the middle of the street. It appeared an eagle had picked it up and dropped it there. It was a unique atmosphere with bald eagles flying around, roosting in trees, and fish parts lying in the street. People in the area told stories about catching 140-pound fish as if it was common.

The adventurers found a nice little restaurant for breakfast. It was a quaint, privately owned type of place. As they were sitting at their table, a man, his beautiful wife, and two small children stopped to talk. They were on a family vacation. The husband asked the adventurers several questions about their motorcycle trip. He told them he had previously owned a Harley Davidson Road King. They conversed for some time about motorcycle riding while his wife and children waited. At the end of their conversation, the husband exclaimed that he really wished he was riding with them instead of doing what he was doing (vacationing with his family).

His wife's face fell and you could see the disappointment in her eyes as she thought he would rather be riding with them than spending time vacationing with his family. Trevor was sure the poor fellow didn't mean it that way but nevertheless, he was glad he didn't have to deal with the aftermath of that comment. That type of comment can easily ruin a family vacation.

The plan was to take a ferry from Prince Rupert to Port Hardy British Columbia, which is located on the north end of Vancouver Island. They hadn't reserved a spot on the ferry but knew that one was scheduled to leave the next morning. Little did they know that one of the ferries traveling to and from Port Hardy had missed a course change, hit a rock, and sank. The vessel was carrying 101 passengers and crew. All except two were accounted for. When a loaded ferry sinks in BC, a person would think that it would have been newsworthy in the US but none of the riders knew about it.

That evening Jim called the ferry terminal to schedule a ferry to Port Hardy and they told him he would have to wait several days to get one. Since the ferry went down, reservations needed to be reserved a week in advance. After much conversation, Jim informed the scheduler that they were on motorcycles and maybe they could squeeze them in. The scheduler agreed to try and fit them in at the front of the boat. The scheduler told Jim they would have to be at the terminal at three in the morning. This would allow them to load the motorcycles before any cars came aboard. At three in the morning, they loaded the motorcycles at the front of the ferry. Prince Rupert was great to visit, but it would have been very expensive and quite an ordeal to stay there for a week. Once again, the riders had lucked out.

It was an eighteen-hour ferry ride from Prince Rupert to Port Hardy. The riders were tired considering their early morning boarding. They tried to think of the ferry ride as a cruise ship adventure without the indulgences of gourmet food, shows, swimming, gambling, and nice beds. It was a wonderful contrast to ride the ferry after many days on motorcycles. There weren't any beds, and the seats were uncomfortable so it was very difficult to sleep. The trip down the coast was very pretty because you can see coastline or islands most of the way. The main entertainment was watching for whales. Every so often they could see a whale porpoise out of the water.

When they got to Port Hardy, they unloaded the motorcycles and stayed for the night. The next morning, they traversed the length of Vancouver Island to Victoria, British Columbia. It was a remote area with very tall trees lining both sides of the road. It looked like they had carved a road corridor right out through the trees.

Victoria, British Columbia, is at the southern end of Vancouver Island. It has a lot to do and a lot to see. It was beautiful weather, and in the daytime, they toured the town. It happened to be the first of July, which is the Canadian equivalent to the Fourth of July in the United States.

In the evening they went downtown to play pool and join in the July 1 festivities. They met a group of Canadians and got involved in a very competitive game of pool. Canadian folks are generally very avid drinkers. They asked the motorcycle riders where they were from. When they asked why they came there, Trevor told them they came to show the Canadians how to drink. The party was on.

The game of pool progressed to where Trevor and a beautiful young lady in her mid-twenties were on a team. Sometimes, Trevor could play pool very well and this was one of those times. The two were cleaning up on the other players and developed a great camaraderie. It was easy to tell that Trevor and his partner were very attracted to each other and got great pleasure out of beating the other players. The young lady was gushing and Trevor was eating it up. They were having fun, being a team. They beat every pair of players except one.

The stakes had been for drinks, and Trevor and his partner hadn't lost a game. It came down to the eight ball and Trevor had an easy shot to win the game. If he made the shot, he and his partner would be proclaimed the winning team. It is not uncommon for Trevor to make difficult shots and miss an easy one. Sure enough, he missed the shot. The other pair was left in perfect position and ended up winning the game. The young lady had been getting quite a kick out of beating her friends and acquaintances. A look of disappointment came over her face as she gave Trevor a halfhearted hug. She had the look of a lover who had come a half second away from achieving an orgasm and all hope was gone.

Trevor would never forget the look of disappointment on her face. Her look mirrored Trevor's feeling of disappointment—the motorcycle adventure and his marriage had to end. He couldn't live a lie. He was more likely to respect a murderer than a liar, as it is possible for a murderer to be honest.

Chapter 2

Honesty in Relationships

The relationship counselor had recommended that Trevor and his wife live separately, so Trevor had been residing in Southern California. Now it was time to go home and resolve his marital situation.

Trevor had ridden across country enough to establish certain places to stay. On this trip, he decided to stay at a hotel in central California. The rates were decent and the rooms were nice considering the age of the hotel. He had stayed at this hotel a couple of years ago. It was privately owned by a Japanese lady with a good business head. The last time he had stayed for several days and tried to talk her down on rates. Although he had stayed for a week, he could only talk her down five dollars per day. This time it was going to be a challenge to see if he could do better at getting the rate down.

Trevor had experience in horse trading in his younger days, so he could drive a hard bargain without irritating the other party. It wasn't the money. It was the challenge of a worthy opponent. You always need to have small talk before bargaining. It is something Trevor was good at. He had heard that in the Japanese culture, you need to have small talk before business or you will not be trusted. This was a practice he had incorporated in business dealings.

As it turned out, he didn't do any better this time. She only came down two dollars per night. As mentioned, she was a good businesswoman. The interesting part was that after the price for the room was established, they both joked about the fact that he could only talk her down two dollars. She then went on to relate that she had just returned from her sister's funeral in Japan. Evidently, her sister's only living relative (an uncle), had been killed in the Tohoku tsunami in Japan. Her sister had tried to commit suicide once and then succeeded by hanging herself from a tree on the second attempt. It is interesting how a person can relate such a personal story to a perfect stranger when they may not be able to talk about it to someone close. It must be what was on her mind at the time. Sometimes small talk can lead to opening the flood gates of conversation. Here Trevor was on a carefree motorcycle ride across country. After hearing her story, it put things in a different perspective.

Trevor enjoyed meeting the locals, so after he settled into the hotel room, he headed for the local pub. He had been there before and it was a happening place with people playing pool, dancing to the juke box, and having great fun. This time though, there were only three or four people in the place. Trevor met a fellow named Russ. He had short, cropped red hair and was well muscled. It was evident he lifted weights but was not overly bulky either. Russ mentioned he had been a wimp in high school and was excited to go to his class reunion now that he was a weightlifter and didn't take guff from anyone.

Russ was a sheriff and seemed like a guy who was pretty much black and white about things. He told a story about how he had arrested people that had subsequently done a lot of time in prison following their arrest. Sometimes, he would run into those folks in the pub. Trevor asked him if that was a little uncomfortable, as they might hold a grudge. His reply was that he just asks them if they are keeping their nose clean and they always insist they are.

Russ told Trevor that the pub had changed hands recently and it wasn't the same as it used to be. Then he suggested they go to a neighboring town where there would be more going on. He gave Trevor directions, telling him to go this way, that way, and the other way. Having been in the area before, Trevor knew he wouldn't find the place, as the roads ran every which way. As it turned out, Trevor decided to follow Russ to the pub in the neighboring town. It ended up being about fifteen miles away. It was like a maze getting there.

This pub seemed much like the other one, only there were quite a few people talking, playing pool, and a band was preparing to play. Everyone seemed to know Russ. Russ and Trevor, along with seven or eight others, gathered around a large table to tell stories and drink. Trevor didn't care much about drinking, but enjoyed meeting new folks and learning what he could from them. To be sociable, he would have a drink or two and maybe an iced tea, something non-alcoholic. He knew it was going to be tricky finding his way back to the hotel late at night in a strange town where the roads didn't run straight with the world. They looked like someone had just dumped out a can of worms. Drinking a lot and riding a motorcycle is not a good idea, so Trevor took it easy on the drinks.

Naturally, everyone was interested in Trevor's story. A guy, hundreds of miles from home, riding a motorcycle. He explained that he had been away from home for a while and was on his way back. As the pub became crowded and the band began to play, people settled into conversations with those closest to them.

Robert and Kim, a couple close to Trevor, seemed to take an interest in learning about Trevor and his ride. Robert was of average height and build and was a nice guy. He seemed to take a particular interest in entertaining everyone. He would converse for a while, then get up and dance his way over to another table to find a dance partner. Everyone seemed to know and enjoy Robert's antics. As they settled into conversation, Trevor mentioned he had several interesting experiences in his recent stay in Southern California. In particular, Robert seemed to get a kick out the following story Trevor told.

After playing golf, Trevor was putting his clubs away in the golf course parking lot when an Asian fellow named Li came up and mentioned he had played the same golf course Trevor played two days ago. Trevor thought he must have seen him there, so when Li asked him if he would like to play golf the next day, Trevor agreed. Trevor always liked meeting new people and really didn't know anyone in the area to play golf with. Li asked Trevor for his phone number and said he would make a tee time and give him a call.

As Trevor started to leave, his new acquaintance asked him where he was going. Trevor told him he knew a restaurant that offered free refills on Pepsi and he was going there. His new acquaintance then asked if he could come along and accompany Trevor to the restaurant. Trevor didn't mind, as a little company would be fine. It was a very hot day and Trevor was parched from the combination of heat and golf.

As soon as they both sat down and before the Pepsi arrived, Trevor's new acquaintance immediately asked him where he was living and Trevor told him. The next question was, "Can we go there?"

Trevor replied "No, I like it right here."

Right away Li asked him if he would like a massage.

Trevor replied "No, are you a masseuse?"

Li said "No."

The next question was, "Can we go to your place?"

Trevor was in shock and putting two and two together by now. He started feeling a little cheap. In a hurry, Trevor downed some of his drink and explained he suddenly remembered he had an appointment. He made his exit.

About 8:00 p.m., Trevor's phone rang. It was Li. Trevor ignored the call. Nine o'clock he called again. Ten o'clock he called again. Trevor turned off the alert sounds on his phone. When he got up the next morning, there were eight calls from Li. By now Trevor thought he was home free. Li must have realized he was not interested by now. Nope! At eight thirty in the morning, he got a text message: "Can I come to your place?"

By this time Trevor knew he needed advice on how to handle the situation. He surmised that women know how to handle these things, so he called a female friend for advice. She told him to reply with, "If you haven't figured it out by now, I am not gay. Lose my number." Well, this seemed to work. He received no more messages.

After Trevor told his gay story to his new friends at the bar, he didn't know whether to feel complimented by being hit on or cheap and easy because the guy didn't even offer to buy dinner or drinks. No foreplay at all, just straight to the naughty stuff.

Robert found it entertaining from that point forward to dance around, look at Trevor, use his fingers to slant his eyes, and give Trevor his best come hither look. He was entertaining and the drinks were starting to take effect.

Robert's wife, Kim, was a slender, nice-looking lady. Trevor could tell she wasn't entirely of European descent. As they were visiting, Trevor was trying to figure out her ethnicity. For a while he thought she could be Hispanic, maybe Filipino, or possibly of Asian descent. Figuring out other people's ethnicities was a game Trevor played with himself. If you are going to guess an Asian person's descent, you don't want to guess incorrectly, as there can be a lot of animosity between Koreans, Japanese, and Chinese. On the other hand, if you guess correctly, it can be quite entertaining.

As she was talking, Trevor was doing his best to figure out her descent. Eventually she got up to go to the restroom and Trevor thought he determined her ethnicity based on her butt.

When she returned and conversation ensued, Trevor confessed that he had been trying to figure out her descent. She took the bait and asked him to make a guess. He told her, after much thought and consideration, he had come to a conclusion based on her butt. She seemed intrigued.

"Oh, you have been watching my butt, have you?" she exclaimed.

"Yep, based on your butt, I would say you are part Japanese." Trevor did well. He was correct.

She went on to ask Trevor how he could tell by her butt.

He explained that it wasn't only her butt. It was a combination of the shape of her face and her butt. The dead giveaway though, was that her butt was flat. She didn't seem to be insulted or self-conscious at all, she was impressed. Trevor guessed her alcohol was starting to kick in.

Much to Trevor's surprise, she continued to tell him she actually pads her butt because it is so flat. She had padded it before she left the house that evening. She didn't say whether she used one piece, two pieces, or multiple pieces of stuffing, but she padded her butt with something. First the hotel proprietor told Trevor about her sister hanging herself. Now Robert was dancing around the room entertaining everyone while his wife was telling Trevor about her butt padding.

Russ was telling everyone about how many homicides he was involved in last year, and Kim was taking a lot of interest in Trevor's adventure. Women always seem to be very interested in the relationships of others, so Kim was busy questioning Trevor about his.

Trevor explained that he was on his way home after a separation from his wife. He and his wife had drifted so far apart that there didn't seem to be a way to build a bridge to close the gap.

Kim explained that she had always been deeply in love with Robert, and that he had always been deeply in love with her. Eventually, Robert wandered back to the table and explained to Trevor that their relationship is a very solid, loving relationship. In fact, he went on to explain that a couple of years ago, she had been addicted to drugs and had been hospitalized for her addiction. They talked about how close they were and how their love had gotten both of them through the addiction. They assured Trevor that if a couple were truly in love, they could withstand the worst of adversity. Their seventeen-year-old daughter had been experiencing the dating process. Kim explained that in both their relationship and the dating relationships of their daughter, the most important thing is honesty. Her advice for her daughter was to always be honest in her relationships. She told Trevor that most of what she knew about relationships was from mentoring her daughter through dating. She went into great detail, explaining how honesty had solved each problem in her daughter's relationships. With each situation, honesty was the answer.

Trevor became convinced that honesty is best. He decided to go home and be as brutally honest as he possibly could, believing things will fall in place and honesty will be the solution.

By this time, Robert was back to being funny and entertaining everyone. Kim was smiling and talking about how cute he was. Russ had way too much to drink and was about to fall off his chair. He began talking about getting a taxi. He was having reservations because he would need to leave his little pickup at the bar overnight. He had something of great value in it, and whatever it was belonged to the Sheriff's Department. Kim told Trevor that the main road was a DWI trap, and that there was a back road he should take to get to the hotel. Kim insisted that Trevor should follow them back to the hotel, but Robert didn't want any part of going to Trevor's hotel.

Trevor knew it would be difficult to find his way back. Taking a different route was out of the question. Kim decided she should take her husband home, then show Trevor the way to the hotel. Robert didn't like that idea either. The next thing was another round of shots. Kim began thinking that Robert might pass out. Well, Robert didn't pass out, and he emphatically insisted that Trevor could find his own way.

The evening of storytelling, drinking, and fun was coming to an end. The bar was closing and the sheriff had gotten so drunk he disappeared in a taxi without saying goodbye. Robert was slurring his words and looked like he was trying to put the make on one of the other ladies. Kim was sitting next to Trevor explaining that if she could get away from Robert, she would really like to fuck him.

She looked Trevor straight in the eye and said, "I wish Robert would pass out so we could fuck."

Trevor said, "If we fuck, will you tell Robert?"

Kim replied, "OH GOD NO!"

Well, so much for honesty in relationships. Her statement summed up the truth of the matter. On top of that, Robert had been slanting his eyes, dancing around the room, and making fun of the Asian guy all while knowing his wife was half Japanese.

Chapter 3

Brothers and Sisters

They say women get married thinking they can change a man and men get married believing a woman will never change. Both are wrong!

Menopause had been a significant change in Trevor's marriage. Sex had come to a halt years ago and the symptoms of PMS were not just a monthly occurrence, they were a permanent day to day fixture. As far as Lea, Trevor's wife, was concerned, hormone replacement was out of the question. Her family had a history of cancer and she believed hormone replacement to be a major cause of cancer. The bottom line was that the two were happier when they were apart. The counselor recommended they get a divorce and the couple agreed that divorce would be their best option.

Early one bright, sunny day, Trevor and Jim headed for California. Jim had relatives in the central valley and planned on staying with them. Trevor would try to find a hotel on the outskirts of town. They planned to meet in Redding California. From there, they would continue to Bodega, California, and in two days, they would be in wine country. The ride from Redding heading west is a really nice motorcycle ride but not comparable to the ride down the coast on Highway 1.

Trevor, Jim, and their motorcycle buddies all agreed that the motorcycle ride down the coast (on Highway 1) is probably the best motorcycle ride they have experienced. The road is twisty and winds its way along the coastline. It is not only twisty, but it also has a lot of dips and valleys. Although these characteristics make it a fun motorcycle ride, the scenery is also spectacular.

They met and stayed their first night at a place in downtown Redding. It was clean, a good price, and close to the turn going towards the coast. It was a single-story hotel, which is great because you end up making more trips to a motorcycle than you would if you were traveling by automobile. The other thing about being on the first floor is it makes it easier to keep an eye on the motorcycles. The room had two queen beds, so the cost was quite reasonable, when split between the two travelers.

Later in the night, they heard sirens from several police cars. When they looked out the window, they could see several police cars gathered at the far end of the parking lot. There was a lot of commotion about something. At checkout the next morning, they inquired about the police cars and commotion in the night. Evidently, two women had lured a guy into their automobile by enticing him with sex. When he was in a vulnerable position, a man jumped into the car and the three of them robbed their victim. It made Jim and Trevor wonder how often this setup occurred. Trevor supposed many people would not report it happening to them.

The trip from Redding down the coast was fantastic, as always. If you ever do this trip by motorcycle, it is very tiring, so the recommendation is to do it in two days instead of one.

The next day they were in wine country. The wine industry can be a fascinating study to a novice. An acre of productive farmland in the Napa Valley sells for about $800,000. There are many wineries that grow and produce various types of grapes. A wine is named by the type of grape used to make that particular type of wine. A merlot is made with merlot grapes, and a pinot is made with pinot grapes. The grapes are commonly grown in the vineyard, then picked at a particular time when the sugar is at a precise level for a particular wine recipe.

Although a winery may grow the grapes, much of the processing of grapes is done at a wine processing plant. In other words, the grower grows the grapes, but the processing company determines when to pick the grapes, follows a particular recipe for processing that particular type of wine, and turns the grapes into wine. A processing plant will process and label a number of different brands and types for various wineries.

Hotels are very expensive in the Napa Valley, so it is economical to stay in one of the surrounding areas. Jim stayed with his relatives, and Trevor began the process of searching for a hotel and eventually found a good place a few miles away.

The next day, Trevor and Jim toured the wine processing facility and began learning about turning grapes into wine. In the evening, they visited with Jim's relatives until it was time to retire. Jim's relatives had to work the next day, so they retired early. Trevor, on the other hand, rode his motorcycle out through the vineyards and back to his hotel. He is not an early riser and is used to staying up late. He isn't much of a television watcher, so he decided to go out and meet the locals. Meeting the locals is much of the enjoyment of traveling. It can be very entertaining, but most of all, you learn a lot from people in different areas. One of the best forms of education is travel.

Trevor found a local tavern very close to his hotel. He thought it would be great because he could have a few drinks, visit with the locals, and it would be a short ride back to the hotel. The tavern was an interesting place filled with locals. There was one empty bar stool, so he grabbed it right away. As he was sitting at the bar, there was a man sitting to his left and a nice-looking lady sitting to his right. If there had been a choice of places to sit, and he picked the one next to the nice-looking woman, it would have looked like he was trying to make up to her. This was perfect—the only available seat was next to the good-looking woman. Trevor didn't want to appear overly eager to talk to her, so he passed pleasantries with the guy to his left. If he would have tried to start a conversation with the woman, she would have sensed he was trying to pick her up. He knew if he ignored her for a while, she would eventually start small talk. If she started the conversation, she would be initiating the seduction. She would be the one striving to maintain his interest. All he had to do was be charming and she would try to reel him in.

Trevor understood the psychology of this situation very well. When he was in his late twenties, he had been to the doctor about an issue with his privates. The doctor took samples and ran tests, but it would be a few days before the test results came back. In the meantime, the doctors had told him he shouldn't have sex because he could have something contagious. The last thing

Trevor wanted to do was get involved with a woman.

After Trevor saw the doctor, he and his friend decided to go out to one of the nicer restaurants and have a good meal. On the way out of the restaurant, there was an area with pinball machines and a pool table. They decided to play pool and before long, they were mixing and mingling with others in the game area. They had a few drinks and eventually there was an accumulation of about fifteen people.

Out of the mix of people, there was one female who stuck out as being particularly attractive to Trevor. She seemed very nice also, not a pretentious person by any means. She had a perfectly curved body, bubbly personality, big bright blue eyes, dark hair, and a very strong sex appeal. Every male except Trevor was ogling her or hitting on her. Trevor was just happy playing pool. The last thing he wanted was to hook up with someone.

The evening marched on and the circus of guys plying for her attention continued. Eventually, the bar closed, and it was time for all to leave. During the evening, Trevor had passed pleasantries with the beautiful woman but for the most part, he had ignored her.

The bar closed. On her way out, she asked Trevor if he would take her to buy beer. If a bar closes and a gorgeous woman asks if you would take her to buy beer, it doesn't matter what your health conditions are—you are headed for the convenience store.

After purchasing beer, they headed for the park. The park ran along the river and consisted of camping areas and an occasional barbeque site. It was a good, secluded place to park at three in the morning.

The next thing Trevor knew, they were sitting in the car at the park, drinking beer. Trevor was trying to avoid getting physical. He sat there for a short time trying to make conversation.

Before long, the hottie looked over at him and said, "Let's just cut the shit."

Trevor was afraid to tell her about his health issue, so now he was in a pickle. There they were, sitting in a sports car with bucket seats.

She reached over the console and started unfastening his pants. They kissed and things progressed. Trevor had his pants down and she was playing with his privates. The more she played with his privates, the more excited she became, the more excited he became, and Trevor just let her keep doing what she was doing. She explained that she hadn't had sex for a very long time and that her ex-husband had remarried that day.

For the first time in Trevor's life, he was a selfish lover. He let her continue until he was satisfied. He hadn't done one thing to please her.

A few days later, Trevor's test results came back and all was well, he wasn't contagious after all. He felt very bad about the way he had treated this woman, so he wanted to make it up to her. He called her right away. He hadn't called her for a week and thought she may not want to see him again. He called her and asked her if she would like to come over. Sure enough, she drove clear across town to see him. He didn't feed her dinner, get her drunk, or do anything except make her very sexually satisfied.

Although there was some psychology to the seduction in this scenario, Trevor would have to acknowledge the fact that there was a very nice chemistry between the two of them. Even though there was a good chemistry, *the reserve to make a woman work for a man's attention was an invaluable learning experience.* This experience would serve Trevor well throughout his life. The fact that he hadn't called her had increased his value. After all, *what is easily available is common, what is scarce is valuable.* Women usually play this to their advantage.

Trevor was remembering this now in wine country, sitting on a bar stool between a man and a nice-looking woman. He had been sitting there for about ten minutes. He had passed pleasantries with the man to his left. The juke box was playing some fantastic tunes. He was ignoring the woman (Lisa) to his right, as she was no doubt used to guys coming on to her on a regular basis.

As they were sitting there, an Eagles song began playing on the juke box. Lisa looked over at Trevor and exclaimed "The Eagles are my favorite group! I played that song."

The ice was broken and this was a good subject for Trevor, as he really enjoyed music. Although he enjoyed music, he was sick of almost all of the Eagles songs. They conversed for a few minutes before Trevor said something about Glen Fry. She corrected him about the pronunciation. It is pronounced Glen Frey. They conversed for a while longer and she corrected him on his pronunciation again. Fry, Frey, however it was pronounced, it didn't suit her. The conversation continued until it got around to the usual disclosure of commodities and currency. Where is Trevor going? What is he doing there? Where does she live? What is she doing there?

Come to find out, she was a soccer mom and she had picked up her kids earlier and took them to her ex-husband's place where they would stay for a few days. Trevor could tell she was very interested in him by the way she studied his face. Alcohol was having a definite effect on her. Trevor was talking and she was studying his face.

In mid-sentence, she interrupted him. "Would you like to fuck?" she asked.

Trevor was thinking, *That didn't take long. This is cutting to the chase!* He searched for words and replied, "That sounds good to me."

She smiled wide and said, "You have to tell me you want to fuck me, or I won't go to your hotel room with you."

Trevor thought quickly and responded by saying in his most seductive voice, "I would love to fuck you."

A fellow that had been talking to some folks a few feet away walked over right on cue, as if he had heard what Trevor said. He introduced himself and said his name was Frank. He explained that he and Lori were neighbors. Frank and Trevor traded pleasantries and visited until Frank left for the restroom. Frank was an average guy in every way: job, build, face, and dress. He was wearing Levis with a plaid shirt. He could easily have been cast in the *Home Improvement* television series. He appeared like a handyman who hadn't shaved or bathed for a couple of days.

While he was in the restroom, Lori explained that Frank was her neighbor and that he helped her out a lot. He was a good neighbor, fixed her car, did odd jobs, and she knew he was romantically interested in her. Although she knew he had romantic intentions, she explained that he would never be more than a friend. Nevertheless, she accepted his favors.

Whether we openly admit it or not, women use sex as a commodity, and men use different forms of currency to get sex. The prettier the woman, the higher the currency. If a man is attractive, charming, and successful financially, he has a lot of currency. A man with these characteristics will have enough currency for one-night stands; that is, if he chooses less attractive women. In a one-night stand, the man will almost always be more attractive than the woman.

In Frank's case, he was using the currency available to him. He was fixing things, watching out for her, and hoping to win her favor. By doing odd jobs, he was getting close to her in the guise of being a good neighbor. She probably made him pie or cookies to show her appreciation and accepted favors in the guise of him just being a good neighbor. Women easily form emotional connections with men they are often around, and if he played his cards right, she would form an emotional connection with Frank.

Trevor, on the other hand, had a different kind of currency. He and his currency would soon be on the road to Southern California.

Trevor and Lori visited for a very short time before the conversation got back to business. Lori asked him to write the name of his hotel and room number on a napkin. Although Lori knew right where the hotel was, he wrote it down for extra measure. He handed her the napkin and she stuffed it in her purse.

She told him she drives by his hotel almost every day and that she lives within a mile of the bar. They planned on her following Trevor to his hotel. When Lori grabbed her car keys from the top of the bar and picked up her purse, Frank was right on cue. He came over and told her she was too drunk and shouldn't drive. She argued that she was alright and it was just a short distance. She didn't want to leave her car at the bar because she would have to come back and get it in the morning. She put her purse down and began visiting with Trevor.

He explained that she could leave her car and ride to the hotel on the back of his motorcycle. The real reason she didn't want to leave her car sitting at the bar was it was a small town, and people would notice if it was left there all night. Gossip in a small town can be wicked.

They finally arrived at a solution. Trevor would leave the bar first so Frank wouldn't think she was going to meet him. Lori would wait for a little while, then drive to the hotel.

Trevor went back to his hotel, took a shower, turned on the television, and contemplated the events of the evening. He was thinking the chances of Lori showing up were about fifty-fifty. Frank could catch her on the way out and insist on giving her a ride to her place. If this happened, she would be afoot. She could end up too drunk to function. In any event, her inebriation may serve as an excellent excuse for Frank to make sure she behaved properly.

Trevor could have gotten her phone number to guarantee their connection, but he really didn't care if she showed or not. On one hand, if she showed up, it could be quite entertaining. But on the other hand, it had already been a fun-filled evening. Trevor went to sleep and Lori didn't arrive. It had been a very entertaining evening interacting with the locals.

The next day Jim and Trevor helped turn grapes into wine. The grapes were tested in the field for sugar content. If they had the correct amount of sugar, they were picked and trucked to the processing plant. They were then smashed and put through processing. Then the juice from the grapes was stored in oak barrels for a specific period before it was bottled and sold. The whole process was very time-consuming and quite interesting.

In the evening, Trevor and Jim's family went downtown for a nice meal at one of their favorite restaurants. They wanted to drink specific wines that they had processed, so they brought three different types. Trevor learned that it was common in this area for people to bring their own wine. He always thought it was bad manners to bring your own drink but found out that it is customary for people to bring their own wine in this area. In return they had to pay a corking fee for the privilege of drinking their wine at the restaurant. The fee was usually fifteen dollars, but could be as much as seventy-five dollars in very swanky places.

Most of the dinner party didn't stay out late because they had to get up early in the morning and get back to making wine. After dinner, Trevor made his journey back to his quaint hotel on the outskirts of town. He didn't have to get up early, so he could stay out as late as he liked. He could go back to the plant whenever he felt like it. There, he was just an observer who helped when he could.

Since the bar was so entertaining the night before, he decided to check it out again. Maybe Lori would be there. He would find out what happened to her the night before.

It was Saturday night, so it was a different crowd than the night before. There wasn't one familiar face from yesterday's gathering. Friday night seemed to be locals, but now it looked like travelers or out of town folks. It wasn't crowded and the juke box was plugged with some of Trevor's favorites. "Hotel California" played first. Of course, people visiting from out of state had to play that one. "Pumped up Kicks" played and "What's Up," was next.

There were two couples dancing. One of the couples was a very nice-looking pair. They looked like they could be of Scandinavian descent. They looked close in age, possibly in their late thirties. Trevor thought they made a good-looking couple. The female was extraordinarily beautiful with a perfect body. She was definitely model material.

Trevor ordered a drink, listened to music, and watched people dance. He began thinking he had made a wonderful choice of places to stay. The good-looking couple started noticing him and began showing off for him. They were doing turns like country dancers, although it was obvious they were not. They were just having fun making shit up. Trevor was amused by their antics and began smiling and laughing at them. It was later in the evening and these folks probably had several drinks by now.

For mutual amusement, strangers seemed to enjoy starting conversations and joking with Trevor. He enjoyed meeting interesting folks and sharing humorous banter. His motorcycle buddies told him people gravitated towards him because he appeared approachable. He was in his element.

Eventually, the good-looking couple finished dancing. When they left the dance floor, they walked straight over to Trevor and said hello. They acted as if they were Trevor's long-lost friends. After introducing themselves, Trevor found out they were there for a wedding. They were from Boston and a friend of theirs was getting married to someone whose family owned a local winery.

The man seemed a bit surly at first, and Trevor didn't know how to take him. As they continued their conversation, he told Trevor his companion was his sister. Automatically, Trevor did not believe they were brother and sister. When you meet people in a bar, they will often misrepresent the relationship between them and their partner for various reasons. Sometimes people do it just for amusement. Trevor put them through a line of questioning and told them he didn't believe they were brother and sister. The couple immediately pulled out their driver's licenses and eventually proved to Trevor that they were in fact brother and sister. This was good news because the sister (Susan) was very attractive and certainly available.

Trevor had noticed bras hanging from the ceiling of the bar. The patrons informed him that ladies would take their bras off and show their breasts. The bra was then hung from the ceiling as a souvenir.

Susan certainly had nice looking breasts. This would be a challenge. The conversation continued as they went outside and looked at Trevor's motorcycle. Susan mentioned that she would like to show up at the wedding on a motorcycle. Things were starting to look good for Trevor as the evening progressed with talking, drinking, and dancing. They were having a great time.

Susan's brother, Rich, was still a little snarky, and every once in a while, he would make a comment about politics or other things that didn't suit Trevor. Trevor made himself a personal challenge to convince Susan to remove her bra and show her breasts. She lived clear across the country, was on vacation, and nobody knew her. This could work out.

As things progressed, Trevor mentioned that Susan should leave her bra as a travel memento. She balked and talked about how expensive it was. She said she wanted to wear it to the wedding the following day. Trevor could tell she was up for the challenge but wanted a little convincing. He told her he would buy her a new one and that they could easily locate a store that sells bras.

Then Trevor said, "There is no time like the present," and "This time will never come again." To further lighten up the situation, Trevor teased her about her Boston accent.

With a little verbal persuasion, she was up to the task. She unfastened her bra and took it off. She actually removed her bra without taking her shirt off. She then pulled up her shirt and showed her breasts to the bartender. She was too embarrassed to show them to Trevor. The bartender knew who convinced Susan to show her breasts and with perfect timing, he told her she had to show them to Trevor also. What a great bartender he was! They were nice sized, round, natural, perfect breasts with large areolas and perky nipples. Susan's breasts were definitely voluptuous gifts from the gods. Trevor wanted to investigate them further. The party continued, but there was one glitch. What to do with Rich?

When the bar closed, Susan wanted a ride on the back of Trevor's motorcycle. At two in the morning after drinking, Trevor agreed to give her a ride. After all, she had really nice breasts and Trevor would have done about anything to investigate them further. There was only one helmet, so Trevor put the helmet on Susan. California has a helmet law that requires all motorcycle riders to wear helmets.

When they told Rich they would see him back at his hotel, he would not have anything to do with letting his sister and Trevor out of his sight. As Trevor and Susan left the parking lot, Rich pulled up behind them in his rental car. Away they went, only one rider with a helmet, flying down the road on a motorcycle at two-thirty in the morning. Rich was in hot pursuit. To add to the challenge, it was a strange town and they had been drinking all night. Susan hadn't ridden on a motorcycle and began shifting around, throwing the motorcycle off balance. They were zooming around corners and flying down the straight-aways.

Losing Rich was not an easy task. He was relentless as they went down the interstate one way, hit an interchange, and went back the opposite direction until they hit another interchange. They then took a frontage road and went through a residential area. Eventually, Rich was nowhere to be seen.

By this time Susan needed to use a restroom, which made a perfect excuse to stop by Trevor's hotel room. They headed through town and wound their way down the side roads. They had to stay where Rich couldn't see them. Susan and Rich were staying at a hotel about three quarters of a mile from Trevor's. Luckily, Rich didn't know which hotel Trevor was staying at.

Trevor parked the motorcycle in front of the hotel and locked the helmet in the trunk. The room was a small one on the first floor and the close quarters were perfect for this situation. In order to get to the restroom, you had to walk right between the bed and the wall.

Susan went into the restroom, and Trevor positioned himself on the bed so he was in perfect position for her to sit next to him when she came out. When she went into the restroom, she left the door ajar, just enough that Trevor could hear the sound of her tinkling in the toilet and the sound of relief when she finished. He was only sitting a few feet away. As she came out of the restroom, Trevor asked her to have a seat next to him. They talked for a moment but they both wanted to do more than talk.

Susan was actually a beautician by trade. She had fine auburn hair with blonde streaks and it was attractively cut at shoulder length. At this point, the most distinguishing feature Trevor noticed was the soft look of her skin. He had noticed her skin earlier when he helped her put on the motorcycle helmet. Her skin looked so soft and delicate it made him excited just looking at it. He thought about how soft her skin felt when his hand had gently brushed her neck while fastening the motorcycle helmet strap for her.

As he was noticing her skin, she leaned in and they kissed. Susan was a good kisser with lips that were not too full and not too thin. She knew how to work them in the most sensuous of ways. They kissed for a while until Trevor thought about how sensuous her neck was. He started kissing her on the neck. Trevor knew of a certain spot on the neck that is extremely sensitive to women.

It is an erogenous zone that all women seem to possess. This area is so sensuous he can give women goose bumps by lightly kissing it.

Susan had the softest, smoothest, most sensuous neck imaginable. Sure enough, he kissed her on the neck, located the erogenous zone, and kissed it lightly. Goose bumps appeared on Susan's arms. Trevor located the erogenous zone on the other side of her neck. He kissed her on that side of her neck and again, goose bumps appeared on her arms. For a while he would kiss her on one side of her neck then he would switch and kiss her on the other side. He did this for a while until he was sure it was time to go to the next level.

He moved his kisses further down and his hands moved further up. Getting Susan to leave her bra at the bar had been a splendid move. Susan was definitely excited. She made sensual moaning sounds of approval. Her excitement was obvious as Trevor caressed her protruding nipples. Now she even had goose bumps on the undersides of her breasts. It was time to move downtown.

As a teenager, Trevor had learned to take it slow. When he was younger, he tried to get inside the pants at this point. He soon learned it is better to fool around on the outside before moving indoors. So, Trevor moved his hand downtown as they laid down on the bed. He was feeling her excitement and warmth as she started to make small whimpering sounds. Susan mentioned that she hadn't had sex in a long time. Trevor was thinking she was telling the truth.

All of a sudden, the sound of an automobile horn exploded just outside Trevor's hotel room. The sound of an automobile horn blasting in front of your hotel room door at three-thirty in the morning is not something you can easily ignore. There was a hotel full of people trying to sleep. Rich was parked directly in front of Trevor's hotel room while he was continuously pressing on his automobile horn. It wasn't just the people on the first floor trying to sleep. The rooms on the second and third floor were fully occupied also. A normal person might start by honking their horn intermittently. Rich was not normal, plus, he had been drinking all night. He pressed down on the horn non-stop. It doesn't matter how well your love making is going—a car horn blaring outside your door makes it very difficult to proceed. The fact that you know the blaring horn is waking everyone in the hotel makes it even more difficult.

Susan walked out and talked to Rich. He told her he would not stop honking until she got in the car. When she was done talking to him and walking back towards the hotel room, he began to continually push on the horn. Susan gave Trevor a hug, climbed into Rich's car, and off they went.

To find Trevor's motorcycle, Rich must have searched every hotel parking lot in the area. Trevor lay in bed waiting for a knock on the door. He was expecting a very displeased hotel clerk to inform him he would need to find somewhere else to sleep for the night and probably the rest of the week. The knock didn't come and nobody said a word about the blare of the horn in the middle of the night.

Trevor was amazed that Rich would go to such an extent to keep his sister away from him. Although Rich may have been over-protective, it was obvious he had a feeling of unconditional love for his sister.

Trevor surmised that men who have sisters develop a broader understanding of how women relate to others. Women study men with the utmost of scrutiny. One of the primary characteristics a women will observe in a man is how desperate he appears. If it appears he is trying hard to circulate or hitting on many women, they will label him as desperate or just trying to get laid. Desperation does not look good on either sex.

Chapter 4

Kristy and Katy

Now that Trevor was a single man, he became very nomadic, continued to tour by motorcycle, play golf, and look for a new place to live.

When Trevor saw Kristy for the first time, he was totally taken with her. As he entered the restaurant, he had noticed her talking to three young fellows sitting at a table. When he walked past the table, he noticed another woman, whose name was Katy. He had met and briefly visited with Katy in the past. He walked over to say hello.

Katy and her friend Shelly were sitting at a table drinking beer. Shelly worked at one of the most exclusive golf courses in the area, so Trevor bought her a drink and went to work on obtaining an invitation to play the course. Shelly was a large lady wearing a straw hat, and she was not attractive by any means. She seemed to like Trevor, though. Trevor wondered why big, heavy ladies were attracted to him, as he was only five feet seven inches tall and in good physical condition. Anyway, he was well on his way to securing a golf game at a private, exclusive course.

Little did he know, Kristy (the gorgeous woman he had seen when he entered the restaurant) was an old high school friend of Shelly and Katy's. Kristy had come to visit Shelly and was catching an airplane back to the Midwest early the next morning.

When Kristy finished visiting with the three young gentlemen, she came over to the table. Trevor looked at Kristy and Kristy looked at Trevor. Kristy asked the other two women why they hadn't locked Trevor down and if they were dating him. Kristy said she didn't want to offend the other women, but why hadn't someone locked him down?

Trevor studied Kristy. She looked just like a younger version of his mother. She had the same nose, high cheek bones, facial shape, and hair. Her body and height were also like a younger version of Trevor's mother. She was what you might imagine a petite Irish beauty to look like. She had auburn hair, blue eyes, and a mischievous smile. To Trevor, she was the most attractive woman he had ever met. There is something undeniably attractive about a woman who resembles your mother.

Kristy was giddy and made no bones about how attracted she was to Trevor. She told Trevor her husband had died.

Trevor's response was, "You didn't poison him, did you?"

She laughed and explained that he died of an uncommon and strange illness. She didn't mention that they had divorced several years before he died. I guess it sounds better to tell prospective dates that your husband died rather than you got divorced, then he died. There is not much you can do about your husband dying, but a divorce is like a black mark on your record.

They conversed for a while and Kristy left for the restroom. While she was gone, Shelly told Trevor that he didn't want anything to do with Kristy. Trevor asked why.

Shelly said, "Kristy is a hot mess."

Trevor replied, "Kristy is very cute."

Shelly agreed. Trevor wondered if Kristy had problems, or if Shelly was trying to cut her out because she wanted him. Already, Trevor's brain may not have been functioning correctly.

When Kristy returned from the restroom, Trevor asked her if she would like to see his motorcycle. He took her by the hand and they went out the back door. He told her she could sit on it. She crawled upon the motorcycle and pretended to drive it. She seemed fun!

When they went back inside, they stopped in the hallway and sat on a windowsill. Kristy told Trevor she had only been with two men in her life, her husband and her boyfriend of six years. Trevor explained that she looked like a young version of his mother and that he was extremely attracted to her. They kissed, then they kissed some more. When they got back to the table, Kristy's friends began teasing the two lovebirds.

Katy said she had a business just down the street and she would open up the doors so they could have sex. She mentioned she had some big reclining chairs that would work quite nicely. Trevor agreed. He thought it was a very good idea. Kristy was not game. Kristy and Trevor visited for a while and exchanged phone numbers. Kristy had to catch an airplane early the next morning and Trevor was late for a dinner engagement. They reluctantly parted and said goodbye.

Maybe good chemistry is the key to a long-term relationship.

Chapter 5

Stranded

Trevor was looking forward to playing golf, hiking, and meeting the locals in Southern California. He had stayed winters in the Coachella Valley but hadn't been there when it was warmer. In one of Trevor's former stays, he had met a beautiful woman named Kristy. Now he had arranged to meet her in the Coachella Valley.

Before leaving home, Trevor had his motorcycle checked out by the service department. He made sure the oil was changed and that it was caught up on the service schedule. There had been a recall concerning locking of the rear brakes. He had the recall checked and they assured him his motorcycle was well within the acceptable parameters. He even had the brake fluid changed so everything would be perfect. You don't want to end up stranded on a motorcycle in the middle of nowhere when you are traveling solo.

This trip would be extra fun because Trevor had a new state of the art touring motorcycle with heated seats, heated grips, surround sound, navigation, CB radio, and anti-lock brakes. It was the Rolls Royce of motorcycles. He would be traveling in style.

Trevor left for Southern California in May. It was nighttime and he was about halfway up a mountain pass when snow started falling. He thought about turning around and going back but turning a motorcycle around in the snow on a steep incline would be a problem. Motorcycles are not stable on snow or ice, and it soon became as much trouble to go back as it was to go forward. As snow hit the pavement, it was sticking on the sides and middle of the road, but not where car tires were running. This left Trevor a path to follow either in the right tire track or the left tire track.

The snow became heavier and heavier as he went up the mountain. As he climbed the mountain, he noticed the outside temperatures were dropping. The temperature was sitting around freezing. He decided moving forward was his best option as turning around would be a huge problem. Then he started thinking about going down the other side of the pass. If the temperatures dropped, the snow would freeze on the road. Going downhill on an icy road would be extremely difficult since braking on ice would certainly send the motorcycle into a slide. Just steering the motorcycle would become tricky. Sometimes you are just caught between a rock and a hard spot. All you can do is the best you can. For the most part, turning around was not in Trevor's nature. They say good decisions don't make interesting stories.

Trevor decided to keep going as long as he could. If he got to the top of the pass, the temperatures would be colder and snow would become ice. As he went down the mountain the temperatures would warm up. He meticulously picked his way to the top of the pass. Then painstakingly, found his way down the other side of the mountain. A trip over the pass would usually be about forty minutes but it took him several hours.

It was late at night and his arrival was much later than expected. He hadn't been able to call anyone because he was entirely occupied with getting over the mountain pass. Trevor met his friend in a town located at the bottom of the mountain. After they ate dinner, Trevor's friend walked up to the cash register and one of the customers told him the pass was closed because of snow.

Trevor wanted to say, "It wasn't that bad, I came over it on a motorcycle."

The next morning, Trevor planned to leave for Southern California. He wanted to make it to the Coachella Valley in two days. He would stay overnight just south of Salt Lake City and the following day he would arrive at his destination. Traveling in the dark is the most dangerous time to travel by motorcycle. Animals on the road, combined with a lack of visibility, can make it quite treacherous. That is why Trevor planned to leave early in the morning.

Morning came and it was 35 degrees and snowing. Trevor decided he wouldn't leave until 8:30 a.m., but when that time came, it was still 35 degrees and snowing. He and his friend went out for breakfast, thinking it would be warmer in a couple of hours.

Ten thirty came and it was still 35 degrees and snowing. Traveling on a motorcycle at 35 degrees is very cold when you figure in the wind chill factor. The weather forecast for traveling south was good so Trevor put on his long johns and left for Southern California.

The pavement was wet so Trevor had to be very vigilant about watching for icy spots on the road. The travel of cars kept snow from turning into ice. After all it was 35 degrees, not quite cold enough to freeze. It might be cold and snowy, but it was better than coming over the pass the night before. Sometimes you just have to test your limits to find out what you can and cannot do.

The weather got nicer and nicer throughout the day. Trevor stayed overnight and left for Palm Springs the next day. He went through Las Vegas and took a cut across through the Mojave Desert. The road that cuts across from Las Vegas to Palm Springs is a nice motorcycle ride and approximately 200 miles of hot, desolate desert travel. About the only stop is Amboy, which is halfway between Palm Springs and Las Vegas. You can't get gas or food there, but it is an interesting stop since entire movies have been filmed there. Trevor always liked to stop there because it was novel and a halfway point between Las Vegas and Palm Springs. Whenever he took this cut across, he thought about how horrible it would be to break down coming across that stretch of deserted road. It is hot, not many cars pass by, there isn't any cell service, and it is miles from nowhere. Yesterday he was dealing with 35 degrees and snow, and now it was a scorching 104 degrees as he traversed the Mojave Desert.

Trevor stopped at Amboy, shut off his motorcycle, and walked around to stretch his legs. He gave the motorcycle a good inspection and checked his gauges to make sure all was well.

He continued to enjoy a nice ride across the desert until he came to the town of Twenty-Nine Palms, which lies just northeast of Palm Springs. It was kind of nice to see civilization after coming that far across a lonesome desert highway.

Trevor spotted a Walgreens store and remembered he couldn't find his reading glasses earlier. He went into Walgreens, bought a pair of reading glasses, walked out to the motorcycle and started it up. When he let out the clutch, the motorcycle wouldn't move forward and the rear wheel would not turn. In order to check the wheel for movement, he put the motorcycle on its center stand, put it in neutral, and tried to spin the wheel. It would not move. It was obvious the rear brakes were locked.

This could have happened coming across the Mojave Desert in the middle of nowhere or a hundred miles from anywhere with no cell service at 104 degrees. As luck would have it, there was a dealership that sold and fixed his type of motorcycle about two blocks away. What are the odds? Trevor called a towing company and they hauled the motorcycle to the dealership.

Now Trevor was stuck in Twenty-Nine Palms, California, with no transportation. The dealership had to order parts, so it would take five days to fix the motorcycle. Twenty-Nine Palms had absolutely nothing that interested Trevor. The town consisted of military grunts and elderly people. He stayed there for one night and decided one night was more than enough, so the next day he boarded a bus to Palm Springs. He planned to stay there until the motorcycle was fixed. There was a lot to do in the Coachella Valley, and he could always catch a taxi.

In Palm Springs, Trevor rented a cheap hotel room and began searching for monthly rentals. This was a slow, difficult process, as it was expensive and unhandy to travel by taxi.

Trevor decided to call Katy, since she was about the only person he knew in the area. Katy explained that she planned to take her mother out for dinner since it was her eighty-second birthday. She invited Trevor to accompany them for the celebration.

This would be fun! What a fantastic break from motorcycle travel and rental searches. It would be great to see them again. Trevor had met Katy's mother in an interesting turn of events. One Sunday afternoon, he was sitting at a bar when he noticed an elderly lady sitting in the restaurant area watching him. She kept looking at him so he lined his head behind the post that was between him and her. This way she couldn't see him and he couldn't see her. He was acting like he didn't notice her staring at him. Eventually the elderly lady told the bartender she would like to buy Trevor a drink. The bartender said he couldn't do that. Well, with a little convincing, he finally agreed to complete the transaction. When a lady buys a man a drink, he is definitely going to thank her for the drink. Especially a little old lady who is old enough to be your grandmother.

When the drink arrived, Trevor thanked her for it. The little old lady walked over and asked Trevor if she could sit by him. Introductions and pleasantries were exchanged and casual conversation ensued. Trevor was polite and very considerate as she was an elderly lady who deserved respect. She looked like an Italian Betty White with dark eyes. Her hair was styled and perfectly colored. In fact, she had just come from the beauty shop. She was primped, styled and prepared for the hunt.

During the conversation, Trevor deduced that the elderly lady was Katy's mother. What are the odds? Trevor actually enjoyed the conversation but sensed that exiting as soon as his drink was finished would be the most prudent method of escape. As Trevor finished his drink, he explained that he needed to go. The elderly lady informed Trevor that she didn't have a car and needed a ride home. Trevor had come on his motorcycle and it wouldn't suffice to take a little, old, drunk lady home. Here was a drunken elderly lady who said she needed a ride home. Who could refuse to help her? He couldn't just leave her on the street.

Trevor decided it would be best to have Katy handle her mother's situation so he walked the elderly lady to her daughter's store. As Trevor and Katy's mother entered the store, the look on Katy's face was priceless. Trevor explained the situation, but Katy had no sympathy for her mother's predicament. She was emphatic that her mother was entirely capable of getting home on her own. Trevor mentioned getting her a taxi but Katy explained that she would probably get the taxi driver to drop her at a bar along the way. Trevor told Katy he would take her home if he had access to an automobile. He was thinking Katy might offer her car. Katy laughed and told Trevor he could take her home if he really wanted to. She was insinuating that Trevor would take her home and sleep with her.

After the insinuation, Trevor thought it best to let family matters be handled by family. As he walked away, Katy's mother was standing on the sidewalk asking him to take her dancing. That was the last time Trevor had seen Katy or her mother. This would be an interesting dinner.

By the time Trevor arrived, Katy and her mother (Gina) were already at the restaurant. This must have been Katy and Gina's hangout as Trevor had met each of them for the first time at this same establishment. The hostess sat them at a high table. One side of the table was up against a wall, which left three sides to sit at. Trevor sat at one side of the table with the wall to his left. Gina sat directly across from him, with the wall to her right. Katy sat facing the wall with her mother on her right and Trevor on her left. The bar stools were comfortable with high backs. Trevor had previously enjoyed conversation and banter with both Katy and Gina. Although he was looking forward to dining and visiting with them, this was going to be the perfect opportunity to find out more about Katy's friend Kristy.

Katy was always thinking one step ahead. She was a good thinker with a perceptive personality. She was sharp enough to know Trevor was going to pump her for information about Kristy. That is probably why she owned a thriving business that was very successful. In contrast, when Trevor met Kristy, she was unemployed. Although she had a college education, Kristy had previously worked as a receptionist/bookkeeper in a doctor's office. Katy was well kept and in good physical condition. She had dark eyes and olive skin. She was attractive but not by any means as attractive as Kristy.

Kristy, on the other hand, was exactly Trevor's type. During dinner, Katy explained that her husband had passed away a couple of years ago. She also indicated that they had an excellent relationship and that she still wasn't over her husband. They had been married since their late teens so it wasn't easy for her emotionally. By the expression and manner in which Katy described her marriage, Trevor believed it was probably a very caring, close marriage. Katy had a great sense of humor and appeared to have it all together. Gina mentioned that a suitor had recently proposed to Katy. Evidently Katy had told the suitor that she could not sleep with him because there would be three people in bed.

This was her way of indicating she was not over her husband.

As Trevor listened to Katy talk about how wonderful her relationship had been with her deceased spouse, it made him wonder if the relationship was really that good or if she just chose to remember it that way. It occurred to Trevor that widows always tell about how wonderful their relationship was with their deceased spouse. Maybe they think it makes them sound like they are good prospects for future relationships. Anyway, there isn't a spouse to tell the other side of the story.

They began dinner with wine. After all, it was a celebration of Gina's birthday. The three were enjoying a fun filled dinner full of conversation and laughter when Trevor commented that Gina looked very good for her age.

Gina looked across the table and fired back at him "For my age, what do you mean for my age? I either look good or I don't look good." She was very indignant and extremely hostile.

Trevor began searching for the right words to heal his faux pas but all he could think to say was, "I didn't mean it that way."

The tension lingered for a while but after several glasses of wine and much conversation, all was forgiven. Trevor was visiting with Katy and trying to learn about her relationship with Kristy. He became very conscientious about how he spoke as he didn't want it to appear obvious that he was bleeding Katy for information about Kristy. As he was visiting with Katy, he started to feel something moving up and down the calf of his leg. Katy was engrossed in conversation, talking about how she graduated from the same high school as Kristy and Shelly.

As Trevor was listening to Katy, he noticed a mischievous expression on Gina's face. As he put two and two together, he realized that Gina was running her foot up and down his leg.

After several glasses of wine, they were sitting at a table and Gina was running her foot up and down the calf of Trevor's leg. Katy was talking away and Trevor was trying to keep a straight face. One thing was for certain, Trevor would never, ever, tell a lady she looked good for her age again. If you tell someone they look good *for their age* it is not a compliment!

They began to close the restaurant and it was time to go. Trevor was afoot and needed to get a taxi. Gina would be staying at Katy's house, so she and Katy would be going back to Katy's place. After a little discussion, Katy invited Trevor to her house for a nightcap. After all, it was Gina's birthday celebration.

Katy's apartment was kind of long and narrow like a row home. It was comfortable with two bedrooms, a dining area and couch, it was well stocked with alcohol. Gina was tired and immediately went to bed. Trevor and Katy had several night caps one after the other and eventually switched from wine to beer. It was hot outside and the swimming pool looked very inviting. There was some discussion about skinny dipping.

Katy left for the restroom and when she returned, she found Trevor naked in the pool. He tried to get Katy to join him but all she did was laugh. Trevor was intoxicated enough he didn't notice the neighbors could see him if they looked out their window. He swam for a while and eventually Katy brought him a towel. The next thing they knew they were both naked, rolling around on the living room floor, hugging, kissing and playing around. Katy had great skin, nice hair, a good figure, and the body of a woman in her late twenties. Each woman has a certain physical quality that sets her apart from others. It can be a quality of sexiness that is not really describable. The quality can be her breasts, smile, expression, butt, stomach, or legs. Katy's redeeming characteristic was not any of the aforementioned, but she had a very fine quality that only a few will ever appreciate. She was intelligent, so she knew what to do and when to do it.

She would make someone a terrific partner. She just wasn't Trevor's type.

When things settled down and they felt relaxed, Katy mentioned feeling guilty about being intimate with Trevor when her friend was coming to see him in a few days. Trevor knew that in the afterglow of love making, the walls come down and there is a period of uninhibited openness and honesty. Trevor concluded that this may be a good time to find out what Katy really thought of

Kristy.

He asked her, "What do you think of Kristy?"

She replied, "She seems a little dingy." When she realized she had said something negative that could be repeated, she recovered with, "I don't really know her."

Trevor had caught her at the right moment to get an honest opinion. He understood *that people would say they do not know someone when they don't want to give an honest opinion.* It was an out that Trevor had used many times.

Morning was not as awkward as it usually is in this type of situation. By the time Gina woke up, Trevor was resting on the couch and Katy was asleep in her bedroom. Katy had to go to work soon, so she quickly got ready and took Trevor back to his hotel. It had been a fun-filled birthday party.

In a couple of days, Trevor received a call from the motorcycle shop indicating that the work had been completed on the motorcycle. It was ready to go. He called Katy and she agreed to give him a ride to the motorcycle shop. During the trip they agreed they would like to do a replay of the birthday celebration.

As it turned out, the bill for fixing the motorcycle was covered under recall and the factory warranty. The only out of pocket expense was getting it hauled to the dealer. First of all, Trevor felt lucky that he broke down next to a dealership and not out in the middle of the desert. Secondly, he was fortunate that the expenses for getting it fixed were fully covered and the factory warranty was only a few days away from expiration.

Most of all he felt extremely fortunate to have met and enjoyed the company of Katy and Gina. It was the human connection and openness that Trevor valued and enjoyed. In the afterglow, Katy had told Trevor that Kristy was dingy, and Kristy and Katy's mutual friend had told him she was a hot mess. Were these ladies trying to cut Kristy out of the picture or was something wrong with her?

One thing was for certain. Trevor would never again tell anyone they looked good *for their age.*

Chapter 6

Porsche vs. Motorcycle

It was much easier for Trevor to look for a rental now that he had wheels. Rentals were plentiful and cheaper in the summer months at about half what they would be during the high season. Eventually he found one that was conveniently located. He could go north, south, east, or west for golf and entertainment. The negative side was that he had to ride the motorcycle to get to any of these activities. There really wasn't anything located within walking distance.

The Coachella Valley consists of nine municipalities, with the most notorious one being Palm Springs. It was one of the earliest areas to be settled and is probably the most widely recognized because a lot of movie stars settled there. Each municipality has its own unique character. For example, Rancho Mirage seems to be old money. Indian Wells is new money, and Palm Desert has become a playground for the wealthy.

The altitude in the valley is about sea level and a portion is actually a little below sea level. The San Jacinto Mountains run along the west side of the valley and rise to 10,800 feet. At times, winds can be an issue. The winds come across the Pacific Ocean, which lies to the west of the mountain range. When they reach the mountain, they sweep up the side of the mountain until they are deflected off the atmosphere. This results in the winds slamming down on the other side of the mountain (Coachella Valley) in full force. The wind in that area is evidenced by the plethora of wind turbines located along I-10.

Upon arriving at his rental, Trevor met his new neighbor. His neighbor was very proud of the brand-new car he had just purchased. He showed Trevor his car and they visited for a few minutes. Trevor mentioned he was going grocery shopping but would shop light, because he needed to pack his groceries on the motorcycle. The neighbor handed him the keys to his new car and asked him to take it. He said the only thing he wanted him to do was shut off the air conditioner before turning the car off. Trevor always did this anyway, so it was an easy request.

Trevor was amazed that his new neighbor gave him the keys to his brand-new car after knowing him for just a few minutes. Not only could he get a car full of groceries, but it was 110 degrees and the car would be more comfortable. To repay his neighbors, Trevor made sure to buy a twelve pack of beer. He planned on having his most hospitable neighbor and his wife over for drinks.

Trevor settled into playing golf, riding motorcycle, and hiking. Life was good, but he needed to maintain a social life. Kristy had agreed to come and stay while he was in the valley. He had kept in contact with her from time to time, so he decided to give her a call. She had always been excited and positive, but now she was apprehensive about coming. She said she was nervous and scared. Trevor assured her she didn't have to stay with him. She could have her own place or stay with her friends. He just wanted to get to know her. The trip would be like killing two birds with one stone. She could visit her friends and get to know him, also.

The next day Trevor called Kristy to see about her coming and again, she was apprehensive. The more Trevor tried to convince her to come, the more she made excuses. Trevor could have traveled anywhere but had chosen to come here because it was convenient for Kristy. It was the place she had chosen to meet and she had always been very positive and excited before.

Trevor finally became so exasperated with her he just asked her point blank if she was coming or not. Yes or no. She said she was not coming. Trevor told her he was sorry to hear that and ended the phone call. After all, this was what he was looking forward to—getting to know Kristy. He was a proud man and felt let down. He told himself he would never talk to her again.

Well, he had his rental for the month. He was enjoying golf and going on some great motorcycle adventures. Now that Kristy was out of the game, there wouldn't be anything for anyone to feel guilty about. Trevor called Katy and they decided to go for drinks.

The next night they were back at the hangout where they first met, where Trevor had met Katy's mother and where they had celebrated Gina's birthday. It was a restaurant/bar combination, and Trevor enjoyed the atmosphere. They were seated at the center of a u-shaped bar with tables behind them. It was a weeknight, so there weren't a lot of patrons. Trevor and Katy laughed, joked, and conversed until the restaurant started closing.

Katy mentioned she had to work the next day and needed to get going. Trevor mentioned that he should go with her, but she insisted she wouldn't be up for work the next day if he went along. They both knew they would be up all night. Nevertheless, Trevor tried to convince her to take him home. As Katy looked around the bar, she told Trevor he could have any of the women in the restaurant. Of course, Trevor's response was that they would not be her.

Trevor looked around and there were four nice looking women at one table. He surmised they were out of the question. *You can't separate one from the herd. You need to seek out the stragglers.* There might have been some men in the bar but Trevor didn't notice them. There was a nice-looking woman sitting two chairs down on the other side of Katy. He started to wonder if she was correct in her statement. Could he really have anyone in the restaurant?

Trevor walked Katy to the door, then exited to the restroom. As he was standing in front of the urinal looking down at the sanitary pellet, and he noticed his aim was a little off. He was weaving from side to side. As he was standing there targeting the pellet, he began pondering Katy's statement and a little smile came across his face. That was a very complimentary thing for Katy to say. Could he have anyone in the restaurant?

Upon exiting the restroom, Trevor walked by the four women sitting at a table on his left. They were in a heavy discussion. He knew it was impossible to cut one of them from the herd. To his right was the bar. As he walked around the bar in route to his seat, he noticed a straggler (woman sitting alone). She was watching the television, located behind the bar. A football game was on, so Trevor asked her if her team was winning. That was all it took to start the conversation.

A big smile crossed her face. It was the kind of smile that expressed naughty thoughts. It was not just the smile but the look in her eyes, her expression, manner, and demeanor, that let him know she was very interested in him. She gushed and asked Trevor about his girlfriend. He explained that Katy was a friend but not a girlfriend. He knew that *women favored a guy who was liked by other women, so having another woman of interest raised his value.* It would create competition and she would work harder for Trevor's attention. The conversation was easy and the drinks went down quickly. Trevor learned that she was a professional body builder and had a home in a gated community. Her house was located about halfway between the restaurant and his rental. They had a few drinks before the cleanup crew began cleaning the restaurant.

The bartenders insisted that Trevor and the body builder (Sara) should remain until they were finished cleaning. By now Trevor had developed a rapport with the bartenders and they were working in his best interest. Bartenders can be a very valuable asset when picking up women, so he didn't want to overstay his welcome. Trevor mentioned to Sara that they should go so the cleanup crew wouldn't have to clean up around them.

The town probably closed down early because the majority of the population is elderly. Many folks probably get up at 6:00 a.m. and go to bed by 8:00 p.m. This area can be very busy early in the day or evening, but by this time of night the streets were empty.

The town was pretty much closed at this time of night, so going home was about the only option. Trevor explained that he had a lot to drink and didn't like to ride a motorcycle after drinking that much. On the other hand, he wasn't about to leave the motorcycle in the lot overnight. Sara told Trevor she was in worse condition than him, however, she was going to drive home. That was a fact—she was more inebriated than he was.

Trevor told her he could make it to her place since it was halfway between the restaurant and his rental. Sara smiled as if to say, *Nice try, but you can't stay at my place.* Trevor asked her how she got to the bar and she explained that she drove her sports car. He could tell she was very proud of her car.

The conversation continued outside the bar. It went something like this: Which is the most agile and maneuverable in town, a Porsche or a motorcycle? Of course, Sara insisted her Porsche was, and Trevor insisted his motorcycle was. When push comes to shove, there is only one way to settle a debate such as this. The bet was on and the wager was placed. Trevor didn't know where Sara lived, only that it was about halfway between the restaurant and his place. If he didn't keep up with the Porsche, he would be out of the picture and she would be gone. On the other hand, if he could keep up with the Porsche, Sara had promised she would be his.

Both parties had too many drinks and shouldn't have been driving but there they were. The game of cat and mouse was set to begin. The Porsche was parked on the street in front of the restaurant and the motorcycle was parked behind the restaurant. Sara sat in her car waiting for Trevor to pull out onto the street. When the motorcycle entered the street, it would be Sara's cue to begin the race.

Trevor was thinking she would be a little careful because she had several drinks and would not want to get picked up for drunk driving. He was wrong! When the motorcycle entered the street, she punched the pedal to the metal. She knew the streets well and had no intention of losing the wager. She was a competitive body builder and a very competitive driver. Her honor and pride in her car were at stake. Her strategy was to do a lot of U-turns in hopes of losing the motorcycle.

The Porsche raced down the street and flipped a U-turn. It went down to the end of the street and took a left. After a couple of blocks, she took another U-turn. It was only five miles to Sara's house, but she wasn't headed straight to her place. She planned on losing Trevor by taking a long, indirect route. She headed down one street, back on another, and kept flipping U-turns.

She definitely had a good strategy! Flipping U-turns on two wheels after a night of drinking is not entirely sane; four wheels were a definite advantage. The race continued for some time, back and forth, U-turns, turning corners, and flying down the street. It was a ten-mile trip to get to a destination five miles away. If there wasn't a divider (curbing) in the center of the road, Trevor could hang back a little and take a short cut across the center line when Sara pulled a U-turn. This strategy considerably improved his ability to keep up. The adrenaline rush for both Trevor and Sara had to rank right up there with auto racing, sky diving, and bungee jumping. The thrill of the race, the risk of getting caught by the police, and the fact that they were going to have sex, if the motorcycle kept up, made it a thrill like no other.

Both Sara and Trevor were bundles of excitement by the time the game of cat and mouse came to an end at the entrance to Sara's gated community. The high-speed maneuvering had been a bonding experience. They had shared the thrill of the chase!

At the gate entrance, Sara pulled over to the right side of the entry allowing enough room for cars to pass between her car and the gate entry keypad. If a car happened to come along while they were parked, it would be able to go between the Porsche and the keypad and the driver would be able to reach out his window and operate the keypad. The guard station was located directly behind the keypad and was unattended at this time of night.

Trevor pulled his motorcycle in behind the Porsche and as he climbed off of the motorcycle, Sara exited her car. They came together alongside her car with an enormous hug and a passionate kiss. The game had been like foreplay. Both of them were having an adrenaline rush that resulted in a very passionate make out session. *Experts say that women kiss to increase bonding and men kiss to create or increased stimulation.*

At this point they were both stimulated and bonding. Trevor moved Sara's hair back, kissed her neck, and began searching for erogenous zones. Trevor soon discovered that Sara had very sensitive ear lobes. It may not be that her ear lobes were that sensitive but kissing and nuzzling them turned her on. Trevor was kissing her neck and nuzzling her ear lobes. As her breath pattern started to change, he could tell she was getting more and more excited. Trevor mentioned going to her house. Sara insisted that they should remain where they were. It appeared that having her didn't include having her in private. Maybe she could still be convinced.

Trevor had Sara pinned against the side of her car, kissing and caressing her. It was time to up the game and move to the next level. Trevor moved his hands inside of Sara's blouse and felt her well-shaped stomach and sides. She was sculpted. She acted as if it tickled as he moved his hands up and around her back so he could feel underneath her bra strap. She seemed to like it, so he unfastened her bra and moved his hand around to her breast. As his hand slid around the baby soft under side of her breast, he noticed that she was very sensitive there.

He softly caressed the underside of her breast while gently brushing her nipple. Sara's nipple was rock hard. Trevor then became curious as to whether her other breast was stimulated or not. As he moved his other hand from her butt to her other breast, he discovered that it was in need of attention. Now he had each of his hands up her blouse stimulating her breasts as he was passionately kissing her. Trevor was thinking that stimulating both breasts at the same time probably felt twice as good.

Every event seems to be about timing. A car pulled into the gate entrance between the Porsche and the guard shack. The guy in the car was one of Sara's neighbors and probably had a key fob he could use to open the gate, but nevertheless, he took the opportunity to stop and say hello to Sara. As he exchanged pleasantries, it was evident he had the hots for her and was pleased to break up the soiree.

As they were passing pleasantries, Trevor looked over at the guard shack and noticed a camera on the corner of the building. Sara and Trevor were being recorded or viewed by a video security service. So, what should he do now? If he told Sara about the camera, it would be the end of the make out session. If he continued making out with Sara it would be recorded and viewed by the security service.

When Sara's neighbor pulled through the gate, Trevor decided to do what any drunk, horny, excited man would do. He kept his mouth shut and didn't mention the cameras. Once again, Sara and Trevor began kissing and making out. It was time to step up the game. Trevor put his leg between hers and again she was pinned against the car. She seemed to enjoy it so he concluded that it was time to move to the next level. He slowly moved his hand in between his leg and the hot, wet area between her legs. He slowly started massaging her as she began writhing and moving her hips.

Trevor moved his hand up and unfastened her pants. He had easy access now as Sara moved back and forth making small whimpering sounds. Trevor continued kissing and massaging her until she eventually gasped and her knees buckled. It was a good thing Trevor offered her support by pinning her to the car. At this point her body was limp and relaxed.

Trevor discovered that if the stakes are high enough, a Porsche cannot out-maneuver a motorcycle.

He also realized that Katy had given him the confidence and incentive to seduce Sara. Even so, Trevor understood that *it is not just a matter of confidence that determines the success of an introduction, it is the art of being tactful and indirect.* Trevor thought of the time he asked a woman what kind of mileage her little red car got. When shopping at a grocery store, he had commented about a bracelet the checkout lady was wearing. With each of these ladies, Trevor had opened the floodgates of conversation by asking them about something they were obviously proud of. In each of these instances, he could have commented about how nice the ladies looked, which would have been a fatal error in opening a conversation. Asking Sara if her team was winning had been the perfect ice breaker.

The next time Trevor talked to Sara, he couldn't resist asking her if she ever noticed the security cameras at her gate entrance.

There may not be anything more attractive to a woman than a man who is attractive to other women. A man will raise his value if he keeps company with attractive, young, successful, ladies.

Chapter 7

Dinner Conversation

Lena

»

Lena was of Spanish descent and had grown up in Mexico. She had pretty brunette hair with natural blonde streaks. Her facial features were petite, along with a narrow nose and piercing dark eyes. Her appearance reminded Trevor of the pretty flamingo dancers he had seen in Mexico. Although she was a little plump, her sexy Spanish accent compensated for her extra ten pounds. Her accent was very similar to that of the actress Penelope Cruz.

As Trevor and Lena were sitting in the vehicle en route to a swanky Italian restaurant, they began discussing the menu and drinks. They talked about what they were hungry for and what they might order. They had been on several dates, and Trevor knew Lena enjoyed fine dining but more importantly, the best tequila. After they settled on what type of food they might order, Lena started talking about the types of tequila available at the restaurant. She was a tequila expert and appreciated the finest and most expensive tequila. Lena asked Trevor if the restaurant had a certain type of tequila that costs about twenty dollars a shot.

From past experience, Trevor knew it wouldn't be one shot and that each shot would lead to another. In his head, he started calculating the cost of the tequila. Then he started thinking about how much money he had already invested in dinner, drinks, and tequila on their previous dates. He concluded that he had invested close to a thousand dollars with absolutely no return on investment. It wasn't that Trevor minded spending the money, but there comes a time when a person gets a feeling that they are being used.

As Trevor was driving along, he looked over at Lena and said, "I don't mind buying dinners, but you have been as cold as a cucumber. There could come a time when a person feels like they are being used."

Lena said, "So, I have been as cold as a cucumber. I will use you."

Trevor didn't want to spoil the evening so he let the subject drop.

At the restaurant they ordered an exquisite meal with a perfect bottle of red wine. The restaurant had a fine selection of tequila, so it would be the best tequila along with chocolate cake for dessert. The two laughed, visited, and enjoyed a wonderful meal. They were sitting across from one another enjoying a decadent meal when a smile came across Lena's face as she gazed across the table littered with food and drink. She looked Trevor in the eyes and uttered in her sexy Spanish accent, "I want your sperms inside me."

As mentioned before, each woman has a bedroom quality that separates her from the rest. Later that evening, Trevor discovered that Lena had not only one, but two unique bedroom qualities. About every six months or so, Trevor enjoys a refresher on those qualities

Chapter 8

One Good Roundhouse

At this time of year, temperatures are very warm in the Coachella Valley. The high temperatures are about 110 to 115 degrees Fahrenheit. Many things are cheaper at this time when the weather is hot and the snowbirds have retreated to the North Country. A golf course that usually costs $200 to play can be on special for around twenty-five to thirty-five dollars. At these temperatures, only the very serious, crazy, or bargain golfers will be playing.

One morning Trevor was reading the newspaper and noticed an ad to play one of the high-end golf courses for twenty-five dollars. It was a course he would like to play, so he jumped at the opportunity to play it for a cheap price. Of course, to get the cheap price he had to play it in the hottest part of the day.

When Trevor initially started riding his motorcycle to the golf courses, he would wear athletic pants over the top of his golf shorts. When he arrived at the course, he would remove his athletic pants and his golf shorts would be underneath. After doing this many times, he eventually stopped wearing athletic pants and just rode to the course in his golf shorts. For the most part it seemed cooler with the wind blowing on his legs and up his shorts. It also cut out the hassle of putting on and taking off athletic pants.

Typically, golf courses have a big igloo-type water cooler about every third hole. The coolers are filled with ice and water. As the ice melts, it keeps the water cold for the duration of the game. Trevor brought a bottle of water with him. His plan was to drink the water in the bottle then continue filling it from the coolers. This way he would be able to drink cool water all day long.

Trevor was looking forward to a fun filled day of golf. He put his golf shorts on, grabbed his bottle of water, and mounted his motorcycle. He was anticipating an inexpensive round of golf on a high-end golf course.

It was a fifteen mile ride to get from his rental to the golf course. When he arrived, he had the course to himself. At a high temperature of 115 degrees, everyone else seemed to be smart enough to stay home. Trevor relished the idea of having the course to himself. He would be able to concentrate on his game and play at his own pace.

When Trevor registered for golf, the cashier told him the ice machine was broken. He didn't need ice, so he wasn't concerned about the ice machine not working. He had his bottle of water and there would be water coolers at every third tee box.

The course had a nice layout and a variety of characteristics that made it interesting to play. It was fun, but the bottle of water was empty by the second hole. At the end of the second hole, Trevor removed the cap on his water bottle, placed it under the spigot of the igloo cooler, and opened the water cooler valve. As the water made contact with the water bottle, it was so hot it distorted the plastic bottle as if it was placed next to a hot fire. Evidently there wasn't any ice in the coolers because the ice machine was broken. The intense, direct sunlight had heated the water to the extent that it instantly melted the water bottle upon contact. It was way too hot to drink. Evidently there hadn't been enough golfers to warrant a beverage cart, so it would be six holes of golf at 115-degree heat before Trevor would be able to get hydration at the club house.

Trevor enjoyed playing golf but was parched by the time he got to the club house. There he selected a couple bottles of Gatorade to keep him hydrated on the back nine. The problem was that there wasn't any ice in the golf cart cooler. After two holes of golf, one of the bottles of Gatorade was gone and the other was too warm to drink. Gatorade has a very sickening taste when it is warm.

Since there wasn't anyone playing golf in front or behind him, Trevor was able to play two balls for the rest of the day. Playing two balls took longer but he was able to get in some extra practice on the beautiful course. Trevor enjoyed his time on the course and played until he was extremely tired and thirsty. He was relying on getting hydrated and out of the heat when he got back to the club house, but by the time he got to the club house, it was closed. There were so few players, the workers had gone home. There wasn't anywhere to get out of the sun, and there wasn't anything to drink.

Trevor parked the golf cart and mounted his motorcycle, thinking he would stop by a little wine bar about halfway between the course and his rental. There he could get a cold drink and reprieve from the sun. He didn't have pants on, just his golf shorts. When he was riding down the road when it was 80 or 90 degrees outside, shorts felt good, but at 115 degrees, the direct sunlight was scorching his legs and it was very unpleasant.

As Trevor pulled up to the wine bar, he noticed his head was aching. He realized this was an early warning sign of heat stroke. He walked up and pulled on the door of the wine bar, and it wouldn't open. The wine bar was closed for the season.

He headed for a beer garden about a mile and a half down the road. By the time he got to the beer garden, he had a throbbing headache, felt drained, and was dehydrated. The beer garden was a welcome sight. He was able to get fruit drinks, food, and ice water to replenish his system. Although he hadn't eaten since breakfast, he wasn't hungry. There were televisions with football games and cheering fans. It was cool inside and the air conditioners seemed like they were turned down to 60 degrees. Trevor stayed at the beer garden for several hours before he felt like he had recovered enough to continue the ride home. He stayed there until dark, so the ride home would be much cooler.

Trevor had been the recipient of cheap golf on an exquisite golf course. It may have been cheap but in the end, it was not a bargain. The physical effects lasted for three days.

Once Trevor had recovered from bargain golf, it was time to socialize. He had been practicing at the driving range and had a nice lunch with a golf instructor. On his way home, he decided to stop by a swanky place for a glass of wine. After all, it was happy hour and wine would be half price.

This was not a place Trevor knew well. It was a popular hangout for professional tennis players when they came to town for the BNP Paribas Tennis

Championship in Indian Wells. The BNP Paribas Open is the largest tennis tournament in the United States with 438,000 people in attendance in 2016.

The only other time Trevor had been in this establishment was during the Paribas. He had drank, laughed, joked, and had a big time hanging out with some of the biggest names in tennis. Trevor didn't know a lot of big names in tennis, so they were just people to him. Maybe the ladies had thought Trevor was a big-time tennis player also. He was on a roll with the ladies, so the tennis pros started teasing him about being good looking and accomplished with the ladies. Before the night was over, he had established a nickname among some of the most skilled tennis players in the world, "Wingman." Trevor had so much fun the last time he was there, he wondered what kind of adventure awaited him now.

Since Trevor was returning from golf, he was wearing shorts, flip flops, and a golf shirt. Most people in the restaurant would be dressed in slacks, suits, and dresses. Trevor didn't care for pretentiousness and being underdressed didn't bother him at all.

When he arrived, there were only five or six people at the bar, so he chose a barstool at the far end of the bar. To his right were empty seats, to his left was a serving area. It was good real estate. He could visit with folks when they placed orders, and the empty chairs to his right allowed people to sit by him, if they wished.

Trevor ordered a drink and checked his emails while people started drifting in. Smartphones are great for looking occupied when you are alone at the bar. When people are looking for a place to sit, they are more likely to sit by someone who looks occupied. If you are just sitting there watching people, they feel more conspicuous sitting next to you. *If a pretty woman comes in, she will feel more comfortable sitting next to someone who didn't notice her.*

There was a piano in the corner of the room and it wasn't long before a musician started to play. As Trevor was occupied on his phone, a couple of people sat on the bar stools to his right. The person closest to him sat down with a plop. It seemed like the type of movement that was designed to draw attention.

That type of sitting down movement seemed designed to say, *I have had a long day and I need a drink.* Next was the search for a place to put a purse. The two people settled in and ordered drinks. They started conversing as they drank wine.

    Trevor was acting engrossed in his phone when in fact he was just reading jokes his friend had emailed him. Trevor could tell by the conversation that two women had sat next to him. After he was done reading jokes, he exited his phone and placed it on the bar as if he just finished something important. He looked over at the ladies sitting to his right and they were engrossed in heavy conversation.

    The woman further away was attractive with auburn hair and a nice complexion, although she was a little thin. She had a way about her that was appealing but not irresistible. She was probably getting close to forty years old; thirty-eight was Trevor's best guess. The woman sitting next to Trevor was about the same age. She had long natural blond hair, no makeup, and casual clothes. She was a natural beauty with a perfectly sculpted figure and face. Trevor thought back, trying to remember a woman more attractive than the woman sitting next to him. The Coachella Valley is well known for high maintenance women with plastic surgery, fake boobs, and huge lips. Many look pretentious or ostentatious with just the right clothes, purse, jewelry, and makeup. This woman had a wholesome look about her. She looked down to earth. If Trevor had commissioned an artist to paint a picture of his ideal woman, she would have easily fit the bill. He was particularly fond of her bright blue eyes. The only woman he had known to be more attractive was Kristy. Something indescribable had attracted Trevor to Kristy. With one look at the lady sitting next to him, Trevor knew every man had tried to get in her pants since she was twelve. He knew he had to play it cool.

    Now that Trevor had assessed the ladies, he switched his attention to the piano player. He noticed that the ladies had finished their first glass of wine and were now ordering another. This was a good sign because he knew they would begin to loosen up after the first glass. Now that they would be staying for a second glass, there would be plenty of time to start a conversation.

Out of the corner of his eye, Trevor noticed that the women had looked at him a couple of times. Now they were looking in his direction often. He knew they were wondering why he hadn't engaged them. After all, every man since they were teens had craved their attention.

The piano player was located behind and to the left of Trevor. So as Trevor was observing him, he was facing mostly away from the ladies. Eventually Trevor decided it was time to break the ice. As he turned around to the bar he looked over and made eye contact with the ladies to his right.

The one further away looked at Trevor and said, "My name is Cindy and this is my friend Sherrie."

He knew at this point the game was on. He had waited until they were the aggressor. They were now vying for his attention. All he needed to do was maintain their interest and they would do the rest. The ball was in Trevor's court.

Sherrie was a Coachella Valley resident and Cindy was an old friend who was visiting her. They were both from Oregon and had known each other since high school. Cindy was married and she and her husband owned and operated a couple of gambling establishments in Oregon. She had been enjoying warm weather and time with her friend. Cindy was down to earth and business-like. Sometimes she tended bar in their establishments. No wonder she felt comfortable in the bar room atmosphere. The fact that she was married explains why she was the one to do introductions. She was acting as her friend's wing woman.

Sherrie grew up in a remote logging area in Oregon. She came from a family of loggers, which explained why she seemed down to earth. She told how she had driven logging trucks and enjoyed working in the back country. She seemed proud of being from Oregon and growing up in the woods. She enjoyed telling stories about her childhood in Oregon. After a few drinks and several stories, she talked about how she had felt outcast in the logging community where she grew up. Trevor thought it was odd to hear a beautiful woman talk about feeling outcast in the logging community where she grew up. He could only imagine how she would be doted over and spoiled by everyone. How could such a beautiful woman ever feel outcast?

As the conversation continued, Trevor learned that Sherrie longed to live in the northern states. Her husband had brought her to the Coachella Valley because of his employment opportunities. Although they had divorced a couple years ago, she was now rooted in the Valley. Her daughter lived and worked there and she was established. She resented the fact that she now lived in the desert because of her ex-husband.

The conversation continued until Trevor had to leave. He told the ladies he had to go back to the North Country tomorrow and that in the summertime, he would stop by Cindy's restaurant for a visit. He also explained that next year, he would be back in the Valley. They exchanged phone numbers and said their goodbyes. As Trevor was walking away, Sherrie was saying *Call Me! Call Me! Call Me.* She sounded like an excited little girl trying to get the attention of an ice cream truck coming down the street.

When summer arrived, Trevor and his friend traveled through Oregon. Trevor made a special effort to stop by the restaurant Cindy owned and operated. Of course, they had to call Sherrie and let her know they had connected. As soon as dinner was ordered, Trevor called Sherrie and explained that he was eating in Cindy's restaurant. Trevor and Cindy had a short conversation with Sherrie, teasing her about how fun it was visiting and eating at Cindy's place.

Trevor promised Sherrie that he would call her when he came to the desert the following year.

A year had passed and Trevor had lost out with Kristy, hooked up with Katy and Sara, played golf in the heat, and had some fantastic motorcycle adventures. It was time to call Sherrie.

Trevor called Sherrie and explained that he was in town and would like to take her for drinks. She protested about going out until Trevor mentioned that all he wanted to do was visit and have drinks. He explained that he didn't want to pressure her and that it would be fun. It was obvious she wanted him to talk her into drinks. As Trevor ended his phone conversation, he noticed his phone had somehow changed to FaceTime. He could hear Sherrie fixing her hair but the camera was pointed towards the ceiling and the video wasn't very entertaining. Trevor disconnected from FaceTime not wanting to be a voyeur. After he thought about it for a while, he regretted turning FaceTime off. Sherrie had probably changed the phone connection to FaceTime on purpose. That could have turned into a very entertaining video.

    Trevor and Sherrie drove separately and met at an Irish pub. They hugged and ordered drinks. Trevor and Sherrie felt totally comfortable in each other's presence. It wasn't like the folks that meet online, get together at a coffee shop, and tell each other how rich they are. They settled right into interesting conversation. Time went by and they had another drink, then another. Eventually they had several drinks. For most of the time, Sherrie was like a housewife who had come home from work after a long day and needed to vent. She had been talking continuously, as if conversation had built up inside of her like a repressed volcano that had now erupted and begun spewing forth.

    As Trevor and Sherrie were conversing, they were sitting at a table on the outer perimeter of a concrete, outdoor patio. The other customers were located between their table and the door leading into the bar. There were about five or six other customers sitting on the patio, but most of the patrons were sitting inside the bar. While Sherrie was talking, Trevor noticed three females who all appeared to be gay. Eventually one of the ladies kissed the other. As time went on, they became increasingly amorous.

    One of the three moved over to a table next to Trevor and Sherrie. She was now sitting between the entrance to the bar and the table where Trevor and Sherrie were sitting. Trevor had been listening to Sherrie for a long time when she noticed he looked bored. She looked at Trevor and asked him if he was bored.

    Trevor replied, "I am." Thinking she would gain his interest back, Sherrie asked Trevor if he would like a lap dance. That was a no brainer. Trevor said he would love a lap dance. Trevor turned so he was facing the entrance to the bar. At the next table between Trevor's table and the bar entrance sat one of the three apparently gay females. The two amorous ladies remained off to his right and towards the corner of the patio.

Sherrie proceeded with a lap dance. Originally, she was facing Trevor, sitting on his lap and moving around in a most seductive fashion. She began grinding on him but the arms on the chair inhibited her from getting in close enough to be in key position. Eventually she turned around, facing away from Trevor so she was able to sit in Trevor's lap and grind away. Trevor was having a good date. He was sitting on the patio getting a lap dance. Sherrie was grinding on him as two lesbians were kissing and making out in the corner.

Since Sherrie was facing the other direction, he had full view of the two women in the corner and the woman sitting directly in front of Sherrie. Sherrie was grinding away. It was a very sensual situation with the visual of two women making out while Sherrie was starting to make little whimpering noises. The woman sitting directly in front of Sherrie was watching and staring at Trevor. Of course, Trevor looked at her with a look that said, "You are cute, pleased to be of service, I know you are enjoying the show." Trevor was taking in the moment thinking this is the way life should be. *Why couldn't life always be like this?* He thought, *Maybe I will get kicked out for lewd behavior.* Fines, jail time, whatever, it would be worth it.

After this went on for a while, Sherrie stopped and looked up as if she had just noticed the lesbians. One of the two in the corner got up and headed into the bar. The woman sitting directly in front of Sherrie said, "Your boyfriend likes other women."

Unfazed, Sherrie stood up, walked across the patio, and up to the lone woman whose lover had just gone inside the bar. She looked at the woman in a seductive manner and exclaimed "You aren't lesbians," as if she was using reverse psychology to make the woman prove she was a lesbian. At the same time, she began using her finger to trace the tattoo on the lesbian woman's chest. It was a large tattoo which covered her chest and most of her breasts. The woman didn't seem to mind. She just stood there while Sherrie continued to talk and run her finger across her chest. Sherrie had the expression of a little girl amused with an art project. Trevor was thinking, this was her best effort to entertain and alleviate his boredom. For whatever reason, this date had become quite intriguing.

Sherrie was standing there, running her finger across the woman's chest and talking softly when the lesbian's partner came out of the bar. Her partner walked right up to Sherrie, clenched her fist, and gave her a right hook to the jaw. Like a fighting drill that had been practiced and rehearsed, Sherrie took a step back and countered with a roundhouse kick to the mid-section. The lesbian hit the floor and began flopping around like a fish out of water, gasping for air. The other lesbians looked at Sherrie like they wanted to take her out but were scared shitless.

The bartender exploded out of the bar and told Sherrie to get out. Sherrie was pissed off and told the bartender where he could stick it. She called him every curse word you can possibly imagine. Her final statement to the bartender was, "Go fuck yourself!" It was evident at this point that Sherrie had more than enough to drink. She had evidently pre-lubed with a few drinks before she arrived at the bar. She was wasted at this point!

The problem now was that everyone knew she had too much to drink. They told her they would call the police if she drove. She was pissed beyond belief as she crawled into her Ford Explorer and tore out of the parking lot. The bartender and the lesbian gals were in the parking lot jotting down her license plate number as she left. Trevor was barely able to get a word in edgewise but he managed to tell Sherrie he would follow her.

Sherrie had split. Trevor got on his motorcycle and left in pursuit of the Ford Explorer. They were headed down the street fully loaded with alcohol, knowing the lesbians had reported her for drunk driving and called in her license plate. Sherrie would have to stay at Trevor's place for the night. The police would probably be waiting if she pulled into her driveway. At least Trevor told her they would.

They arrived at Trevor's place and all was well except for the fact that Trevor was totally on edge. He was curious about how Sherrie had so easily dispatched her opponent. Sherrie explained that when she lived in the mountains, she had known someone who had studied martial arts. The martial artist had told her she only needed one technique to defend herself. That technique was a roundhouse kick. Sherrie was an athletic Tomboy type, and she had enjoyed practicing the roundhouse kick. It had been perfected. There is an old adage in martial arts that says, 'You are better to have one excellent technique than a lot of techniques that are unrefined.' Sherrie had proved this to be true.

Although Trevor had made the perfect seduction and accomplished getting the beautiful maiden to his bedroom, it was not his finest moment in the bed chambers. It became blatantly apparent to Trevor that *the most beautiful woman is not attractive if she has the wrong personality.* Sherrie remained at Trevor's place and ran around naked most of the following day. Trevor kept thinking to himself that there should be a dating rule requiring your date to go home before noon.

As Sherrie left, she once again sounded like an excited little girl chasing an ice cream truck down the street. *Call Me, Call Me, Call Me!!* She sounded just like the first day she and Trevor met.

The month had gone by quickly. It was an extraordinary adventure but it was time to head home. Every one of the beers Trevor had purchased to share with his most generous neighbor still remained in his refrigerator. Before Trevor departed, he gave the beer and all of his leftover groceries to his very kind and most generous neighbor.

Kristy called asking why Trevor hadn't called her. He thought it was obviously because she reneged on coming to the desert. All he could say was that he had been busy. Kristy went on to explain that she would be in Las Vegas in a few days and that Trevor should meet her there. It was on his way home. He thought maybe he should visit her in Las Vegas.

Men do not select women, women select men. After a man has chosen his real estate at the bar, it is best if he remains somewhat stoic, orders a drink, and patiently waits for the drama to unfold. It is best to pass pleasantries, particularly with men, as this demonstrates that a person is cordial and not just seeking the attention of women. Women meticulously scrutinize one's interactions with men, as well as women.

Chapter 9

Birds and Panties

As the sun was coming up, Trevor mounted his motorcycle and headed north. It was a gorgeous morning in the desert as he passed the large, white wind generators that inhabit the landscape like giant, formidable objects deployed upon a chessboard. What a wonderful, free feeling to be back on the road. He couldn't help but feel emotional as he cruised down the road, thinking about the people he had met, spent time with, and enjoyed. He knew he could always come back to the Coachella Valley and feel right at home. One lonely tear left his eye as the desert slowly disappeared in his rearview mirror.

Trevor was looking forward to riding the Angeles Crest Highway, as it was touted to be one of the most prominent motorcycle destinations in the United States. It was one of the most popular, if not the most popular, motorcycle destination in California. The Angeles Crest Highway is a very scenic highway that runs through the San Gabriel Mountains. It is sixty-six miles long and runs from North of San Bernardino, California, to East of Burbank, California. It has moderate curves along with beautiful mountain scenery. It is part of California State Route 2.

It was perfect timing for traversing the San Gabriel Mountains. As Trevor headed west and up the east side of the mountain, the sun was coming up behind him. With the morning sun at his back, the desert landscape was lit up in the most vivid of colors. The weather was perfect and the turns were sweepers instead of hairpins. The road was an easy ride, as it didn't demand attention for long. Although it was a nice ride, it was probably considered one of the best because there was a large population base nearby. Therefore, a lot of people were aware of its existence. Some of the best motorcycle roads are located in remote areas such as Idaho, Washington, Oregon, Montana, Northern California,

British Columbia, and Arkansas. Motorcycle riders are not aware of their existence because they are not close to a largely populated area. The Angeles Crest Highway was certainly a nice motorcycle destination, but Trevor preferred roads like Rattlesnake Pass in Oregon or Highway 1 along the California Coast.

Even if you take the long way around, it doesn't take long to get from the Coachella Valley to Las Vegas. It would be a couple of days before Kristy got to Las Vegas. In order to accommodate her schedule, Trevor needed to occupy a couple extra days. So, he decided to tour Death Valley. As he was touring Death Valley, he kept close contact with Kristy. It was hot and there wasn't a lot to see but it was the most enjoyable way he could think of to kill a couple of extra days. As long as he was on the motorcycle, life was good.

To accommodate Kristy's schedule, Trevor had delayed his trip by a few days. He needed to get home after being gone for a month but nevertheless, he wanted to get to know her. Kristy would be visiting her sister in Las Vegas, so she would stay with her. Trevor researched hotels and found one relatively close to where her sister lived.

Trevor was situated in his hotel and Kristy was situated at her sister's place. The hotel had a nice little Irish bar, so it was the perfect place to have drinks and visit. When Kristy arrived at the bar, she was well dressed with high heels, slacks, and a sweatshirt. It was not a combination that most women could pull off, but she looked absolutely stunning. She had big dimples and could be best described as a cute Irish hottie. She was a natural beauty whose nose, cheek bones, and facial structure was identical to Trevor's mother's. She was also the same size and shape. Her hair was auburn with a lot of blonde mixed in. If it was dyed, it was not evident. In personality, she was alive and quick-witted. Her personality was much different than Trevor's mother's. His mother never wore a sweatshirt, drank alcohol, left the house without makeup, ate meat, or cursed. His mother had been a model most of her life and could be accurately described as pretentious. Trevor liked the fact that Kristy's personality was the opposite of his mother's. She seemed down to earth. When Trevor first met Kristy, she had a few drinks under her belt. It was going to be interesting visiting with her when she wasn't fueled by alcohol.

Trevor knew Kristy liked beer and the bar had a good selection. As soon as they were seated, Trevor searched the beer menu and quickly decided on a Hefeweizen. Kristy explained that she had to drive home, so she wouldn't be able to drink. When Trevor offered to get her a cab, she said she had to give her relative a ride, also. She explained that she couldn't stay too long because her friend would be waiting for a ride. Trevor and Kristy had a marvelous time talking, joking, telling stories, laughing, and dancing. It was a fun evening which lasted from 6:00 p.m. to 12:00 p.m. When twelve o'clock rolled around, they were having a wonderful time.

Without warning, Kristy stood up and exclaimed she had to go. At that moment she walked out of the hotel like her tail had caught on fire. Trevor just sat at the table astounded as his jaw dropped at her maneuver. In a few minutes he received a text message from Kristy explaining that her head was spinning and that she had a marvelous time. Trevor explained that he would have to leave the day after tomorrow, so they should get together the next day.

Kristy explained that she couldn't meet tomorrow, she had things she had to do. It was evident that she wasn't that busy, she was playing a game. Trevor explained that he had delayed his return home by several days just to meet with her. He would be leaving day after tomorrow. The whole evening Kristy had not ordered a drink.

Over the years, Trevor had spent a lot of time in Las Vegas. It was not an enjoyable place to him, and he was itching to get away from the sound of slot machines and hubbub. He resented the fact that he had wasted time waiting for Kristy to get there, spending time in a place he despised, and the fact that Kristy hadn't been considerate enough to allot time to accommodate his efforts.

The next day Trevor investigated Las Vegas, went to a nice seafood dinner, and prepared for the return trip home. Once again, Kristy had been a major disappointment.

Trevor got up at daylight the next morning, took a shower, and headed north. It was a relief to leave the city of lights and sound behind. It was a beautiful day as Trevor cruised down the road, enjoying the music playing through his helmet speakers.

He had gone about 150 miles when he decided to get gas. As he filled the tank, he checked his phone for messages. It was about 11:00 a.m. as he looked down and discovered a text message from Kristy.

"Are you at the hotel?" it read. Trevor texted Kristy and told her he was 150 miles away and headed home. He stuck his phone in the motorcycle and continued down the road. The next time he stopped and checked his phone, Kristy had left another message explaining that she had misdialed and that the message was meant for her sister. Now why would her sister be at the same hotel Trevor was staying at, when she lives in Las Vegas?

Kristy was a pain in the ass. Trevor may have been highly proficient at hooking up, but he was a miserable failure at dealing with this type of inconsiderate maneuvering. He surmised that Kristy had expected him to follow her out of the restaurant when she jumped up and left without warning. He was supposed to act like a character in some romantic movie. Evidently, she had expected him to extend his trip another day, also. Kristy had been single for seventeen years. Maybe she was a professional game player. Life sure was peaceful and uncomplicated cruising down the road with Kristy and her shenanigans left behind. How could Trevor be such a fool as to be deceived by Kristy once again?

Going north from Las Vegas is a desolate drive, no matter which road you take. The desert road has its own unique character, so Trevor preferred taking it rather than the interstate. The desert road heading north was a two-lane road, with a seventy-five mile an hour speed limit. Sometimes you can look down this road for miles and see it going straight into the horizon.

Since it is a very long distance between gas stations, Trevor carefully planned his stops for gas. When a driver passed Trevor at a high rate of speed, he would fall in behind and follow them. He preferred getting behind a pickup, because a pickup is big enough that a patrolman won't see a motorcycle hidden behind it.

Trevor fell in behind a pickup that was ripping up the road at ninety-five miles per hour. Stops were few and far between, so he followed the pickup, mile after mile, at ninety-five miles per hour. The road was straight and Trevor became tired. The pickup eventually turned off the road without Trevor noticing.

He was on cruise control, streaking down the road at ninety-five miles per hour, when he suddenly found himself up close behind a highway patrolman, directly in front of him. At that rate of speed, he had closed the gap between him and the patrolman like nothing flat. The next thing Trevor knew, he was hitting his brakes to keep from slamming into the rear end of a patrol car. He had about three car lengths between him and the rear end of the patrol car when the patrolman flipped his lights on, slowed down, and pulled a U-turn.

As Trevor passed by him, the patrolman stuck his arm out of his car window, moving it up and down as his index finger pointed towards the ground. He was mouthing the words slow down. Trevor nodded as if he understood and continued down the road, at the posted speed limit, for the rest of the day. After driving ninety-five miles per hour for a considerable length of time, seventy-five miles per hour felt like creeping down the road. That ticket would have cost a pile of money.

There aren't many roads to choose from when traveling north through Nevada, but when you get into Oregon or California, there is a variety. Trevor liked to take windy two-lane roads and especially enjoyed taking roads he hadn't already traveled. This way, each trip became a new adventure.

When Trevor got into Oregon, he stopped at a small town to study his road map. As I have said, Trevor liked to stop and meet the locals along the way. As he was going down the street, he noticed a tavern that looked like a good place to stop. He was thinking that the locals would know the roads. If he had any questions, they would be glad to answer them.

He grabbed his map and headed into the tavern. It was the middle of the afternoon and there was a sparse gathering of patrons. About halfway down the bar sat a pretty woman with dark hair and a nice figure. Of course, Trevor was partial to the company of ladies. Trevor planted himself a couple of stools down from her and spread out his map. He was checking various routes when a conversation ensued between him and the pretty lady at the bar.

    Amy was thirty-three years old and happily married. She worked part time holding traffic signs during road construction. She was also a bookkeeper struggling to learn Microsoft Excel. Trevor had some experience using Excel, so they shared information about the program. Amy described various roads in the area. She had great ideas about which ones would be the most fun.

    Amy talked about her husband and how she grew up. She talked about her family life and life in general. It would be fair to say that she and Trevor hit it off very well. When Amy finished her beer, Trevor offered to buy her another. She explained that she didn't want another, she would prefer to share Trevor's. She smiled as she talked about sharing the beer. She didn't need to say so but Trevor knew she wanted to share because it seemed intimate. Trevor smiled at her because she knew that he knew she wanted to be more intimate by sharing the beer. It was plain to see that Trevor and Amy had a good connection. They conversed for several hours and from time to time, Amy would text her husband to let him know where she was. He seemed to be impatient for her to come home.

    It was evident that Amy would have to leave for home before long. She and Trevor had a very nice conversation and had connected in a way that could be best described as a connection of spirits. Amy explained to Trevor that she loved her husband, and she valued her relationship with him. She went on to explain that she was also extremely attracted to Trevor. She mentioned that she wouldn't want to do anything that would damage her marriage. She said she would like to have Trevor's phone number and then asked if it would be ok if she were to call him from time to time.

    They exchanged phone numbers and continued to visit a while longer. Amy hadn't seen Trevor's motorcycle, so he asked her to guess what it looked like. When they went outside, Trevor showed her his motorcycle. Amy said it didn't look anything like she had imagined.

    About that time, Amy's husband called and she told him she had met this really nice guy and would like to bring him home so he could meet him.

That didn't go over well. It was obvious he did not want to meet Trevor. She hadn't asked Trevor if he would go to her house. Trevor would have been totally embarrassed if she would have asked her husband in person. Since she asked him over the phone, Trevor was saved the embarrassment.

Trevor didn't think Amy's invitation was about sex and he didn't think Amy was by any means promiscuous. It was his impression that she was a genuinely nice person, who was just being sincere about her feelings and the situation. Trevor could tell by the phone conversation that Amy's husband was not pleased, about her wanting to bring Trevor home.

As they were talking on the phone, Trevor began thinking about times when he had been out with a married couple and the wife would ask if she could take him home. It is highly embarrassing to hear a woman ask her husband if she can have sex with you. In the back of your mind, you are thinking the husband may come unglued and want to beat the shit out of you. If you do the deed with his wife, you always wonder if the husband is going to get pissed afterwards. You may end up looking over your shoulder for a very long time.

Trevor didn't know anything about bees but he was quite familiar with birds. People used to think male birds were the big cheaters. This was probably because the studies were conducted by men. Recent studies, however, indicate that females do as much cheating as men. Recent studies and the use of DNA tests indicate that up to 70 percent of the eggs found in some nests are fertilized by a bird other than the mate (one who helps her build the nest and raise the babies). A recent study indicates that on average, 40 percent of the eggs are fertilized by males other than their mate.

When it is time to build a nest, the female will look for a suitable, steady fellow that is willing to help her build a nest. This male will help build the nest, help with raising babies, and be her social companion. When the nest is built, she will hook up with a handsome dude with colorful plumage and nice long tail feathers. The typical scenario is that she will hook up with the neighbor next door. When the deed is done, she will preen a little and head home. Studies indicate that it is the female who is the most opportunistic and she doesn't have to look far for a male to fill her needs.

Interestingly enough, the babies that are hatched from the neighbor dude are the strongest and healthiest of the babies. These babies also obtain preferential treatment from the female, which gives them a head start in life. She will hatch them earlier, which will be advantageous to them throughout their lives. The diversity of their genes will also work to their advantage.

Trevor used the term *Nesting Syndrome* to describe those who secure a mate, build a nest, then take up with a mate of higher value.

We know that most birds mate for life, which seems romantic. The truth of the matter is that some birds do mate for life but a lot of them mess around.

When Amy got off of the phone, it was time for her to go home and Trevor to head down the road. It was a fantastic afternoon, enjoyed by two people who shared a connection, beer, and each other's company. Sometimes you have a connection without sex and it is great. Sometimes you have sex without much of a connection and it is ok. Sometimes it is better to have a connection without sex complicating it. In fact, relationship experts claim that *women are more jealous of their spouse having a strong emotional connection with another female than if he has sexual relations with her.*

The eventful afternoon with Amy reminded Trevor of a time when he was younger. He had heard there was a good band playing at a local bar. Trevor had been dancing, visiting, and making new acquaintances when a couple walked into the bar. He knew the couple and had done business with them in the past. The husband was tall and lanky; a blue-collar working-class type of guy. It is difficult to say what a woman finds attractive in a man but most would agree that the wife was more attractive than the husband. His wife was well built with an attractive face.

Although her face was attractive, she was not stunning. Her body was kind of the same as her face. It was fit and shapely with nice breasts and a great butt. She was the type of woman who men would be actively pursuing but they would not be falling all over her.

The couple liked Trevor and over the years they had developed a business rapport with him. They were anxious to visit with Trevor on a personal basis since their relationship had previously been strictly business. The couple and their two female friends joined Trevor at a table. The two female friends were thin and average. They were plain but not homely. The female friends talked with the husband from time to time but remained to themselves. The wife (Stacy) spent most of the evening visiting with Trevor. They visited and danced while the rest of the party remained reserved.

Stacy had asked Trevor to dance a couple of times and eventually, they were on the dance floor for several dances. Trevor and Stacy worked up a heated sweat and there was a large crowd of people adding to the mugginess of the area. Toward the edge of the dance floor was an air duct that blew cold air into the room. Trevor and Stacy would make it a point to stand under the air duct at the end of a dance session. The cool air blowing on their heated bodies was stimulating and refreshing. It added to the sensuousness of the event.

While Stacy and Trevor had been dancing and having fun, the rest of their party had been visiting. After a long session of dancing and a refresher under the fan, Trevor and Stacy returned to their seats. Everyone in their party was seated at the table, talking and visiting, when without warning, Stacy looked over at her husband and asked him if she could take Trevor home.

Needless to say, Trevor was shocked at Stacy asking her husband if she could take him home. Not only was he shocked, but he was nervous that her husband might be totally pissed about the suggestion. She hadn't said a word to Trevor about her plan for a little nooky at her place. Trevor sat there as her and her husband worked out the details. They decided that Stacy would ride with Trevor to her house and the husband would stay with the other ladies. Stacy left her car with her husband and rode to her house with Trevor. This way, her husband would have a vehicle to drive home after Trevor left.

When Stacy and Trevor arrived at the house, Trevor was still a little on edge about the whole situation. In the back of his mind, he kept thinking the husband may have second thoughts and decide to come home. Stacy reassured Trevor that her husband would not be home until Trevor was gone. Since they had a long night of dancing and having fun, Stacy took a shower while Trevor got naked and snuggled in under the covers. As he was lying there, all he could think about was whether the husband was going to show up or not.

Eventually Trevor needed to use the restroom; after all, he had been drinking all evening. He knocked on the door that had been left part way open and asked if he could use the restroom. Stacy was in the shower and replied that it was fine. Trevor used the restroom and Stacy stepped out of the shower about the time he finished. A conversation ensued and Stacy continued with her personal hygiene routine. This included douching in front of him. As she performed the ritual, she explained that she had never let anyone watch her do this but she felt comfortable in Trevor's presence. As Trevor was observing Stacy, he was thinking her husband probably hasn't watched her perform such a private task. Eventually they settled into the covers and all was good. Stacy knew what she wanted and was not afraid to ask. She was excited to have a cool dude in her nest.

When things relaxed and the afterglow was in full effect, it seemed like a good time to discuss why the couple had an open relationship. Stacy explained that when she was younger, men or boys didn't pay much attention to her. She got married and started to fill out and they all wanted to fuck her. She and her husband had started a business that was successful. They both worked in the business. She kept the books and placed orders while he did the work. They worked as a successful team and had one child who was well cared for but obese. She went on to explain that she had needs her husband could not fulfill and that he was smart enough to realize that the open relationship allowed them to keep the business going while keeping her sexually satisfied.

Trevor inquired about how many sexual partners she had. He was nervous about having sex with a woman in an open relationship. He didn't have to worry about getting her pregnant, but a promiscuous woman could have a variety of sexual diseases. Stacy explained that there were two other men she had sex with while she was married to her husband.

Trevor was curious about what the husband would do while he was waiting for him to get done with his wife. Stacy said her husband definitely would spend the evening begging for sex from the other two women. Trevor said he was not attracted to either of the other women and would not take either of them to bed. To this day, Trevor still wonders why that statement didn't set well with Stacy.

After the deed was done and the afterglow had passed, Trevor once again became nervous about Stacy's husband coming home. He may or may not be hostile, but it would be uncomfortable to try and make small talk after being with his wife. As Trevor pulled on his clothes and got ready to go, Stacy thanked him and explained that she had really needed that. She further explained that if he wanted to do it again, she would be available. Whenever a woman thanked Trevor for sex, it made him wonder if her former lover had not been a generous lover. Trevor had no comprehension of how a man cannot be considerate of the sexual needs of a woman.

Trevor got in his car and fired it up as if his tail feathers were on fire. He flew the coop and never returned to that nest again.

The trip home was very fun! The roads Trevor and Amy had decided upon had nice curves and fantastic scenery. When Trevor arrived home and sat in his favorite chair, he felt like he was still moving. After a long day of riding motorcycle, this is a common phenomenon.

Now that Trevor was home and caught up on things, he was eager to play golf in the nice 80-degree weather. What a change from playing golf in the triple digits of the California desert.

It was great to enjoy the outdoor patio at the golf course. Trevor had been paying six dollars for a beer in Southern California. Here, he purchased a beer for two dollars and played golf on a very nice course in perfect weather. It was great to be home, play golf, and enjoy relaxing afterwards.

As Trevor was sitting on the patio drinking beer, he was contemplating the travels and events of his most fantastic adventure. He reflected upon his race with the Porsche, Katy, her mother, near heat stroke, and Kristy. For some reason, Kristy had an effect upon Trevor that he couldn't quite figure out. She did look a lot like his mother, but her personality was much different. She had failed to come to the desert as they had planned, and on top of that, she bailed on him in Vegas.

Trevor was sitting on the patio, drinking his beer and contemplating why he had been such a sucker for Kristy when he suddenly noticed he was staring at a woman sitting across the patio. He had been deep in thought when he realized he had been staring at the woman's crotch. The lady had been sitting in her chair like Sharon Stone in *Basic Instinct*. She smiled at Trevor and shifted positions. Trevor then realized he must have looked quite forlorn as he was sitting there in contemplation, not realizing he was staring between her legs. He was sure she had noticed the forlorn look on his face and sensed his emotion. Sometimes women have an uncanny ability to read a person's emotional state. She didn't seem to be at all offended by Trevor getting caught looking between her legs. In fact, she soon changed her position so Trevor could once again see her white panties with little red strawberries.

Trevor's mood was now changing. Instead of sitting there deep in thought, he was enjoying the flirtations of the lady across the patio. He would take a drink of beer and act as if he didn't notice her nice shapely legs, short golf skirt, perfectly rounded, perky breasts, and of course, her nice little white panties with red strawberries. She would converse with the man on the other side of the table as she changed positions from time to time. She very well knew Trevor was looking forward to each time she shifted her position to give him a better look. She would posture herself in a way that was seductive to Trevor and she knew it.

This game of flirtation continued for some time. Eventually she positioned herself in a most seductive way, looked over at Trevor, and smiled in an incredibly seductive fashion. Trevor smiled back. The cards were on the table. They had now admitted to each other that they knew what was going on and that they were having fun with it.

It was time to break the ice. As Trevor smiled, he said "What a great day for golf."

Tanya replied, "You should come over and sit with us." They introduced themselves and passed pleasantries. Trevor learned that the couple was celebrating their wedding anniversary and that they had just finished playing golf. Tanya was definitely an attractive woman and her husband was a handsome man. They were a nice-looking couple. However, Tanya's husband was twenty years older than her.

This was the beginning of a close friendship that still exists today. Trevor and Tanya's husband are very good friends. The relationship between Tanya and Trevor became that of a brother and sister and they still refer to each other as brother and sister to this day. Over the years, Tanya often mentions the initial attraction between her and Trevor. This usually occurs after drinks and in front of her husband, family, and friends. Everyone laughs and smiles as she tells the story, but neither Trevor nor Tanya mentions the white panties with little red strawberries.

Unlike birds, man has reason and there is a moral line that should exist between a man, his wife, and a friend. The value of a brother-sister type of relationship can be extraordinary.

Chapter 10

Disappointment

Time passed and Trevor would think of Kristy from time to time. They had texted a couple of times but hadn't visited with each other since their meeting in Las Vegas. In her texts, Kristy mentioned she loved to travel and she hadn't been to Canada. Trevor had planned a trip to Canada, so he invited her to meet him there. She said she would love to go but money was tight. The plane tickets weren't expensive, so Trevor offered to send her one. Trevor didn't want Kristy to back out at the last moment, so he had her buy her own ticket with the understanding that he would reimburse her. Since she purchased her own ticket, Trevor wouldn't be out his money if she backed out.

Kristy was really excited about the adventure and mentioned she was very low maintenance. She would pack light and Trevor could pick her up at the airport. When Trevor prepared for his journey, he was very particular about bringing just the right type of wine. He carefully wrapped the $150-bottle of wine and placed it in a cubby pocket under the back seat of his automobile. The cubby pocket was not common to many vehicles. You had to get the top of the line in this make and model to get it.

Trevor had been to Canada many times, so it was a routine trip. As he went through customs, they asked him various questions. The border patrol asked him if he had any alcohol. He didn't want them to confiscate his $150 bottle of wine, so he answered "No." The border patrol then looked at Trevor's passport and told him to pull over in the search area.

When he pulled into the search area and got out of his vehicle, the border patrolman told him his passport had expired the day before. He would have been in the clear if he had come one day earlier.

Trevor was standing in the customs building watching the agent search his vehicle. The agent was very thorough. He watched him as he searched the paperwork in the glove box, went through the contents in the console, and looked under the front seats. As he was watching, he was expecting the agent to open the cubby containing the bottled wine. He was wondering if they were going to let him into Canada now that he had lied about having alcohol. It would be an inconvenience if he couldn't get over the border, but worst of all, Kristy would be stuck in Canada by herself. Maybe they would let him into Canada but they would more than likely confiscate his expensive bottle of wine.

The whole search took about thirty minutes. The agent came back into the office and went behind the counter as if he was contemplating something very serious. Trevor was certain it was bad news. Maybe the agent just wanted him to sweat a little bit.

The agent looked up at Trevor and said, "Enjoy Canada."

Trevor must have looked befuddled as the agent smiled at him and explained that Trevor really didn't need to have a passport, all he needed was to convince the agent that he wasn't going to be a problem in Canada. The agent made a humorous comment, Trevor laughed, got in his vehicle, and headed down the road. That was a relief! He still had his wine and he was going the meet Kristy in Canada.

The next day, Trevor was sitting on the couch at his friend's place when Kristy called. When Trevor answered the phone, Kristy explained that they wouldn't let her into Canada. She couldn't get into Canada because she had a DWI on her record. Not only did she have a DWI on her record, she had two. Trevor had no idea she had a DWI or that you cannot get into Canada if you have one. This was a shock! Trevor had anticipated that she might get cold feet and chicken out but this added a new dimension to the situation. She had paid for a ticket with the understanding Trevor would reimburse her. Kristy was again a huge disappointment. Who would pay for the plane ticket?

Trevor visited his friends and took care of business. He had planned to stay in a very picturesque, small town with Kristy. Even though Kristy hadn't panned out, he decided to stay in the quaint little town as a treat to himself. He was feeling let down about Kristy not coming and a nice night in a good hotel would be just the ticket.

He got a nice room, took a shower, and decided he might as well drink the expensive bottle of wine. He didn't want to contend with bringing it across the border on his way home. He opened the bottle of wine, poured himself a glass, drank half the glass, and thought to himself, *Who can drink alone?* Trevor was a social drinker and never drank when he was alone at home. In fact, he didn't drink unless he was at a social function where others were drinking. There was no reason to drink a bottle of wine by yourself if you aren't going to enjoy it. He left the open bottle of wine on the counter and headed down the street.

Although it was a misty evening, Trevor decided to go for a walk. It was drizzling as he walked down the street with his hands in his coat pockets. He walked down Main Street and turned a corner. About halfway down the block, a very pretty, vivacious young lady about twenty years old was standing on the sidewalk talking to a couple of other people who were also about her age.

As Trevor started to walk past, the young lady asked him where he was going. Trevor replied, "I don't know where I am going. Just enjoying the drizzle, I guess." They all laughed and a conversation ensued. Trevor was surprised that the young lady would start a conversation with him. He was a stranger in town and probably older than her father. Trevor was intrigued that the young people would be curious about him strolling down the sidewalk. Maybe Trevor had looked like a lost puppy walking down the sidewalk. As mentioned previously, women seem to have a sixth sense about these things. The group was emphatic about Trevor joining them for drinks and conversation. Trevor estimated that he was the only person in the bar over twenty-five years of age.

The group made Trevor think the world is going to be a better place with such fine young people coming up to take the reins of leadership. Most of them seemed to be flying by the seat of their pants. Typically, they worked at the ski run in the winter and at the lakes in the summer. They were enjoying life and this was party night. They drank beer, downed shots, and told stories. They were a jovial group, and Trevor knew times had changed by the music they played.

One young lady had programmed the juke box to play the song "Discovery Channel" over and over. She knew every word to the song and chimed in with the juke box as she sashayed around the room. The lyrics went something like this:

"You and me baby ain't nothin' but mammals, so let's do it like they do it on the Discovery Channel."

The lyrics went on to describe various ways animals have sex. Trevor remembered how his father had a strong distaste for Beatles music. He thought their music was corrupting society. How would he react to the song "Discovery Channel?" Trevor couldn't help but be amused.

Kristy had once again been a disappointment, but if she had come, Trevor wouldn't have had the opportunity to drink, laugh, and share with the group of young people. The evening with them was irreplaceable and an experience Trevor would never forget. Trevor poured the expensive bottle of wine down the sink.

Yep, he also picked up the $500 tab for Kristy's unused airline ticket. Little did he know that he had not seen the last of Kristy.

Chapter 11

Girlfriends and Jealousy

Now that Trevor had time for motorcycle rides, golfing, hiking, and other outdoor activities, he moved to a warmer climate.

Since he rode motorcycles, several people told him he needed to go to a local, outdoor hangout that was very popular with motorcycle riders. He didn't know why they told him he needed to go but he thought he should find out.

It was a short but nice ride, and he soon learned the destination had live music along with awesome hamburgers. He was enjoying a hamburger and drinking water when some folks from the Midwest sat next to him. He was drinking water because he was in an unfamiliar area and just wanted to enjoy a short motorcycle ride. As he sat and visited with the folks from the Midwest (Dan and Patty), they began drinking beer.

They offered to buy Trevor one, and to be sociable, Trevor took them up on their offer. Patty would get up and buy beer as Dan used his smart phone to retrieve the latest football scores. Each time Patty got up to retrieve beer, the men would ogle her and Trevor began teasing her about all the attention she was getting. Of course, Patty liked being teased about the attention.

Soon, two pretty young gals and a boyfriend entered into the conversation. One of the young ladies was a recently divorced brunette. The other one was a cute blonde who had her boyfriend tagging along. They were in party mode. At this point, Trevor had been reserved about drinking. He only had two beers over a considerable length of time. Eventually, the two young ladies and the boyfriend invited everyone to go to a local dance establishment. How could Trevor pass up an invite to go with two pretty ladies and a boyfriend? As usual, Trevor was visiting with the locals and making new friends.

Before long everyone was at the dance establishment doing shots.

Trevor didn't want to drink, but if a couple of pretty young ladies want you to do shots, it is difficult to say no. Besides, the boyfriend was buying. As the shots went down and conversation continued, Trevor and the pretty blonde (Nikki) became engrossed in heavy conversation. The boyfriend was flitting around and Trevor noticed the brunette kiss an unattractive looking guy with a cowboy hat. He wasn't a real cowboy. He was just some dude dressed up to look like one; an imposter.

Even though the brunette was a nice-looking gal, Trevor ruled her out when she kissed the guy with the cowboy hat. She might have been newly divorced and ready for action, but her kissing that dude totally turned him off. Nikki, on the other hand, was sweet like a delectable treat. Trevor and Nikki became immersed in conversation and every so often, another shot appeared. They downed the shots as if they were a formality, cheers and down the hatch.

The conversation continued and after a while, Nikki began leaning into Trevor indicating she wanted him to kiss her. Trevor wanted to kiss her but was afraid her boyfriend would come unglued. He put his arm around her and she snuggled in.

Trevor had a flashback to when he was eighteen years old. He had graduated from high school when he was seventeen and at eighteen years old, he was living in a remote mountain area. It was Saturday night and he had come to town to enjoy the locals, dance, and have a good time. As he was socializing, a young lady asked him to dance and before long, they were in a lengthy conversation. They danced and talked until her boyfriend became jealous. The boyfriend approached Trevor and told him he should find his own girlfriend and that this girl was his. The boyfriend was about six foot three and outweighed Trevor by about eighty pounds. He was not a handsome man.

As the boyfriend was talking, Trevor's friend noticed the dissension between the boyfriend and Trevor. Trevor's friend walked up to the boyfriend, placed one hand upon his shoulder, and said, "Don't mess with my little buddy."

If you have watched reruns of the *Gilligan's Island* television series, you would easily recognize the manner in which he spoke.

Trevor's friend was a handsome man who had a free ride college scholarship playing football. He was ten years older than Trevor and had a lot of experience carousing. Everyone knew who he was and nobody wanted to get on his bad side. Not only did his reputation as a football player precede him, but most were aware that he liked to fight. If he was drinking whiskey, he would usually find someone to fight with.

Trevor knew he was in the clear now because his friend was looking for an excuse to fight and this fellow had played into the perfect scenario. If a fight broke out, it would be because Trevor's friend was defending his little buddy from the big jealous boyfriend. The jealous boyfriend knew he was in a catch-22.

The boyfriend turned and walked away, although from time-to-time, Trevor would notice him lurking in the shadows. Eventually, Trevor didn't notice him anymore. He may have been lurking in the crowd, but Trevor was too busy entertaining his girlfriend (Kirsten), to notice. He knew his buddy would keep him safe from the boyfriend. Things progressed with Kirsten and as she sat on Trevor's lap, they would gently kiss. They were young and their hormones were in high gear.

When the bar closed, the boyfriend was nowhere to be found. Trevor imagined he had become enraged beyond belief and gone home. This was good! Certainly, Kirsten wouldn't want to ride home with him after she had latched onto Trevor. That would have been a very uncomfortable situation. All had fallen into place. Trevor had to drive Kirsten home.

Trevor lived about eighteen miles from the bar and in the same direction as Kirsten. She lived at her parents' house in the mountains. To take her home, it would be an additional forty to fifty miles.

Trevor took her to his little cabin in the woods where they proceeded to continue the activities they started at the bar. They kissed, caressed, and enjoyed each other's bodies for a few hours. As I mentioned, they were young and their hormones were surging. They made love, looked at the stars, talked for a while, and made love again. Two young lovers had found each other and they were enjoying the view of the night sky, the sound of crickets, and the magical touch of each other's caress. Trevor was glad he was a man and she was a woman and that they could enjoy each other. Trevor thought of his father telling him there was more to life than women. Although he didn't reply, Trevor remembered thinking there may be more to life but the rest didn't matter.

Eventually, Trevor and Kirsten embarked upon the journey to her parents' house located far away in a remote mountain area. The trip consisted of eleven miles of dirt roads with the remainder being well-paved, two-lane country roads. They may have been well-paved and two-lanes, but they were extremely twisty and narrow. The road didn't stop at her parents' driveway. It continued down the other side of the mountain and back into the valley.

The young lady snuggled in close to Trevor as he was driving her home. They had made love several times and they were in an afterglow of sorts. Time passed and they started to get amorous again. As Trevor drove, Kirsten unfastened his pants and started playing around. Trevor unbuttoned her blouse and began playing with her breasts. She was playing with Trevor and Trevor was playing with her. Things continued to escalate. Trevor slid down in the seat and helped her slide his pants down. She now had proper access and proceeded to give him a blowjob. She probably had timed it out to get one last hurrah off as they entered her parents' driveway. As she was sliding her lips up and down and pumping Trevor's shaft, she looked up every once in a while, to make sure he didn't miss the turn to her house.

Eventually, she popped her head up, looked over the dash, and said, "Turn right at the next driveway." Instantly her head was back in Trevor's lap as she began moving faster and faster. Trevor was about to climax and explode as they entered the driveway.

As Trevor entered the driveway, he looked to his left and there was a beautiful Plymouth GTX about twenty yards away. The car looked brand new. It was a very cool looking car and it was built for speed. The next thing he noticed was two guys standing on the other side of the car. *Oh shit!* One of the guys had a hunting rifle laid across the roof of the car. He was looking right at Trevor through the scope of the rifle and Trevor was looking straight into the barrel of the gun. The shooter was using the roof of his car to steady the rifle and maintain a perfect line of sight.

Trevor was familiar with hunting rifles. At this distance, he knew the guy could just shoot his ear off or he could easily shoot him in the head. It was a high-powered rifle and if he shot him in the head, it would blow his head completely apart. He knew his head would explode if the trigger was pulled! Trevor could not duck; he could not hide. He was at the mercy of the guy with the rifle. He was a sitting duck. So, there he was, parked in the driveway with his pants down as Kirsten was pumping away on his shaft. Her tongue began swirling around the head of his penis as he looked straight down the barrel of a high-powered hunting rifle pointed straight at his head.

Trevor recognized the fellow standing beside the person aiming the gun. It was Bill. Trevor had met Bill at a house party two weeks earlier. Bill was four years older than Trevor and he was also somewhat larger. Trevor had been standing in the living room at the party when Bill entered with his friend. The friend seemed to think it was a big deal that Bill was older than the other folks at the party. He also began bragging about Bill being a good fighter. Trevor recently had problems with his girlfriend and was in a bum mood. He listened to the bragging and it rubbed him the wrong way. He looked at Bill and his friend and said, "He looks like a wimpy cocksucker to me."

That didn't go over well. Of course, Bill had to defend his honor. Nobody wanted to mess up the house, so plans were made for Bill and Trevor to fight it out at the turn around past the bridge, at the edge of town. As it turned out, Bill wasn't as tough as he thought he was. Trevor ended up coming out on top. It must have been a humiliating experience for Bill. The whole incident had been totally out of character for Trevor and it was the first and last time he behaved in such a manner.

Trevor was parked in the driveway, a high-powered hunting rifle was pointed at his head, his pants were down, and Kirsten was pumping away on his shaft as her tongue was swirling around the head of his penis. To add to the hostility of the situation, the person standing alongside the guy aiming the rifle was someone Trevor had recently humiliated in a fight. Both of these fellows had cause to shoot him. The sun was coming up but it was still difficult to make out the face behind the gun. Although he couldn't clearly see his face, Trevor was certain the person aiming the gun was Kirsten's boyfriend.

As long as the shooter could shoot and not injure Kirsten, Trevor was in an extremely vulnerable position. When Kirsten sat up, her head lined up with Trevor's. Trevor surmised that the shooter wouldn't shoot now that both of their heads were in line with the rifle. Certainly the boyfriend liked Kirsten or he would not have gone to this extent.

If he shot now, the bone fragments from Trevor's skull would certainly kill Kirsten. Although she had been just as guilty as Trevor, in pissing off the boyfriend, their only hope was that he had feelings for her and wouldn't kill them both.

Now, it was a Mexican standoff; if the shooter fired, he would kill both Trevor and Kirsten. If Trevor put the car in reverse and hit the gas, the gunman would most likely get excited and start shooting. Kirsten understood that she was Trevor's only line of defense and she didn't try to make a run for it. She was a trooper and stayed right there, solid. Trevor asked her if she thought he would shoot her and she said she didn't think so.

A moment that seemed like an eternity went by. Trevor was sitting there with his pants down and Kirsten was snuggled in tight. If Trevor moved enough to pull up his pants, he was afraid the shooter would get a clean shot.

It would be difficult to say how much time had passed when the man aiming the gun and the man standing beside him traded positions. They carefully maneuvered to keep the gun aimed perfectly at Trevor's head throughout the entire transition. Now that they had changed positions and Bill was holding the rifle, the boyfriend walked around the back of the GTX and started towards Trevor's car.

As he walked toward them, Trevor was trying to fix his pants so his genitals weren't showing. The boyfriend walked up to the car and Trevor rolled down his window.

The boyfriend looked at Trevor and said, "Old Bill over there has the 270 pointed right at your head. We need to talk."

Trevor said, "Yeah, that sounds like a good idea. I will let her out of the car."

The boyfriend started walking back toward the gun and Trevor opened his car door. In an instant, Kirsten crawled across his lap and out the door. Trevor knew the shooter would have a clean shot as soon as Kirsten exited the car. He surmised that Bill's grudge was probably not as strong as the boyfriend's, so this would be the best time to make a run for it.

Trevor slammed the car in reverse and hit the gas. The car ripped through the gravel as it sped backward up the driveway and onto the paved road. This caused a huge amount of dust, which may have been a good thing, as it would be difficult to get a clean shot through the dust.

As Trevor flew down the road, he was watching his rearview mirror to see if he was being followed by the GTX. Sure enough, there they were right behind him. How did they get in the car and on the road so fast? They were about a quarter of a mile behind him. As Trevor watched his rearview mirror, he could see their car go around a curve every so often. To stay ahead of the GTX, he had to give the windy road his full attention. He put the pedal to the metal as he flew down the road trying to stay ahead of the GTX.

Needless to say, Trevor was wired as he was ripping down the road. He became paranoid that the two fellows chasing him may know where he lived. They wouldn't be able to find his place, but they could take a shortcut and intercept him along the way. He decided to take a different route home. The alternative route would be an extra thirty or forty miles, but it would be worth it. It would increase his odds of not being caught or intercepted by the crazies chasing him.

Trevor's car exited the mountains and hit the interstate as if its tail was on fire. He was racing down the interstate at 105 miles per hour when he looked over and saw a highway patrolman going the opposite direction. The patrolman instantly flipped on his lights and siren. Trevor had been spotted by the patrolman and clocked at 105 miles per hour. The GTX was nowhere in sight, and he couldn't imagine trying to explain his situation to the cops. No one would believe his story.

Well, Trevor noticed there was a fence dividing the interstate. This meant that the patrolman couldn't get to Trevor's side of the interstate until he reached a crossing between the two sides of the interstate. Trevor estimated that by the time the patrolman got turned around, he may be able to reach the next town. At his present rate of speed, the probability of the cop finding a crossing and catching him was very, very, low. To increase his odds, Trevor decided to punch it down to 115 miles per hour. Realizing he couldn't beat a Motorola (police radio), Trevor knew he would have to get to the next town before the patrolman could radio ahead for another patrolman. Trevor would have to hide out in the next town as soon as he got there.

Trevor took the first exit into the next town and worked his way around the side roads until he found the house of an acquaintance. He pulled into the driveway, laid down in the car seat, and went to sleep.

Trevor was reading the newspaper a few days later when he came across an article about Bill totaling his beautiful GTX on the mountain road the night he and the boyfriend were chasing him.

A couple years later, Trevor was weighing trucks for a friend when the boyfriend pulled up on the scales and came inside the scale house. The boyfriend seemed huge as he towered over Trevor in the tiny little scale house. To say the least, Trevor was a little unnerved as he weighed the boyfriend's truck. Trevor recognized the boyfriend, although the boyfriend didn't seem to recognize him. The boyfriend had plenty of cause to hold a grudge. Trevor had stolen his girlfriend, humiliated his friend, and been the cause of totaling a beautiful car. Trevor was relieved when the boyfriend left the scale house and drove off in his truck.

It is needless to say that with the turn of events that occurred during Trevor's eventful evening with Kirsten, phone numbers were not exchanged and they never saw each other again.

Now, Trevor was sitting in the dance establishment with Nikki, the gal he had met while hanging out with Dan and Patty. Her boyfriend was visiting with other people, and Trevor knew she wanted him to kiss her. Although Trevor knew he would enjoy kissing her, he realized that she and her boyfriend both had kids. Actually, each of them had a special needs child, which created a commonality between them. There certainly wasn't a future for Trevor and Nikki. It was better to let her and her boyfriend explore the possibility of a future together.

Without warning or a word, Nikki's boyfriend swooped in, grabbed her by the hand, and pulled her out the door.

After a few beers and a multitude of shots, it was time for Trevor to go home. He went outside only to discover that there was a motorcycle rally going on and that a policeman was directing traffic a few feet away from his motorcycle. Trevor needed to devise a plan to get past the policeman without him noticing his inebriated condition.

Trevor went back inside the bar and contemplated his situation. He drank a few glasses of water, went back outside, walked up to his motorcycle, and pulled on his helmet. He put it on right away, so the policeman wouldn't see his eyes and notice how inebriated he was. He casually walked around his motorcycle, as if he was checking it out. He wanted to make sure the policeman wasn't suspicious of him before he got on the motorcycle. He started the motorcycle and sat there until he was sure the policeman wasn't watching him. The patrolman was looking the other way, so Trevor pulled out, went down the street, pulled a U-turn, and rode back past the policeman.

As he passed the policeman and pulled up to a four-way stop, he thought about a story his friend had told him. The friend had been so drunk, he forgot to put his feet down when he stopped at an intersection. He and the motorcycle just tipped over. Trevor reminded himself to put his feet down.

A Chevy Blazer pulled into the intersection from the road on the right. This was good because Trevor could follow the blazer and it would be easy to keep a steady speed. Since he was behind the blazer, it would be difficult for the police to see him.

He had followed the Blazer for about a block when a patrol car pulled up at a ninety-degree angle from an adjoining road. He turned on his patrol lights and pulled the Blazer over. The Blazer hadn't done anything wrong. It must have been a random stop. Trevor felt extremely lucky that he had pulled in behind the Blazer, otherwise it would have been him getting picked up.

He had only made it three blocks and now there was no one to follow. It appeared the police were just heavily patrolling the motorcycle rally and once he got out of town, there was very little traffic. Trevor went for a couple of miles, took a left turn, and discovered he had entered onto a street going the wrong direction. It was a four-lane street with two lanes going one direction and two lanes going the other direction. Because of the divider, he had not noticed the other two lanes. He quickly pulled a U-turn and began heading in the right direction. This was bad— going the wrong way down a street—plus he could have been picked up instead of the guy in the Blazer. Trevor made it home safely, parked his motorcycle, and never drove that inebriated again. Well, almost never.

That night, as Trevor laid in bed in his inebriated state, he was at peace, home safe, and relieved that he wasn't in jail. He thought of Nikki's face, her warm smile, the twinkle in her eyes, her laugh and her fun, flirtatious spirit. He thought about how enjoyable Nikki had been and he couldn't help but smile. It wasn't the possibility of looking down the wrong end of a high-powered hunting rifle that had deterred him from kissing her. It was the fact that there wasn't a future for the two of them. Trevor couldn't imagine how heart wrenching it could be for Nikki's boyfriend if he had kissed her or taken her home. *Sometimes the most caring thing you can do for someone is to do nothing.*

Chapter 12

A Conflict Between the Heart and Mind

People will purchase an automobile that costs thousands of dollars. It will be decorated with emblems and license plate holders advertising the dealership. Many people leave the advertisements on the automobile for as long as they own it. Trevor didn't like to leave dealership emblems on an automobile. He also got rid of the license plate holders that advertise the dealership. For resale value, he left the emblems that describe the make and model of the vehicle.

In some states, you are required to have a license plate on the front and back of your vehicle. In other states, you are only required to have a license plate on the back. Since Trevor was living in a state that didn't require a front license plate, he removed the apparatus that holds the license plate along with the plate itself. This cleaned up the front bumper and added to the appeal of the vehicle. When the plate and apparatus were removed, it left two small holes in the bumper. To make the vehicle look extra clean, Trevor decided to buy two small plugs to fill the holes.

He went to the hardware store and purchased just the right type of plugs. He placed them in the bumper holes and was thinking the vehicle looked much better without the apparatus, license plate, or holes in the bumper. Trevor was quite particular.

Trevor had recently returned from visiting Dan and Patty in the northern states, where he had met a very nice woman named Alex. He sent Alex a plane ticket and she came to visit. Trevor took her on motorcycle rides and they toured the area. She was a very nice, well-adjusted person. Trevor sometimes commented that she didn't seem crazy. Trevor was impressed by the fact that she would always create a rapport with the waiters and bartenders, and upon exiting an establishment, she would always shake their hands.

Trevor had made it clear that he wasn't interested in a long-term relationship, and she was okay with it. She probably thought she could change his mind though. Even though Alex had an excellent personality, was intelligent, and created a good rapport with everyone around her, she just didn't have a wow factor chemistry. Trevor wondered if a good chemistry wore off eventually and then a person might as well have stayed with the one who didn't have it in the first place.

As Trevor was driving back from the hardware store, he was thinking, *Life is good.* His vehicle was looking good and life was as it should be. It was not complicated. He had money to travel, he could do as he pleased, and he had the company of a woman when he wanted. Life was simple when not committed to a relationship. If life continued as it was, all would be grand. The worst that could happen is that he would meet a woman and fall head over heels.

He was almost home when he thought about stopping by a quaint little bar to have a beer. Life was good and it would be befitting to have a beer in celebration of a content, uncomplicated life without being committed to a relationship.

The little bar was a community bar, a gathering place for many in Trevor's community. It was not a particularly nice bar; it was just located close to a densely populated area. People patronized it because it was close to home.

As Trevor entered the bar, he noticed a good place to sit at the far end of the bar. It was good real estate because it was close to the restrooms. Being on the end of the bar, there wouldn't be anyone on one side of him, which would allow him extra seating space. The other thing that made it such a good location was that a musician was playing at that end of the room. It would be easy for Trevor to request songs and hobnob with the musician.

Trevor sat down, ordered a beer, and turned so he could see the musician. The musician was singing rock and roll songs while playing guitar. When Trevor turned to look at her, she was also looking at him. She looked out of the corner of her eye, slightly tilted her head, and smiled with her eyes. Her eyes were flirting with him. If Cicero was correct, in saying the eyes are the window to the soul, her soul was saying "I like you!" There was a twinkle in her eye and a smile ran across her face as she sang and played. The musician (Tracy) had long, natural blonde hair and blue eyes. Although she had a perfect figure, Trevor only noticed her face and expression. Not only did Tracy have a wholesome look about her, she had a wow factor, sex appeal, and chemistry.

As Trevor turned back toward the bar, he moved his arm across it, sending his beer crashing to the floor. The glass broke into a hundred pieces as it hit.

The bartender said, "No problem, I will get it." He proceeded to get a broom, clean up the glass, and mop the floor. After the cleanup was done, Trevor asked what he owed for his clumsiness.

The bartender said, "No charge" as he sat a fresh drink upon the bar.

Trevor turned back toward the musician. She was singing rock and roll songs from the 70s. She was an excellent singer and a very good guitarist. She wasn't just a strummer. She had an uncanny ability to play notes, strum, and switch between the two. Some musicians have a cheat sheet or an iPad they use to remember the words. Not Tracy. She knew the words without fail. She didn't know every song requested, but it was very difficult to think of a song she didn't know.

Trevor knew that some people have a natural talent for music. Many people will practice music all their life and not be a good musician. Others have God given abilities and will become exceptional musicians with little effort. It was evident that Tracy was a natural talent. She was one of the best individual musicians Trevor had ever heard. He may have heard better singers and maybe better guitarists, but there were very few who could sing and play on par with Tracy.

Trevor requested "Fire and Rain" by James Taylor and Tracy did one of the best renditions he had ever heard. He requested another song and she pulled it off like clockwork. Trevor knew women sometimes communicate by song. He thought that he should think of the perfect song for their meeting.

Then he requested "Wicked Game" by Chris Isaak. The lyrics to the song are about not wanting to fall in love with someone. This would be the perfect song because Trevor was thinking about how good his life was without commitment to a relationship. He also realized he was really attracted to Tracy. She thought for a little bit, played several notes, hummed the lyrics, and said she used to play it but didn't remember it.

Tracy had a contingency of groupies at the bar that evening. There were a few women who looked butch and several gentlemen about ten years older than her. That put them in the same age group as Trevor. Although they were in the same age group, they were not attractive men. They were all overweight and seemed to have given up on themselves years ago. They all seemed to adore Tracy.

When it came time for Tracy to take a break, she walked over to her admirers and began socializing with them. As she walked across the floor, Trevor could tell she was self-conscious in regard to him. As she conversed with her admirers, Trevor knew she would walk by him to grab his attention. Trevor began thinking about the best way to start a conversation when she walked by. Sure enough, she walked by and a conversation ensued.

They found out that they grew up in the same state and both liked to ride motorcycles. Trevor also mentioned that he liked to play golf. Trevor asked Tracy if she would like a drink and she said she didn't drink. Trevor laughed and said he would drink hers for her. His brain kicked in gear and he realized that everyone had probably tried to buy her a drink.

He noticed she had CDs for sale and inquired about them. Trevor asked her if she would play a couple of songs from her CD. She agreed. There isn't an artist alive who doesn't want people to appreciate their accomplishments. The request would endear him to her.

During the next set, Tracy played a song from her CD. Trevor didn't care for the song. He asked her if she would play a different song from the CD. She played the second song and it was amazing. The lyrics were great and the arrangement was superb. Trevor wanted to buy the CD out of curiosity. He also realized that every dude probably tried to endear themselves to her by buying her drinks. He understood that it would be more endearing to buy a CD from her than a drink for her. By buying a CD, he would have something to show for his money, also.

Trevor drank another beer and Tracy finished her set. She had two heavy speakers, her amp, and some other paraphernalia to load. Tracy rolled up her cables and gathered them, then grabbed the small stuff. As Trevor was observing, he noticed, that none of the men offered to help her with her equipment. He knew the groupie dudes would love to endear themselves to her but they sat there like fat bumps on a log while she tore down the equipment. Trevor helped her with the heavy speakers, pushed the cart out to her car, and assisted in loading her equipment.

When they finished loading, Tracy said "What now?" Trevor thought she might go to dinner if he asked her. He didn't want to rush things. He had been thinking about the fact that a lot of dudes were probably hitting on Tracy all the time. They probably asked her out to dinner and tried to buy her drinks on a regular basis. He had to be smarter than the average bear, so to speak. He thought a better approach would be to mention that he knew a place where she could probably arrange another gig. This was not asking her out, it was helping her out. Trevor told her about two places he believed she could get gigs. He would go with her and they would see what they could do.

The next night they met at the first location, had dinner, and left contact information. They went to the second location, had dessert, and left contact information. They had good conversation, talked about music, their home state, and life in general. Every day for several days, they did things together. Tracy would always come to Trevor's place or they would meet somewhere. Trevor and Tracy immediately formed a tight relationship. Both of them were night owls, which worked out perfectly.

Trevor always thought women got touchy, leaned in close, or gave some other kind of signal indicating they were ready for physical contact. He couldn't remember being rejected for a kiss since high school. He also could not remember how or what happened before he kissed someone. Most of the time, he could not remember how a kiss started. It was just that nature took over and kissing began.

When Trevor and Tracy were spending time together Trevor noticed that the only time Tracy touched him was if he touched her first. She seemed to like it when he touched her. He consciously wondered if she had given him a signal for a kiss and he had missed it.

Tracy mentioned she would like to go on a motorcycle ride to a small town about eighty miles away. Trevor was delighted to take her on a ride. They left after dark on a Sunday evening. When they got to the small town, everything was closed except for a gas station. At the gas station, they bought a couple of health drinks, sat on the curb, and downed their drinks.

As they prepared to get back on the motorcycle, Tracy was standing still with a blank look on her face. Trevor wondered what she was thinking. In retrospect, Trevor wondered if that was her way of getting a kiss. Maybe in her mind, she thought it would be romantic to have the first kiss in a small town in the middle of the night. If so, she wasn't giving much of a signal.

They headed for home as soon as their drinks were finished.

Although it was an eighty-mile ride in the darkest of night, it was a splendid ride. The stereo was blasting and the curves were superb. As they pulled into Trevor's driveway, one solitary drop of rain landed upon Trevor's hand. By the time the motorcycle was parked and covered, torrential rain was coming down. They had left at night for a 160-mile trip and returned just in time. In just a few short minutes, the roads were impassable by motorcycle. In an hour, even cars were stranded.

Trevor and Tracy sat on Trevor's porch and watched the rain come down like sheets of water. The sight and sound of the rain coming down was foreboding. Trevor and Tracy were sitting there, enjoying the rain, and Trevor was wondering if Tracy would like a kiss but didn't want to be obvious.

Eventually, Trevor made his bold move. He stood up part way, leaned across the table and gave Tracy a kiss. He guessed right; she had been waiting for that. She didn't seem too intent on kissing but the kiss led straight to the bedroom.

Since Tracy was a professional musician, she would play gigs three or four nights per week. Trevor would meet her at the gigs early enough to help her set up. He would pack in the big, heavy stuff and set it up while Tracy organized the small stuff. Tracy would be singing and playing while Trevor socialized with the patrons or bartender. Tracy's followers would consistently show up at her gigs, and Trevor became acquainted with them also.

This scenario was quite interesting because the income from gigs consisted of three parts. First of all, the musician was paid by the bar, restaurant, or private party that hired them. This was generally the larger percentage of income from a gig. Secondly, there were tips, and thirdly, there were CD sales. The business that hired the musician expected the musician to have a following. The musician maintained a following in order to get better gigs and tips.

In the old days, it was much easier to maintain a following. When DWI laws became stringent, people began patronizing musical events and bars that were closer to home. This decreased the odds of getting a DWI. If they taxied, it wasn't as expensive to travel a short distance rather than a long one. Since people didn't travel long distances, the musician would maintain a few followers who traveled, but most of them would only attend performances close to home. These days, most local musicians don't maintain a large group of followers. However, those that do have an advantage when it comes to getting bookings. The bar makes more money if the musicians bring in a group of followers. The musicians also make more money because the followers contribute consistently to the tip jar. So, the variables in the industry were getting gigs that pay well and maintaining a good following. The sale of CDs was relatively consistent.

Tracy played a gig every Saturday at a swanky little restaurant downtown. Without fail, she had the same friend and follower in attendance. He was about fifty-eight years old, seventy-five pounds overweight, and retired. Every so often, he would walk across the room and drop a five-dollar bill in the tip jar. He did this to remind other patrons to tip the musician.

For Tracy, it served two purposes. First of all, she got the tip, and secondly, it spurred others to tip. It was easy to see this fellow was making his best effort to endear himself to Tracy. He had been attending her gigs every Saturday at the same restaurant for a couple of years. He only came a few times after Trevor entered the picture. After he quit coming to her gigs, Tracy would call him and he wouldn't respond. The odds of him entering Tracy's romantic picture had been less than zero but he had been giving it his best shot.

Tracy asked Trevor if he thought the fellow, had romantic intentions.

Trevor replied with "Uh, yeahhh."

She seemed appalled. She had thought of him as a friend. Tracy hadn't heard from him for a couple of years when, out of the blue, he suddenly appeared at one of her gigs. That evening he earned the nickname "Nipples" because he ran his hand up his shirt and played with his nipples as he watched Tracy sing and play.

Trevor got in the habit of making an obvious walk through the center of the restaurant to drop a tip in the jar. Sometimes, Tracy would use Trevor's tip money to buy dinner for the both of them. At times, Trevor asked Tracy for money to seed the tip jar, so it wasn't all coming out of his pocket.

Each gig, Trevor made it a point to place ten dollars in her tip jar without her knowing it. Sometimes, he would ask a small child or someone sitting close to deposit the money for him. His favorite maneuver was to have a cute child put money in the tip jar. They would be too shy to deliver the money by themselves, so Trevor would help them. This made a production that everyone noticed and people would become conscientious about tipping.

Although their sex life was fantastic, Tracy was not particularly touchy outside of the bedroom. This seemed unusual to Trevor, considering she was in a new relationship. She always wanted Trevor to attend her gigs, but it was evident that she didn't want it to look like she and Trevor were attached. Trevor surmised she would get better tips if men thought she was available. Since they didn't know Trevor was her lover, it made it very interesting to watch men try to endear themselves to her.

The men playing up to her was a curiosity in itself. Typically, they would want to buy her drinks. Some would put hundred-dollar bills in the tip jar, but very few were smart enough to buy a CD. Trevor was well entertained between her music, her followers, the bar flies, and the dudes plying for her attention. This was entertainment at its finest.

Trevor and Tracy had been sleeping together for about a week when Tracy mentioned she had issues. Trevor pressed her for what she meant by "issues." She wouldn't comment further. All she would say is, "I have issues."

Until then, she had been a real sweetheart. She had a quality that was very seductive. She was sweet and a little timid. Everyone that met her seemed to adore her. There was something unusual about Tracy though. Trevor couldn't really put a finger on it, but there were a couple of things out of place. The first time they made love there hadn't been a buildup to sex. It went from kiss to bedroom. Coffee in the morning was not one or two cups, it was several cups. Walks in the evening were not moderate walks, they had to be five-mile walks, no matter what time of night. There was no moderation. If it was something she enjoyed, it was in excess. Music was no exception; it was her entire world.

For the third time in Trevor's life, he had what he considered a prophetic dream. This type of dream is different than any other type of dream. When it is over, you wake up and every hair follicle on your body is stimulated. It is like goosebumps or a chill. Visually, everything is in the highest of definition. Mentally it is as if you are in a higher state of awareness. If you have this type of dream, you will never forget it.

Trevor's first dream of this nature did not involve a person he knew. Trevor's second prophetic dream had occurred shortly after his father's death. During the dream, his father had given him a piece of business advice and Trevor followed it. The advice turned out to be extremely beneficial a few years later.

They say there are two types of parents: *nurturing* and *critical*. Trevor's father was a nurturing parent. His method of punishment was that he would be disappointed if you handled yourself in a way that he would not approve. To Trevor, his disapproval would be worse than any other type of punishment he could possibly receive.

In Trevor's dream, he and his father had been working side by side for three days. His father had not spoken to him during this time. Trevor began contemplating why his father would not speak to him. He hadn't done anything wrong and his conscience was clear. Certainly, his father must be upset about something. For the life of him, Trevor could not figure out why his father was upset. To confront his father, Trevor had to think of just the right approach because he didn't want to make matters worse.

When Trevor's father turned towards him, Trevor explained that they had been working together for three days and he hadn't spoken to him during that time.

Trevor's father looked him straight in the eye and said, "You know why." In that instant, Trevor knew his father was disappointed because he had been seeing Tracy. To his father's statement, Trevor replied, "It's okay, I can get out of that anytime I want."

Trevor's father disappeared. Trevor woke up and looked at Tracy lying there sleeping. He knew deep down that his father was right and a time would come when he and Tracy would have to part. Trevor had never been in a relationship he couldn't walk away from unscathed.

After her gigs, Tracy and Trevor would walk late at night. They rode motorcycle, hiked, and swam. They liked doing the same activities and seemed to enjoy any type of physical activity. Tracy seemed quiet at times and when Trevor would ask what she was thinking, she wouldn't have an explanation. He could tell she was thinking of something unpleasant.

Tracy's father had been on his death bed and passed away about two weeks after Trevor and Tracy met. All this time, Trevor had not been to Tracy's home. Trevor did not know why she hadn't invited him there, but he had surmised that her place wasn't as nice as his, and she was self-conscious about it. Tracy was alone at her place the night she received the call informing her that her father had died. Over the phone, she told Trevor her father had passed away. Trevor didn't want her to be alone and offered to go to her place to be with her. Tracy agreed that he should come and keep her company.

Chapter 12

Tracy's house was in an older part of the city. It was not a bad part of town, but it was close to the undesirable areas. For a woman on her own, it was commendable that she owned her own home.

Trevor knocked on the door and Tracy let him in. The house was organized for the most part, but it was the house of an artist or a musician. It had bright colored walls and music paraphernalia all around. It would be safe to say it could use a good thorough cleaning. The odd thing about her house was that the batteries in a couple of the smoke detectors had gone out and the detectors were chirping. Then there was a small dog and a bird without feathers. It had wing feathers and tail feathers but it didn't have feathers on its body (chest). So, this was Tracy's house. Trevor visited and comforted Tracy but remained a little on edge. Tracy was sad and mourning the loss of her father. When Trevor left, he complimented her on her house by saying "It is a nice house."

Tracy replied, "No it isn't."

On his way home, Trevor was uneasy about the alarms going off and the bird without feathers. Trevor was particular and would not have a bird without feathers and certainly the alarms would have to be silenced immediately. He told himself he would never go back to that house again. As Trevor contemplated the events of that evening, one thing was for certain. Tracy needed help.

What was the right thing to do? If someone needs help and you don't help them, what kind of person are you? Alarms were going off in Trevor's head just like they were in Tracy's house. Tracy must be going through a horrible depression. Although alarms kept going off in his head, Trevor was very fond of Tracy and couldn't turn his back on her. Maybe helping her was his way of justifying the fact that he was already very fond of her and couldn't cut her loose.

A couple days later, Trevor found himself at Tracy's house replacing the batteries in her smoke detectors. The thought of her smoke detectors chirping was driving him crazy and he wasn't even staying in the house. When Trevor installed new batteries, he noticed her back yard was also a mess. Grass had grown up around a couple of old bicycles that were laying in the corner of the yard. The swimming pool had turned green, and there was a large dead tree at the corner of the patio. It wasn't even Trevor's place, but he couldn't stand the sight of the yard.

Trevor and Tracy went to work on the yard and within days, the dead tree was hauled off, the grass was trimmed, and the swimming pool was balanced and clean. The two of them made a great team when it came to doing manual labor.

Tracy was a hard worker. Some like to think of stubbornness as a negative thing, but Trevor liked to think of it as willpower. Tracy had an extreme amount of willpower. Another thing Trevor liked about her was that she wasn't overly concerned with money. She wasn't materialistic to the extent that she had settled for less than most.

At times, Tracy acted very happy, then without incident or notice she would go quiet, as if she was having an argument with herself within her own head. She wouldn't comment on what she was thinking, but she would sometimes admit to having a lot of insecurities. You wouldn't think a beautiful musician who performed on stage would be insecure. In fact, she had no realistic sense of self. Her self-image changed drastically from one moment to the next. Trevor came to believe that she validated herself through her musical endeavors.

Even though Tracy had lived in the same city for over twenty years, she hadn't been to any of the lakes in the surrounding area. She hadn't ventured out and her world was very small. Her world was totally the opposite of Trevor's in this regard. One by one, Trevor took Tracy to each of the surrounding lakes. She was like a little girl on an adventure but for half of the adventure she was withdrawn. It was a real joy for Trevor to see someone so sheltered get out and see the world.

In time, Trevor and Tracy rode together to her gigs. They would be riding along in Tracy's car and she would play a song about being abandoned. Trevor asked her if there was a particular reason she liked the song. Tracy went on to explain that sooner or later, everyone abandons her. Trevor thought that was pure honesty. Who would admit to such a thing? He definitely wouldn't.

Trevor asked her why everyone abandons her.

She said, "They always do. You will too."

Tracy had previously met Trevor's neighbor. One morning as she was leaving Trevor's place, the neighbor asked her if she left Trevor happy. That was it for that neighbor, she wrote him off as a serial killer or something. In Trevor's reality, the neighbor was a good person with poor social skills.

Trevor's friend was coming to town to stay with him and play golf for five days. Trevor explained to Tracy that he and his friend would be playing golf for the next five days, but when his friend arrived, he would take the three of them to dinner so they could become acquainted. Trevor also wanted her to understand that she could spend time with them anytime she liked. It would be fun because his friend would also enjoy going to her gigs.

Trevor text messaged Tracy when his friend arrived and she didn't respond. Trevor took his friend to dinner in an area halfway between his place and Tracy's so she wouldn't have far to travel. When he called Tracy, she was livid. She thought Trevor and his friend were out on the town chasing women. She got hysterical and Trevor told her he was turning his phone off. He turned it off and turned it over on the table.

After dinner was over and they started home, Trevor noticed there were thirty-six hang-ups from Tracy. When Trevor got home and went to bed, he called Tracy. She explained that she thought Trevor and his friend were doing this and that. Trevor wrote it off, thinking she was upset because she wasn't the primary focal point of his attention since he was spending time with his friend.

Tracy had been trying to sell an old automobile without success. She had agreed to sell it to someone for half of what it was worth, but the young fellow couldn't raise the money. Trevor went to work selling her automobile. She also had a list of stereo equipment she would like to sell. Within a week, Trevor sold the pickup and stereo equipment for full value.

The assistant pro at the golf course challenged Trevor to a four-day play off. Whoever won would be treated by the loser to a steak dinner at the restaurant of the winner's choice. The first day of the playoff was at a golf course close to a restaurant Tracy played at in the evening.

They set a tee time so they could eat and listen to Tracy after golf. What an excellent way to top off a day of golf; dining and listening to music. Trevor was sure the assistant pro would enjoy it.

When Trevor and the assistant pro arrived at the restaurant, Tracy looked sad. Every song she sang was sad. Trevor wondered how the patrons in the restaurant kept from crying in their food; it was so sad! Tracy looked pissed. When her break rolled around, Trevor tried to give her a kiss and she pushed him away. She explained that she didn't think Trevor was playing golf and thought they spent the day at a strip club. Just by their attire and sweat, it was evident they had been playing golf all day. Besides, Trevor had no interest in strip clubs. Since he met Tracy, he had zero interest in any woman other than her. Tracy wrote off the assistant pro, saying he was bad.

In many ways, Trevor and Tracy were perfectly matched. They both liked the way they looked individually. They liked the way they looked together. Physically, they enjoyed each other with an unbridled level of intimacy. They had a chemistry that was like nothing Trevor had experienced. Both of them enjoyed the same music. There wasn't one song one liked and the other didn't. Tracy would learn and play any song Trevor liked; if she didn't know it, she would learn it. She could easily learn two or three songs a day if the arrangements weren't extremely difficult. She could listen to a new song while driving to a gig and perform it upon arrival. It would sound as if she had been playing it all her life.

A friend of Trevor's had a business venture that Trevor was interested in, so he was going to be out of town for three days. When he told Tracy he was going to be gone, she went ballistic. She thought Trevor should take her along. By now, Tracy had alienated every friend Trevor had introduced her to. He could just imagine taking her on a business venture and having a blowout. It would not make for a productive business trip and Trevor would need his wits about him. He couldn't take the chance.

When Trevor returned from the trip, Tracy accused him of abandoning her. She seemed to think that Trevor had a thing for his friend's wife and that is why he went on the trip.

Well, all got back to the routine. Trevor helped Tracy set up for her gigs, visited with her followers, and enjoyed her shows. Trevor and Tracy spent time together almost every day and they almost always spent the night together. It was like a roller coaster of events with Tracy.

Another friend of Trevor's came to visit and stay with him for a few days. By now Trevor realized he needed to prepare Tracy for his friend's visit. He explained to her that his friend was coming and they would spend most of their time golfing. Even though they would be golfing, Tracy was welcome to come along. Everything would be as usual, except they would have Trevor's friend around for a while.

Trevor's friend (Justin) was a lot of fun. Actually, his ability to drink large quantities of alcohol was his greatest talent; however, he was a big teaser. He had a gravy job and made a six-figure salary, but he was down to earth and liked to joke and play golf. He liked to refer to himself as a smartass.

The evening Justin arrived, Tracy and her band were playing at a dive bar. It was not the worst of bars; it was a middle-of-the-road kind of place. The crowds at these venues can be eclectic to say the least. Tracy had a following of lesbians, gay guys, overweight folks, and of course, there was an anorexic.

When Justin and Trevor entered the bar, the band was already playing. A couple sitting at a large table, asked them to join them. It was the anorexic gal and her boyfriend.

Justin ordered drinks, looked around the bar, and said "Jesus Christ, we have arrived at Dysfunction Junction." It was an accurate description! The anorexic gal took a liking to Justin and proceeded to tell him the most intimate details of her life. He listened intently, as if he was sympathizing with her. Trevor and Justin played shuffleboard until it was time for the band to break.

When the band took a break, they went back to their table. Trevor introduced Justin to Tracy.

Following the introduction, Justin looked at Tracy and said, "I will give you five thousand dollars if you take your guitar and smash it to pieces on the stage."

Tracy said she wouldn't do that for any amount of money. Later, Tracy told Trevor that she didn't like Justin at all. What a horrible thing to say that "He would pay me to break my guitar." She had no comprehension that he was kidding her. This was the fourth one of Trevor's friends she had alienated.

During Justin's visit, it was a constant concern that Tracy was getting as much attention as Justin. He was a guest and Trevor made sure he felt as welcome as possible, but it was difficult having someone competing for attention.

Trevor wondered if there was something he should be doing when he had friends around. Did he not include Tracy enough? Did he not give her enough attention?

It was evident that Tracy had issues. What had caused her feelings of insecurity? Was she born this way, or had something happened to her along the way? When Trevor would ask her what she was thinking, she wouldn't say. She did say that she was afraid to say because Trevor would use what she said to hurt her later. If Trevor could figure it out, he could help her overcome her fears. If her difficulties were a product of her past, they could certainly be resolved.

It had been eleven months since they met and the roller coaster had its ups and downs. It was soon to be Tracy's birthday, so Trevor planned a trip to the coast. They would celebrate in a very nice hotel along the water. They drove for several hours to get to their destination. The hotel, its surroundings, and the weather were beautiful. Since she had hardly been out of the city she lived in, Trevor was elated to take her on an adventure.

As soon as they settled into the hotel, Trevor suggested they take a walk along the water. Most people would like to investigate the area but not Tracy. As soon as they got there, Tracy wrote a song about Trevor, herself, and the area. The trip was immortalized in song.

At dinner, Trevor sensed something was off. They discussed it later and Tracy said she thought something had been off also. The rest of the evening went well and the two made passionate love, as usual.

The next morning was Tracy's birthday. They woke up in the beautiful hotel room, all excited about a day of adventure. They talked and agreed to stay an extra day. Trevor walked to the lobby and paid $250 for another night of lodging.

When he came back to the room, Tracy's phone rang. It was a swimming pool store owner, asking her to play at his store. After the gig, he wanted her to go to dinner with him. Tracy commented to Trevor that she should have told him her boyfriend would come also. She laughed.

Trevor laughed and said, "I couldn't have said it better. The perfect answer. What did you tell him?"

Tracy had told him she would let him know. They both knew the gig was the pool store owner's way of setting her up for a date. It was her he was after. Tracy said she didn't want to do the gig. She asked Trevor what he thought she should do. Trevor said she should tell him she would do the gig but her boyfriend would be there also. The conversation went downhill from there. It wasn't that Tracy was interested in the pool store owner. The problem was she didn't have boundaries. She ended up cancelling the gig.

That started the ball rolling. It was her birthday, and Trevor hadn't given her a card or present and she was hurt. Evidently, she was expecting a ring or something. Trevor had planned on taking her to a certain shop where she could pick out her own present. He was thinking it would be a special token from their adventure. He also thought she would appreciate the fact that he had spent a lot of money to take her on the trip.

When Tracy got upset, it was as if someone had cheated on her with her sister or as if he had killed someone. She became hysterical. The whole day was in shambles.

When it came time to go to bed, Tracy was still angry. Even though it was a king bed and they could sleep without touching each other, Tracy chose to sleep in the vehicle located in the parking garage. She didn't take a blanket, pillow, or anything else. She just slept in the back seat, wearing her jeans and t-shirt on. Later, Trevor took a pillow to her but she was sound asleep by the time he arrived.

The next morning when Tracy returned to the hotel room, Trevor had already showered and packed. He was ready to go home. One thing was for certain: he wasn't doing another day of this nonsense. He offered to buy Tracy a ticket home. He certainly didn't want to ride home with her and all of her drama. He told her his drama bucket was completely full, and in fact, it was overflowing. He didn't have room for any more.

Tracy wouldn't hear of taking a bus or plane home. All day in an automobile with her drama was an experience Trevor did not want. Since she wouldn't go back on a plane or bus, there was no other choice. She was going back with Trevor.

Neither Trevor nor Tracy said much until they were out of town. Bitterness was dripping from every pore of Tracy's being as they left. She started coming up with every grievance she could possibly think of. Trevor listened for a while, trying to keep the peace. After all, it was a long ride home. Evidently, Tracy had realized she had been unreasonable and she needed to find blame with Trevor to justify her behavior. She mentioned a few grievances and Trevor didn't confront her, although his patience was wearing thin. Why should he listen to her bullshit without saying anything? It wasn't worth taking this kind of abuse just because it was a long ride home.

Tracy had been complaining for some time when she mentioned that Trevor had an old girlfriend's picture on Facebook.

Trevor replied, "Well, that could be, but it isn't near as good as the pictures you have of your old boyfriend. My favorite is the one with you in the sheepskin coat."

At this comment, Tracy went hysterical and started grabbing for the door handle as if she was going to bail out of the vehicle. She seemed so upset, she was having trouble locating the latch but grabbed it and cracked the door open. Tracy looked back at Trevor and the look in her eye told him not to call her bluff. She had the wild look of goodbye in her eyes.

Her eyes told him, he would not see her alive if he didn't take action. In that instant, he imagined her rolling out of the vehicle and hitting the embankment. He thought of how horrible it would be to see her lifeless, broken, dead body. Her seat belt was unfastened, the door was open, and she was absolutely hysterical.

Trevor had been anxious to get home, so they were rolling down the interstate at eighty-five miles per hour when he hit the brakes. As the vehicle started to slow it appeared that Tracy decided not to jump and shut the door. The vehicle came to a stop.

They stopped on the edge of the road and Trevor assessed the situation. The look in her eyes told Trevor she had completely flown the cuckoo nest. She may have bailed out had he not stopped. Her normally beautiful blue eyes had a deranged look about them and all color had fled from her face. She looked as white as a ghost.

Trevor asked her if she wanted to get out of the vehicle and she said "No." He asked her if she was going to do that again and she said "No." He asked her if she wanted to continue down the road and she said "Yes." It was as if she had a moment of realization, an epiphany, that she had almost made a tragic mistake. Trevor had a reputation for being stable under pressure, but this had been an adrenaline rush he never wanted to repeat. The whole event was so bizarre, it would have been laughable had it not been for the fact that Tracy had almost bailed out of an automobile speeding down the road at eighty-five miles per hour.

They continued down the road at a slower rate of speed for about fifty miles. By the time they got up to speed, they were in the middle of nowhere. It was about eighty miles from the city they came from and forty miles to the next convenience store or gas station.

Tracy had previously told Trevor about one of her former birthdays. For her birthday, her boyfriend had taken her to a cheap restaurant and bought her dinner. When it was time to pay, her boyfriend proceeded to argue with the restaurant management about the cost of the meal. Tracy had mentioned that it had hurt her feelings.

Now, they were rolling down the interstate in the middle of nowhere and

Tracy started mentioning all the things she didn't get to do on the trip. She had wanted to go kayaking and hiking. She began talking about how disappointed she was with the trip.

Trevor was listening to her complain as he thought about the fact that the only thing her former boyfriend had bought her for her birthday was a cheap dinner that he complained about paying for. Trevor had planned a trip and spent over a thousand dollars on hotel rooms, fuel, dinners, and entertainment. Here she was, complaining about Trevor not doing enough for her birthday.

Trevor was thinking about the disparity of the situation when Tracy said, "This was the worst birthday in my whole life."

Trevor couldn't maintain his silence any longer. He said "Well, what about the birthday when your boyfriend bought you a cheap dinner and complained about the cost?"

Tracy instantly became totally irate at this remark! She said, "I never should have told you something so personal. I knew you would use it against me. I knew I couldn't tell you anything personal or you would use it against me. I can't believe you used that to hurt me."

Trevor said he was just trying to use an example to show the disparity between what he did for her birthday compared to what her last boyfriend had done for her birthday. There was no reasoning and all rationale was gone. Once again, Tracy was hysterical beyond belief.

Tracy said, "I want out of here." Remembering the previous incident, Trevor began slowing the vehicle. He thought he should pull over and try to settle things down. Tracy said, "I am taking my guitar and getting out of here." She reached for her guitar in the back seat and had trouble getting it up over the seat.

Trevor pulled to a stop. He asked Tracy where she was going to go. She was in the middle of nowhere. As soon as the vehicle stopped, Tracy opened her door, walked to the back door of the vehicle, and pulled her guitar from the back seat.

Trevor walked around the vehicle while explaining to her that she was in the middle of nowhere and she couldn't walk all the way home. He also explained that a lot of bad things could happen to her if she got out and started walking down the road. The more Trevor tried to rationalize the situation, the more adamant Tracy became.

As a last resort, Trevor grabbed her by the arm and explained that she needed to get back in the automobile. Tracy picked up her guitar and started walking down the road.

Trevor pulled up alongside her, rolled down the passenger window, and asked her to get in the vehicle. Nope, she wasn't having it. Trevor went down the road until there was a crossover between the lanes of the interstate. He crossed over to the other side of the road and went back until he found another crossover between the lanes. He drove until he pulled up behind Tracy and asked her to get in. She wouldn't talk. She just kept walking.

Trevor had to concede that he was not getting Tracy back in the automobile. Down the road he went. He was headed home. Tracy was a good-looking woman and she would get a ride without effort. Trevor was hoping she wouldn't get picked up by the wrong people.

As Trevor was flying down the road, he couldn't help but feel responsible for leaving Tracy in the middle of nowhere. He was going to feel really bad if something happened to her.

He thought about other people that may be able to talk to her. Maybe he was not the only one who felt a sense of responsibility toward her. He traveled for about thirty miles before he came to a gas station/convenience store.

Trevor stopped at the gas station to get a snack and something to drink. He decided to call Tracy's sister, who lived several states away. Maybe she could shed some light on Tracy's behavior, but most of all, he thought she should know where Tracy was and what the situation was. Maybe she would have a solution. Maybe she would call Tracy and be able to talk sense to her. This way, Trevor would not be the only one responsible.

Tracy's sister tried to call her several times but she wouldn't answer her phone. Trevor and Tracy's sister concluded that she may not have cell service in the middle of nowhere. Trevor took his time eating his snack, as he wanted to spend some time pondering the situation. He imagined that Tracy may have gotten a ride by now because it had been over two hours since they parted.

Trevor's phone rang. It was Tracy. Trevor asked her where she was and she said she was along the road. Trevor asked her why she called him and she said she didn't know. Trevor asked her what she was going to do and she said, she didn't know. He asked her if she wanted him to pick her up and she wouldn't answer. He asked her if she needed help and she said she did. He asked her if she wanted a ride and she wouldn't reply. Trevor told her he was a long way down the road and that he wasn't coming back to get her unless she promised to get in the vehicle and go home. She wouldn't respond. He asked her several times if she would agree to get in the vehicle and go home and she would not respond. Trevor asked her if he needed to go to where she was and she said "Yes."

As I mentioned earlier, Tracy had a lot of willpower. Trevor could see that they were at an impasse. Tracy would not agree to get in the vehicle and go home, but she wanted Trevor to come to her. So, what was the mystery? Trevor agreed to drive back and assess the situation.

He was about thirty miles away and it would take a while to get back to where he had left Tracy. She would be on the opposite side of the interstate, so he would have to pass her location and use one of the turnarounds between the interstate lanes. He did have a four-wheel drive, so he may be able to cross without finding a turnaround. He would watch for her on the other side of the interstate.

As it turned out, Tracy was easy to spot. She was sitting on a guardrail with her guitar at her feet. A police car had just arrived. The lights were flashing and two policemen were exiting their vehicle.

Trevor was lucky and didn't have to drive far to find a turn around. He pulled in behind the police car and assessed the situation. What had happened was that Tracy had walked until she came to a long guardrail. She couldn't go around the outside of the guardrail because it was a steep drop off of about 500 feet. It would be too dangerous and narrow to walk on the edge of the highway for the distance of the guardrail. It would be particularly dangerous considering she was also carrying her guitar. She had walked until she couldn't continue and there she sat, with her guitar at her feet, two policemen were interviewing her, and the lights were flashing. The flashing of the police lights reminded Trevor of the chirping coming from Tracy's smoke detectors. Another warning!

As Trevor walked past the police car and towards the two policemen interviewing Tracy, one of the policemen stopped him. They didn't want him near Tracy and they proceeded to interview the two of them separately.

They asked Trevor what his relationship was to her, how long he had known her, what his address was, where they came from, and where they were going. When they asked Trevor what she was upset about, he told them she didn't get to go kayaking. When they asked why she was walking down the road, he told them it was because she wouldn't stay in the vehicle. The policeman seemed somewhat amused by the situation and one of them couldn't help but chuckle. One of the policemen told Trevor next time, he should drop her off in town. Trevor chuckled and told the policeman that he didn't have a choice.

The policeman asked Tracy if she would rather go with him or them. They gave her an ultimatum and she chose to go with Trevor. They asked her if she was afraid of Trevor. She chuckled slightly and said "No." When Trevor, Tracy, and the policeman were together, Trevor asked her if she was sure she wanted to go with him instead of the policeman. She said she would rather go with him. Trevor told her it would be fine with him if she went with the policeman.

For the remainder of the trip, Trevor and Tracy only spoke when it was absolutely necessary.

About halfway home, Trevor became hungry and pulled into a roadside convenience store to get a sandwich. He asked Tracy if she would like anything and she said she couldn't eat. Even though it was well over 100 degrees outside, Trevor turned the vehicle off and took the keys out of the ignition before entering the store. Not only was his drama bucket full, it was overflowing and bursting at the seams.

As the travelers entered the city limits of their hometown, Tracy started breaking the silence. She began talking about how people weren't meant to live alone and finding another relationship was not something she was looking forward to. She also mentioned that she couldn't go home because her pet sitter would be staying at her house. It was clear her mood had changed.

Now she was worried Trevor would take her home and she would never see him again. She was absolutely correct. Trevor had every intention of leaving her at her house and never seeing her again. It was becoming another situation to get her to go home. Rather than have another fiasco, Trevor let her stay the night at his place.

This incident was a good example of how impulsive Tracy could be. She had jumped out of a vehicle in the middle of nowhere, without a thought of where she would go from there. This was how she went through life. She lived in the moment without regard for the future. Like many extremely talented musicians, Tracy was a tortured soul. Trevor could ask her why she had done something and her reply would be, "I don't know why I do what I do." Tracy had stated many times that she was not *normal*. Her musical ability definitely wasn't *normal*; she had an uncanny ability to write, perform songs, and play musical instruments.

The trip had been a gut-wrenching experience for Trevor. That evening as he was lying in bed, he understood the dream involving his father. Excruciating heartbreak was invariably certain. How could something so right be so wrong?

Trevor rode the roller coaster until Christmas. He had been helping Tracy almost every day prior to Christmas. He had taken one day to find just the right presents for her. He wanted to get her new bedding and a nice, thick, warm bath robe. Tracy's bedding was a hodgepodge. It had been cold walking outdoors to the hot tub, so Trevor thought a nice warm bathrobe would be a very thoughtful present. Trevor was very particular and liked a certain type of expensive bathrobe. It had to be very thick and feel nice on bare skin. He looked all day to find just the right bedding and bathrobe. He wasn't enthralled with the bedding but thought Tracy could take it back if she wanted to trade it.

Christmas morning, the two of them unwrapped their presents and all seemed fine, initially. They cleaned up the wrappings and had a nice breakfast. Tracy had gone to the restroom and upon exiting it, she exclaimed in the most sarcastic of way, "I love my presents."

Trevor asked her what she meant by that. Tracy responded by saying that the bedding is just about sex. Trevor told her that her bedding was horrible and he thought she would be glad to have new bedding. The disagreement went downhill from there. Trevor was unbelievably hurt by her complaining about the presents. He had been so busy helping her, he only had one day for shopping. He had spent the whole day looking for just the right presents and now she was complaining. It seemed so ungrateful that he was seething.

They had planned on going for a hike on Christmas day, so they put on their shoes and headed for the mountain. During the hike, Trevor couldn't get it out of his head that Tracy had been so ungrateful about the presents. He had spent the whole year helping her with her business, house, and anything else she needed. Now she had the audacity to complain about her presents!

When the two of them returned from the hike, Trevor asked Tracy to grab her things because they were going to her house. On the way to her house, Trevor explained how he felt about her complaining about the presents and how much it hurt. He left her in her driveway and told her he was getting off the roller coaster. They were finished.

The relationship had been a paradox. It had the highest of highs and the lowest of lows. The overall effect was like that of an intoxicating drug. Trevor had never experienced such an intoxicating chemistry. It had been a relationship of intimacy, passion, and turmoil. Trevor's once uncomplicated, non-committed lifestyle had gone from contentment to emotional chaos in a matter of months. It was obvious to Trevor, that there can be an unexplainable feeling of affection and connection to someone of the opposite sex. *It was also obvious that this type of connection is not always conducive to long term health or happiness.*

What wasn't obvious to Trevor is that this would not be the end of the saga between him and Tracy.

Chapter 13

Bikers and Body Shots

Arizona Bike Week is one of the largest gatherings of motorcycle riders in the United States. Approximately 100,000 motorcyclists converge upon the Phoenix metropolitan area during the first week in April, with the largest concentration of riders gathering in Scottsdale. On a single day, 70,000 motorcycles may pass through Cave Creek, Arizona.

Cave Creek, with a population of about 5,000, lies north and west of Scottsdale and is known as Arizona's drunkest town. It has rock and roll motorcycle bars on one side of the street and country western rodeo bars on the other side. Some refer to it as costume town because motorcyclist on one side of the street are dressed in motorcycle costumes and on the other side of the street folks are dressed like cowboys. It is usually a popular motorcycle destination, but during bike week, motorcycles take over and line the streets.

Concerts are a big part of Arizona Bike Week and most bars will have live music every night of the event. Big name concerts, such as Joan Jett and ZZ Top, are held at Westworld. It is an enormous outdoor concert area. There will also be several big-name bands playing at different venues throughout the area.

Benefit rides can also be a big part of Bike Week. The riders will pay a sum of money (usually about thirty-five dollars) to benefit cancer or some other worthy cause. Then they are organized in a group and follow each other to various bars. One of the more popular rides is the Titty Bar Run. The riders in this group will stop at various strip clubs throughout the valley.

One of the big draws for many people is viewing all of the custom motorcycles on display. It is not unusual for people to have a $60,000 custom motorcycle. The ingenuity and craftsmanship of the custom motorcycles are amazing.

There is a large diversity of people attending Bike Week, with the majority being weekend warriors. Weekend warriors are motorcycle riders who sometimes ride on weekends but are not really long-distance riders. They typically have a higher-than-average income, enjoy putting on leather clothes, riding to bars, and socializing with others who are doing the same. These folks may have a five-year-old motorcycle, which is typically a Harley Davidson with about 4,000 miles on it. If these folks come from out of town, they will generally bring their motorcycle in a trailer.

Another class of riders are the ones who love to ride. They will ride their motorcycle from anywhere and everywhere because they love to ride. Their enjoyment is not in the motorcycle event and socializing, it is about the journey to and from the event. Typically, these folks will ride a touring motorcycle or a sport touring motorcycle such as a BMW or Honda Goldwing. These days, adventure-type motorcycles are quite popular. This type of motorcycle accommodates longer distances, along with an ability to traverse off-road situations.

Some ride motorcycles as their only mode of transportation. These folks may use their motorcycle in everyday life as a cheap form of transportation. They usually don't ride long distances. For some, riding a motorcycle as their only mode of transportation creates an image. These people will typically have cruisers or crotch rockets (sport bikes). The cruiser riders are typically older folks who have chosen motorcycles as their favorite mode of transportation.

Crotch rocket riders are usually younger riders with a need for speed and cheap transportation.

Then of course, there are the one-percenters who became known as one-percenters because they represent one percent of the population who rides motorcycles. Typically, these riders have three-piece patches on the back of their coats. They utilize Bike Week as an opportunity to demonstrate to the public that they are misunderstood, nice, tough guys and that they are misrepresented as being involved in criminal activity. Only the gullible or ignorant would fall for this façade, as there is a plethora of evidence to the contrary.

The Phoenix area is a melting pot where people move and vacation from all parts of the country. It seems a large portion of the population comes from the Midwest. In April, much of the population consists of snowbirds. The climate is hard to beat and if you live there, people from the northern states love to visit you in the winter.

Trevor and his friends have mutual friends who visit each year during Bike Week and it is always entertaining. Before their friends come to visit, Trevor tries to find a good ride that is suited for everyone. He tries to find a new route that will be scenic and just the right distance. It is fun for him to ride the roads in search of the perfect route.

The couple (Reese and Lisa) from the Midwest arrived in Phoenix, where it was sunshine and perfect weather. Reese and Lisa always reserved a motorcycle at Harley Davidson. Needless to say, they were excited to attend Bike Week and soak in the sunshine. Trevor's other friends, Dan and Patty, keep a motorcycle in Phoenix and they were also excited to ride.

There are so many people renting motorcycles during Bike Week that it is necessary to reserve a motorcycle months in advance. If you don't have one reserved beforehand, you will be out of luck.

Trevor thought he found the perfect route for their adventure. At the end of the route, there was a huge bar with horseshoe pits. It looked as if it would be a happening place during Bike Week. He imagined it to be the perfect ride that all would enjoy.

Everything went well and everyone was on the road following Trevor around the outskirts of Phoenix. The scenery was spectacular and the weather was perfect. Five people enjoying the freedom of the open road. They headed south until they hit farm country and while they were out in the country, Trevor missed a turn, which made the trip longer than he anticipated.

Of course, Trevor had been riding motorcycles off and on over the winter months, so the ride was a short one for him. Since the other participants hadn't ridden in several months and were not really long-distance riders, they were already getting tired of riding. When they got to the bar, there were only five people in the entire place. It was a big place with a large outdoor area that was pretty much vacant. What a disappointment! The patrons all seemed to be locals and it was a Wednesday night. Maybe it was a weekend destination. Everyone had a bite to eat, hung out, and visited for a while. Reese seemed to enjoy visiting with the locals. He was from a small town, so he fit right in. He was also a professional drinker, with plenty of practice.

Well, that place didn't turn out to be much fun and it was time to head home before dark. Patty was thinking about getting back the shortest and fastest way possible. That would be through town, on the interstate, in rush hour traffic. Not fun!

Trevor studied the route and figured out the quickest, most enjoyable way to get home. The trip toward home seemed to go much better since Trevor didn't take everyone out through the farm fields. When they refueled, it was decided to stop at a biker bar on the way home.

The biker bar was a unique one. It was a dive bar but as dive bars go, it was well kept. It was not particularly a hangout for one-percenters but a place where weekend warriors go for drinks and sensual entertainment. The entertainment consists of scantily clad young ladies doing hula hoops on the bar and hanging off of the rafters while performing gymnastic feats. For twenty dollars, the patrons can also buy a body shot.

A body shot is performed by the server of your choice and she is dressed in a bikini of sorts. The server sits on the bar, which is about chest high to the patron. She then rubs lemon and salt on the inside of her leg, just down from her crotch. The lemon is then placed in her mouth and a shot of whiskey is placed between her breasts. The shot is supported on each side by her breasts and the string that holds the breasts together. Now that the shot is between her breasts and the lemon and salt are on the soft, inside part of her leg, she places her legs, up over the patron's shoulders. Then with one hand, she grabs the back of the patron's head, moving it down to the lemon and salt, which he licks off the soft, inner part of her leg. She then moves his head up to the shot glass located between her breasts. With one hand, she controls tipping the shot glass and the other hand guides the back of the patron's head. He downs the shot. She then places the empty shot glass on the bar and moves his head up to her mouth. With his mouth, he grabs the lemon and pulls it from her mouth. With her hand, she grabs the lemon from his mouth and places it on the bar. The scantily clad server then takes both of her hands and places them on the back of the patron's head. She pulls his head forward and places his face between her breasts while she wiggles from side to side with his face between her breasts. This is known as motor boating. The whole event from beginning to end takes about fifty-nine seconds. Time is money and the ladies are very efficient.

Everyone situated themselves at the biker bar. Before long they settled into drinking and conversation. There weren't many people at the biker bar, either.

Reese was a colorful character, to say the least. Your first impression may be that he could easily be cast on the *Duck Dynasty* reality series. This impression is accurate to some degree but not entirely. Reese maintains a short growth of whiskers, is in his mid-forties, and is about five foot seven inches tall. He is a builder or handy man by trade. He is the type of guy who can fix or build anything. In recent years, he had a snowmobile wreck that badly messed up his leg. Doctors advised him to keep the calf of his leg supported with an elastic bandage at all times. Without the bandage, his calf balloons to epic proportions. He also developed diabetes. Considering he had diabetes, along with a leg injury, doctors advised him to stop drinking alcohol. His solution was to switch from drinking beer to drinking vodka. He consistently consumes large quantities of vodka along with a continual dose of medical marijuana. His logic is that neither substance contains sugar.

He is the type of person you would like to take to the golf course and place bets on the game. By his initial appearance and manner, you wouldn't guess that he is an excellent golfer. He plays golf fully loaded with chemicals. The more he drinks and smokes, the better he plays. He may have a high score on the first few holes, but he will finish with birdies and 340-yard drives. After drinking a fifth of vodka and smoking pot, for the duration of a game he has been known to finish with a final score of seventy-three.

Chapter 13

Reese's wife Lisa is a cute petite blonde with lots of patience. As a rule, she is a good, loyal, subservient wife. After they had been at the bar for a while, Lisa began asking Reese to stop drinking. Trevor was not aware of Reese's diabetes and leg problems, so he shared his drinks with Reese. Little did he know the reason she wanted him to quit drinking was because she didn't want him riding the motorcycle home when he had too much to drink. She was concerned about their safety.

The ladies seemed to be tired from the motorcycle ride. They also seemed concerned about getting home safely on two wheels. Everyone except Trevor left for home.

Soon after they left, the bar came to life. Trevor was standing at the bar when he became involved in a conversation with a young man from England. The young fellow was about twenty-three years old and on an adventure touring the United States. The young Englishman was in heaven at the bar with scantily clad women, alcohol, and socializing. A certain server had struck his fancy and he was dying to get a body shot from her. At twenty-three years old, the Englishman probably hadn't seen a lot of naked women, much less had the opportunity to lick salt and lemon juice from the inside of their thighs. As he spoke, it was obvious he was wasted and teetering from alcohol consumption.

The Englishman got the attention of his favorite server. She sat down on the bar with her legs spread apart in front of him. The Englishman asked Trevor if he would record the body shot on his cell phone. There was a low battery warning on the Englishman's cell phone, so they decided to record the event on Trevor's phone. That way, Trevor could send the video to the Englishman after words.

The young man was all smiles as the server spread her legs, applied salt and lemon to her inner thighs, pulled his face down to her inner thighs, and rubbed his face between her breasts. The end of the video was priceless as he turned towards Trevor, smiled with a shit-eating grin, and said, "Man, that went fast." The expression on his face was that of someone who had really pulled off a good one. He was smiling like a Cheshire cat. Trevor was certain it had been one of the most pleasurable fifty-nine seconds in the Englishman's lifetime.

Trevor was standing about three feet from the bar sending the video to the Englishman when the servers carried a galvanized tub by him and placed it on the bar. They filled it with ice and water, then placed a water pitcher upon the bar. Everyone was told that from now on, they wouldn't be allowed to take pictures or record video. A line of women in tee-shirts formed behind Trevor. The women in the line had on t-shirts without a bra underneath. They were bare breasted underneath their t-shirts. There was going to be a wet t-shirt contest and Trevor was in the right place at the right time.

While the video was sending, a beautiful young lady moved past Trevor and climbed onto the bar. She was dressed in a white t-shirt and short shorts. She stepped into a galvanized tub and one of the servers poured cold water over her breasts to stimulate her nipples. She began gyrating in a very seductive, sexually provocative manner. Getting her nipples to stand up and get as hard as possible appeared to be the ultimate goal. This continued for some time.

There was a $1,000 prize for the winner of the contest. Trevor guessed that women willing to get up on a bar and stimulate their breasts with cold water for the pleasure of others were probably very intent on winning the prize money. After all, $1,000 is probably a lot of money to many of these women.

As the first contestant was performing on the bar, the next contestant in the line was standing directly to Trevor's left side. She had long dark hair, dark brown eyes, and perfectly shaped, voluptuous, size D or larger breasts. Her face was gorgeous. She and Trevor were exactly the same height. Trevor and the beautiful young woman were standing side by side, watching the contestant perform upon the bar. As they began conversing, they were eye to eye.

She looked over at Trevor and said, "She is not going to make it."

Trevor replied, "She will need to do better than that." He didn't know what else to say; after all, he hadn't seen a wet t-shirt contest before.

To that she replied, "Her nipples aren't stimulated enough."

Trevor replied, "That's for sure." Trevor was starting to get excited. Not from the woman on the bar, but the sexy contestant to his left. The sexy contestant to his left had a near-perfect face and figure. She was flirting with Trevor. At that point, he was more turned on by her flirting than her sexuality. It didn't hurt that she was standing next to him in a white t-shirt with nothing but bare breasts underneath. He felt a good connection for only knowing her for a minute or so. If she wasn't a ten, he wouldn't know where to take off a fraction. She was a very beautiful young woman and must have liked Trevor or she wouldn't have engaged him in conversation.

As Trevor was talking to her, she began to play with her left nipple. Once again, she mentioned that the woman on the bar was not going to make it. Trevor's brain fired up, and he began to wonder if she would let him stimulate her nipples for her. After all, it is more sensuous to be stimulated by someone else. Maybe it would be even more sensuous being stimulated by a stranger.

Trevor reflected on a time when he had met two ladies in a bar. As he was conversing and getting to know the ladies, another lady entered into the conversation. The third lady had enormous breasts. The woman was about Trevor's height and about fifteen pounds overweight. For a woman her size, she had very, very large breasts.

The conversation went on until it got around to the size of the third lady's breasts. She explained that she wanted to get a breast reduction because her breasts were causing back problems. She claimed that each breast weighed nine pounds. When you think about carrying eighteen extra pounds on your chest, you can understand why she would want a reduction. As the conversation continued, she told the other two females that they could feel them if they wanted. Trevor enjoyed watching the other ladies lift her breast and check them out, but in the back of his mind, he was wondering if she would let him feel her breasts.

Since he was a male and there were other people at the bar, he was certain she wouldn't let him feel her breasts. On the other hand, you never know unless you ask. Nothing ventured, nothing gained. If he asked, he would probably get shot down. If he didn't ask, he would have zero odds of feeling her breasts. After all, much of the enjoyment of sex is about what you can get away with. How seductive you can be and how accomplished you can become. Trevor knew he would need the right approach to succeed in feeling her breasts.

After the other two ladies had felt her breasts, Trevor swallowed and took his chances. "Would you mind if I did that?"

"Go ahead," she said.

Respectfully, Trevor lifted them to feel the weight, squeezed them to see how firm they were, and gently ran his hand across her nipple to see if they would respond. How many men would have the courage to ask if they could feel her breasts in a crowded bar in front of others? He had succeeded.

Now, the young lady to his left was much sexier than the lady with the large breasts. He would not be asking to feel her large breasts. He would be asking if she would like him to stimulate her nipples. The rewards were much higher in this situation. He could ask and most certainly get shot down, or he could take a chance. Should he give it a shot or go home without trying?

Trevor was watching her play with her left nipple when he drummed up the courage to ask if she would like him to help. She didn't reply when he asked her if she would like him to help, so he mentioned that it would be a lot more effective if he did it. She didn't reply. She just looked ahead without response. Trevor thought her lack of response was because she didn't want to verbalize her approval. It is best not to talk about things that have to do with sexuality; it is best to let it happen. She could have said no but she didn't. It was a very, very bold move when Trevor reached over with his right hand and began stimulating her right nipple. It soon became evident that being stimulated by Trevor was more effective than self-stimulation.

As she stimulated her left nipple with her left-hand, Trevor began mirroring her movement as he stimulated her right nipple. As he watched her playing with her left nipple, he learned what felt good to her. Soon her right nipple was harder than her left one. It seemed that Trevor was doing well, so he suggested that he stimulate her left nipple also. Trevor kept both of her nipples hard and at attention until her name was called.

When she stepped upon the bar, she was well prepared for the competition. She was looking good and the other ladies standing around Trevor knew it. The $1,000 prize money could be hers.

Trevor began watching his work in action when a contestant from behind him stepped in front of him and moved in very close. She didn't need words; Trevor knew exactly what she wanted. She wanted the same advantage the contestant on the bar had. She wanted her breasts stimulated also. Trevor was pleased to provide his services. He started caressing her breasts and softly touching her. He was trying to give her goose bumps when another contestant backed up into him.

So there he was, stimulating one contestant while another one backed into him, causing him to get excited, which seemed to be just what she wanted. Trevor became concerned that he had become as much of a spectacle as the ladies on the bar, but it was worth it. These women may have had husbands or boyfriends accompanying them. Whatever, Trevor continued to enjoy his newfound position as the pre-stimulator for the wet t-shirt contest.

Trevor remembered the shit eating grin on the face of the Englishman, as he finished the body shot. He imagined, he had a similar look on his face, after completing his duties as the pre-stimulator for the wet t-shirt contest. Trevor had become so engrossed in his duties, he had no idea who won the contest.

This may be wrong, but likely there are not a lot of guys who have become pre-stimulators for a wet t-shirt contest. This could be one of the most desirable positions a man could possibly have. Trevor thought about the old adage: *It never hurts to ask.*

Chapter 14

A Hot Mess

It had been several years since Trevor and Kristy met. It had been an ongoing saga of cat and mouse. The two had planned on meeting in the Coachella Valley, Las Vegas, and then they planned for another meeting in Canada. Each of the meetings had ended in disappointment. They hadn't spoken for several years, and Trevor became curious about what was going on with Kristy. Trevor did not have intentions of meeting with her. He was just curious about what had happened to her. The last he knew, she had cancelled a trip to Canada because she had two DWI citations and could not enter the country.

One morning as Trevor was fixing breakfast, he decided to give Kristy a call. She was tickled to hear from him and conversed for a long time. Trevor sent her a picture of his breakfast and she sent a selfie. It was as if they were old friends who had missed each other. The next day Kristy sent pictures of the fresh snow in her yard.

Years ago, Kristy had worked as a flight attendant, but she now worked as a receptionist in a doctor's office. Evidently, they did cosmetic enhancements there. With two DWI convictions, she probably wasn't going to be progressing very far up the occupation ladder. Kristy was a very attractive woman but at her age, it wasn't going to buy her much in the job market.

For the next week or so, Trevor and Kristy kept in close contact. The weather was getting colder and Kristy mentioned coming to visit Trevor. She would enjoy getting away from the cold. They discussed her buying her own airline ticket and covering her own expenses. This was the only feasible arrangement because the last time they planned to meet, Kristy couldn't get into Canada and Trevor ended up paying for her airfare. That was not going to happen again! Trevor told her he would pick her up at the airport and she could stay with him.

This was going to be interesting because Trevor and Kristy seemed to have such a wonderful chemistry. When Trevor met other women, he always compared his attraction to Kristy with his attraction to them. She had become a standard for rating attraction. Others just didn't seem to compare.

When Kristy arrived at the airport, she didn't hug and there was no physical contact. Other than that, she was complimentary and pleasant. They both complimented each other on the fact that they still looked the same. Trevor was not being entirely truthful though. Although Kristy was still a very attractive woman, she was not as attractive as she used to be. When he last saw her, she hadn't been cosmetically enhanced. She used to have a perfect facial structure. She had nice cheek bones and the shape of her face was one of her best features. Now her cheeks looked similar to that of a pocket gopher's crammed with food. Her hair used to be auburn but now it was a light-colored blonde. Kristy had been enhanced and lost her wholesome, attractive appearance. However, she was still a very beautiful woman.

The first time Trevor met Kristy, she was very fun, affectionate, complimentary, and interesting. She had sat on Trevor's motorcycle, kissed him, and they held hands. She was drinking and the drinks had affected her. The second time Trevor saw her, they had danced and talked for several hours.

Although they didn't kiss this time, she was warm and friendly. She remained sober and did not drink. Now she was sober and could not drink because of her DWI conviction. Kristy was much warmer when she was drinking.

Kristy had recently been in a relationship with a man who traveled a lot. She told Trevor she had met him while attending AA classes. She referred to AA as a "single bar, times ten." Evidently, she had dated him for two and a half years and now they were broken up. Trevor mentioned that he too had recently broken up with someone he dated for a year and a half.

Trevor and Kristy spent time hiking, swimming, and dining. They always talked about doing a motorcycle ride, so they did that too. Kristy hadn't been to a rodeo or watched bull riding, so they enjoyed that also. Their time together was always pleasant and conversation was abundant and flowed with ease.

When the weekend came, they decided on dining and dancing. They ate dinner and went for a walk. During the walk there wasn't any physical contact. Trevor was starting to get the impression that Kristy was still emotionally involved with her former boyfriend. She didn't touch or show signs of physical affection. On the walk, Kristy mentioned that they should take a picture of the two of them and send it to Trevor's former girlfriend. Trevor told her he thought that would be cruel since he was the one who broke up with her. Later he wished he would have mentioned sending one to her former boyfriend.

At the end of their walk, they came to a bar with a band playing. Trevor was familiar with the establishment and thought Kristy would really enjoy its unique atmosphere. It was uniquely entertaining because the singer would make up comical lyrics to various cover tunes. The singer didn't have a filter and would blurt out anything that was politically incorrect. According to him, all the pretty girls were dates and the men who didn't interact were gay.

As they entered the bar, everyone seemed to notice Kristy and Trevor. The bar was packed, but someone offered Kristy a stool. Trevor had to remain standing because there wasn't anywhere to sit. Someone mentioned that Trevor and Kristy made a striking couple. Kristy seemed to be totally taken with the band and all the people. The singer of the band made a joke and Kristy leaned into Trevor as if she wanted a kiss. Trevor was not going to bite on the first offer. He was a little taken back by how physically cold she had been. He was going to wait until she was more obvious. They danced and listened to the band until the bar closed.

Kristy had insisted that Trevor have a couple of drinks. Even though Kristy could not drink, she wanted to make sure Trevor had a good time. Since Trevor had a couple of drinks, he thought Kristy would like to drive. It wasn't that he was over the legal limit for alcohol consumption, it just seemed that Kristy would be more entertained if she got to drive.

As they were driving home, Trevor asked Kristy how she got her DWI.

She said she had been drinking and was on her way home when she hit a curb and blew a tire. She didn't know what to do, so she called the cops for help. The cops came and arrested her for driving drunk.

Trevor had a flashback to when he first met Kristy. He thought of Kristy's friend telling him that Kristy was a hot mess and that he didn't want to get involved with her. Trevor had replied that Kristy was very cute. The next reflection that entered his mind was that her other friend had referred to her as being dingy. Kristy had not been drinking. It was one thing to call the cops when you are driving drunk. It was another to admit to such a stupid event. Trevor was in a quandary. Which was worse, calling the cops when you are driving drunk, or admitting such a thing to a romantic interest? It was hard to believe that Kristy had a college education.

Trevor and Kristy arrived home safely. At this point, Kristy had been staying with Trevor for several days. They had been on a motorcycle ride, dinners, dancing, and various activities, which all seemed to go well. The one thing that did not meet the picture was the fact that Kristy hadn't physically warmed up to Trevor. She hadn't even offered a hug.

As they sat in the living room after a fun filled evening of dining and dancing, Kristy mentioned things would be different when Trevor wasn't newly out of a relationship. Trevor knew the truth was that *she* was newly out of her relationship and was still emotionally tied to her former lover. That was why she had been physically and emotionally unavailable.

Then Kristy made a reference to moving to the city where Trevor lived. Trevor thought of Kristy's friends referring to her as a hot mess, being dingy, and her admission to calling the cops while driving intoxicated. Here she was, talking about moving to where he lived, but she was as cold as ice. Now that she mentioned moving to where Trevor lived, he couldn't resist asking why she would do such a thing.

He said, "You don't even seem to like me. Why would you do that?"

Kristy said she still had feelings for her old boyfriend.

Trevor asked her why she didn't just stick with him since she seemed to like him.

She said, "There is a problem."

Trevor said, "What is the problem? He doesn't like you?"

Kristy did not want to reply, but Trevor pressed her for an answer. After considerable coercion, Kristy finally confessed that her former boyfriend was married.

Trevor said, "What the fuck? You are telling me you dated a man for three years and didn't know he was married?"

"Yes," she said.

"You must have known he was married but chose to ignore it. How does that happen?" Trevor asked.

Kristy went on to make excuses, but Trevor was thinking her friends were right. She is a hot mess and she is dingy.

Kristy left for home the following day. She and Trevor had a nice breakfast with enjoyable conversation and many laughs. As they were driving to the airport, Trevor asked Kristy if she had been comfortable during her stay.

She smiled and replied that she felt very comfortable and enjoyed her stay very much. Trevor had told her he was thinking of starting a part-time business in the near future. Kristy explained that Trevor should get his business going and she would move to his area the following year. She had to stay where she was for another year because of her DWI convictions.

Trevor didn't know what to say. They had a good time, but she had been very cold. He really didn't expect her to tell him to start his business and that she was moving. He thought it was a little bold and bossy.

Kristy called when she got home. She thanked Trevor for everything and they had a nice visit. A couple days later, Trevor text messaged Kristy and she didn't answer. He went for a long walk but forgot to take his telephone along. It was late at night when he returned and found a return message from Kristy. She said she had fallen asleep and missed his text. Since it was late when he got home from his walk, he hadn't returned her phone call.

The next day Trevor was eating lunch when he received a text message from Kristy. The text said she and Trevor had different lifestyles and she didn't see any sense in pursuing a relationship.

Trevor thought back to the time when she had stood him up in the Coachella Valley and later asked why he hadn't called her. The time he had been with her in Las Vegas when she darted out the door without a word. The fact that she told him she didn't have time to see him the next day, although he had gone to considerable time and expense to see her that day. The time she stood him up in Canada because she couldn't get into the country. Trevor surmised she wanted him to beg her to pursue a relationship. He thought it was another ploy designed for him to show how much he really wanted her.

Trevor simply replied, "I can't win them all."

Trevor thought of a cartoon he once saw. It depicted a woman telling a man he should have listened to her instead of staring at her boobs when she told him she had issues. Kristy's friends had warned him from the start, but Trevor had to find out for himself that *the attraction was not worth the issues*. All attraction to Kristy was gone when he realized that.

Trevor theorized that many extraordinarily beautiful women grow to be very shallow and self-centered because men and women alike dote over them. They experience less adversity and hardship than others. Since people learn from adversity and hardship, their opportunity to learn certain things is stifled. The other contributing factor is *much of a person's personality is formed by how a person is treated by others*. If a person is treated with privilege, they don't have the opportunity to learn and mature like others.

Trevor does not think that all beautiful women are shallow and self-centered. But he does think these factors many times contribute to stifling a *normal* personal growth process.

Most men see a beautiful woman and assume she is secure. Trevor thought about the extremely beautiful women he had met or dated and realized that some of the most attractive had been the most insecure. Trevor reasoned that a large portion of the population is trying to get in the pants of beautiful women, and many are doting over them. In addition, a lot of women are competitively trying to shred her to their level. Plus, many of her romantic partners are jealous of the attention she receives. It isn't easy to remain secure under these circumstances. *The more insecure a woman is, the more games she plays.*

It is not the homely person who gets a facelift, Botox, or fillers. It is the pretty people who are used to the benefits of looking good and want to keep or accentuate their advantage. Homely people make peace with their looks at an early age.

Chapter 15

Did You Meet the Representative?

It is said when you meet someone for the first time, you do not meet the person, you meet their representative. Of course, this is not true for everyone, but it is true of many.

A few years ago, Trevor had moved across country to an area where he didn't know anyone. Like most people, he made friends according to where he went and what he did. Since Trevor played golf, he made friends and acquaintances on the golf course. Sometimes folks turn out to be long term friends and sometimes they turn out to be someone who surprises you.

When playing golf, Trevor became acquainted with a colorful character named Jason. He was about Trevor's age, had long blonde hair, and was educated as an investment banker (so he said). He was an average golfer who didn't practice. He didn't cheat on his score and actually didn't keep track of it. This may explain why he didn't cheat. Playing golf with golfers like him can be more fun than playing golf with folks who are trying to beat others in order to compensate for their shortcomings. Some golfers feel insecure about their lack of accomplishments in life and beating others at golf is how they validate their self-worth. Trevor and Jason enjoyed many rounds of golf because neither was overly concerned with the score.

During their golf games, Trevor and Jason would tell jokes, talk about business, and whatever guys usually talk about. Jason told Trevor he graduated from Harvard. When Trevor would introduce him to other golfers, he would sometimes mention that Jason was an Ivy League scholar who had graduated from Harvard. Jason would light up and of course it would impress his new acquaintance. This would impress people not because he would be seen as an Ivy League scholar, but because his appearance was that of a beach bum. It made him appear eccentric.

When he was drinking heavily, he would talk about famous people he knew. This included actors, baseball players, and politicians. Wherever someone was from, he would know famous people in that area. The famous people were usually one of his personal friends. Although he did not claim to be a personal friend of Eric Clapton, he often told a story about being in rehab with him. He also liked to tell people that he had dated Sandra Bullock before she got married to Jesse James. Since Jason was usually drinking and spent a large amount of time inebriated, Trevor would chide him by mentioning how well rehab had worked for him. Everyone would laugh!

Trevor had overheard Jason tell someone he had purchased seven condos in his condo complex and later overheard him tell someone else he had purchased eleven. Anyway, his mother, sister, and her adopted son lived in one condo and Jason lived in another. They all lived in the same condo complex. Jason's mother had lived in the condo Jason now resides in. His condo still had the same frilly curtains and decorations his eighty-some-year-old mother had furnished it with. An old-fashioned CRT television sat in the middle of an old bookcase located against the living room wall of the one-bedroom condos. It looked as if his mother still lived there. Although Trevor had known Jason for several years, he had only been to Jason's condo one time.

Jason had invited Trevor to attend an annual get together' in Jason's condo complex. Trevor would get to meet Jason's mother, sister, and her adopted son. Trevor was curious about some of the things Jason talked about. He realized Jason embellished but was curious about how far the embellishments really went. When Trevor met Jason's mother, he visited with her about various pleasantries. Suddenly he thought to ask her about Jason's education at Harvard. Rather than mentioning Harvard he asked her where Jason went to college. She told Trevor the name of the college and it was not Harvard. Trevor asked her if he ever attended Harvard and she replied, "There would be too many girls, we couldn't send him there." Why would someone claim they went to Harvard when in fact they did not attend there at all? Trevor felt like a fool because he had been introducing Jason as a Harvard grad.

Sometimes after golf, Jason and Trevor would have a drink at a nice patio bar adjacent to the golf course. The bar drew patrons from out of state and many were from different countries. On this particular evening, there was only one attractive woman on the patio. She was not a ten but was quite pretty. Jason and Trevor found out she was from another state and that her job was to get money and donations for cancer. Trevor began trying to seduce her with wit and charm. Jason began interjecting his two bits along the way, trying to get into the game.

Six or seven men were sitting at another table listening to it all. The young lady eventually went to the restroom and the fellows at the neighboring table began teasing Trevor and Jason about who was going to get the girl.

Jason said, "Watch this. I will show you how to get the job done."

Trevor was up for the challenge. When the young lady returned from the restroom, Jason looked at her and asked how much she usually gets for donations and she told him how it worked. Jason drummed up some bullshit about his company and how it would be a tax write-off to donate $100,000. He said he would give her a check for a hundred grand this evening. He would take it out of his company expenses and write it off on his taxes. Although he didn't explain what it was contingent upon, everyone knew she would have to sleep with him to close the deal.

Her mind was working. On one hand, she could not imagine how someone would make something like that up. She thought he was for real, but on the other hand, she didn't think she would feel good about herself if she went for it. She was thinking and Trevor was turning on the charm. When Jason left for the restroom, Trevor turned up the charm. As he was talking to her, he was looking down her blouse.

The young lady blushed and said, "You just looked at my boobs."

Trevor confessed, saying, "Okay, I did. I like them." He smiled like a Cheshire cat that had just swallowed a canary.

"So, you want to see my boobs," she said as she turned her chair to face away from the other men, pulled up her blouse, and gave Trevor a good look at her boobs. Jason came back and the shit show continued.

Eventually, the young lady looked at Trevor and Jason and said, "I don't know which one of you I like best. I can't decide." She said her goodbyes, grabbed her sweater, and headed for the elevator.

As she was about halfway across the patio, Jason took off in hot pursuit. By the time she punched the elevator button, he was making his last best effort. The guys watching the whole shit show started teasing Trevor and giving him a hard time.

One of them said, "It looks like Jason has it in the bag."

Trevor imagined the conversation at the elevator door to be something like: *This is your last chance at the hundred grand,* Jason would say. *Nope not going to happen!* The elevator door opened, she stepped into the elevator, and Jason returned to his seat in defeat. Trevor was glad the gal was not gullible enough to fall for Jason's tall tale. Although Trevor had her phone number, he never made the call.

Clothing stores and bars have a lot in common when it comes to shopping. You can shop at Kmart, Walmart, Target, Nordstrom's, or Niemen Marcus. It is true that each store has its own personality and identity, the same as each bar has its own unique qualities and characteristics. You can shop at Tommy Bahama in Palm Desert and pay $170 for a sweatshirt. If you shop at Macy's, you can pick up the exact same Tommy Bahama sweatshirt for $75. Walmart and Kmart shoppers stick to Walmart and Kmart, but sometimes they will step up to Target or Bed, Bath, and Beyond. You will not find them at high-end stores. They are not comfortable shopping there.

Most wealthy people do not shop at Kmart and Walmart because they are not comfortable there. In fact, they would not feel comfortable being seen in either Walmart or Kmart. They feel comfortable at Nordstrom's or some other expensive store.

When women go shopping at a high-end expensive bar they are looking for a man with money, position, power, and status. Men shopping at a high-end expensive bar are looking for an attractive, well-to-do female. Men know what women are looking for, so they dress and act as if they have money, power, and status. If a man is exceptionally good looking, he may get lucky for the evening, although he will not be in it for the long haul. Women go all out with just the right hairdo, skirt, shoes, and jewelry because they are looking for a man with money, power, and status. Typically, they are not there to get laid. They are looking for a long-term relationship with a good provider who has status.

For the most, part wealthy men and women do not frequent low-end dive bars because they do not feel comfortable there. Most of the very wealthy wouldn't be caught dead in a dive bar; however, you may find some of them in a middle-class bar. The dive bar crowd does not frequent, enjoy, or feel comfortable in expensive high-end bars.

Jason liked to wear fashionable clothes and hang out in expensive places. One thing Trevor and Jason had in common is that they know how to act and feel comfortable whether they are in a dive bar or a high end tah-tah place. They can put on nice clothes and fit in with the wealthy or put on a t-shirt and hob knob with the dive bar crowd. Both had an upbringing that stressed proper etiquette and both could be well spoken.

Jason was out of town a lot, so Trevor and Jason rarely saw each other, but when they got together it could be very entertaining. By this time, Trevor knew Jason had a tendency towards embellishment, but it had been harmless so far. Nevertheless, Trevor started distancing himself, knowing Jason had lied about attending Harvard.

Trevor and Jason hadn't visited for some time when Jason called and wanted to go to a fancy resort. The resort was very upscale. It is where presidents and other dignitaries stay when they come to the area. Trevor had read about the resort but hadn't been there, so he agreed to go.

Trevor didn't have a suit, so he put on his best slacks, snakeskin dress shoes, and a nice button-down dress shirt. Jason was fashionably dressed. He also liked to wear really huge fashion watches. He had one that was designed to look like a nautical watch. When people asked about his watch, he told them it was a personal gift from a navy admiral who was a client of his. He explained that there were only forty watches of this type made and that every person with this type of watch is a high-ranking naval officer, with him being the only exception.

In reality, you can buy the same watch at JC Penny's for $199.00. The time is always showing on the face of Jason's cell phone, so other than attracting attention, he had no practical use for a watch.

The resort bar was a swanky place with a great view. It was crowded so it took a while for Trevor and Jason to find a place at the bar. They were able to turn their chairs away from the bar so they could look out over the dining area and appreciate the panoramic view of the valley.

As they were appreciating the view, people ordering drinks began to congregate next to Trevor. Jason and Trevor were conversing when they noticed Tucker Carlson from Fox News standing next to Trevor. A lady who appeared to be Tucker's wife was standing behind him. She seemed very sweet and appeared to be about nine months pregnant. Trevor was not really a Tucker fan, but his wife appeared to be very nice. Trevor always felt sorry for celebrities because they don't have anonymity. He didn't try to start a conversation with Tucker.

When Jason and Trevor noticed Tucker, it instigated a conversation about a hot news topic. They were discussing the ins and outs of the topic when Tucker looked like he was ready to chime in.

As Trevor turned to acknowledge him, a pretty Hispanic woman stepped up to Trevor and said, "My girlfriend would like to talk to you. You should really go talk to her."

When Trevor looked down at the end of the bar, her friend, Lisa, was standing there with a *Come fuck me* look in her eyes. Lisa was the right height, had dark hair, nice big blue eyes, larger than D-size boobs, and great cheek bones. She was a pretty woman but there was one thing off. Her hairdo was not as complimentary as it could be. If her hair had been styled differently, she would have been an extremely attractive woman. Both ladies were very well dressed.

Of course, Trevor got up and walked down to the end of the bar to meet Lisa. As Trevor was talking to Lisa, her friend Laura secured a table that would accommodate all involved. As they sat at the table, Trevor learned that Lisa had been a former news caster but her passion was music. She had written, recorded and produced a few country albums with moderate success. At this time, she had a very good job teaching people how to use a particular type of computer program. She was intelligent and a good conversationalist. She was financially stable and not overly concerned with what Trevor did for a living. As she and Trevor became carried away in conversation, Jason and Laura passed pleasantries.

After conversing for a while, the ladies informed the men that they were going to a fancy dance club at the other end of the city. Jason mentioned that he had to talk to a business client at a restaurant across the street. Plans were made for the ladies to meet the men at the dance club after Jason and Trevor had met with the client. Phone numbers were exchanged, and as soon as Jason finished meeting with his client, he and Trevor headed for the dance club.

The dance club was a popular dance place where people would dress in style and put on the dog. The ladies were sitting at a table overlooking the dance floor. Another lady had joined them, so now there were five in the group. The new gal was blonde and extremely attractive. The women said they brought her along to attract men. There was probably some truth to that. When Trevor tried to talk to her, she wasn't very responsive, and Lisa was quick to take over the conversation. Jason talked and danced with the other ladies while Trevor and Lisa conversed.

They say all intimacies start with three Ts: talk, touch, and tease. Of course, the next stage of intimacy is kissing. Trevor and Lisa skipped dancing and went straight to talk, touch, tease, and kiss. Lisa made no bones about her attraction to Trevor.

As talking and kissing continued, Trevor made reference to a bar that was very risqué. Lisa said, "I love that place." It is the type of place patronized by a couple wanting to spice up their love life. A place people go to watch and interact with scantily clad young ladies. Everyone headed for the dive bar.

There was an attractive young couple sitting in one of the booths at the risqué bar. A conversation ensued between Trevor and the young couple. As they were joking and laughing, the attractive young lady sitting next to the young man mentioned quietly that Trevor's girlfriend was feeling left out.

Trevor whispered in her ear, "I know, we are about to make up."

Lisa did not hear what was said but stated that she and Trevor had been married for ten years.

Trevor looked at her and exclaimed, "It gets better every year."

This was followed by a kiss or a make-out session or whatever you would like to call it. The two definitely made up.

When it was time to leave, Jason volunteered to buy a bottle of wine that all could share. He had to have the perfect $150 brand of wine. This was to demonstrate that money was no object. He could have purchased the same bottle of wine at a store across the street for less than half the cost.

After meeting these ladies miles away and halfway across the city, it was a coincidence that everyone lived less than a mile from each other. Trevor and Jason followed the ladies to Lisa's house. Lisa sat on the couch, played guitar, and sang as Jason opened the bottle of wine.

As if they were giving Lisa and Trevor privacy, Jason and Laura soon escaped to one of the bedrooms.

Many of the songs Lisa played were songs that Trevor's former girlfriend had played for him. When she played "To Make You Feel My Love," it was all he could do not to breakdown in tears. Trevor and his former girlfriend had agreed that it was one of the most romantic songs of all time. Lisa could tell he was feeling sad but probably thought it was just her songs. Although Lisa was a talented musician, she was neither as good a singer or guitar player as his former girlfriend. Trevor still loved his former girlfriend. He couldn't have another musician in his life. He would always be comparing her to Tracy.

All musicians want to make the big time. If they succeed, their reward is to ride around on a bus with their band mates and travel from town to town. In such tight quarters, everyone eventually gets on each other's nerves. It is a

Chapter 15

paradox that all musicians would like to be famous but fame is followed by the worst of lifestyles. *The more famous they become the worse their life is.*

Trevor had been trying to unhinge Lisa's bra most of the evening. It was not an easy task because it had four latches and a wide, tight strap. You couldn't reach around and flip the latch with one hand. As Trevor would try to unfasten her bra, Lisa would protest and act coy. In actuality, to remove her bra in public would have caused a public scene. Her breasts were at least twice the size of D cups. Most women with breasts as big as hers purchased them or are chubby and fat. Not Lisa. She was fit and natural. If she went braless, it would not go unnoticed by any human with the ability to see.

Now that Lisa and Trevor were snuggled in bed, Lisa backed into Trevor in a fetal position. Trevor began to kiss her on the shoulder and neck as his fingers proceeded to roam her body. As he moved his hands to feel her breasts, he discovered that not only were her breasts perfect but her nipples were very sensitive. They were not too long, not too short, but rock hard with a perfect smooth areola.

Lisa moved Trevor's hand between her legs as she moved over on her back. As Trevor was stimulating her, she started giving him feedback. She began moaning, groaning and whispering. As time went by, she became louder and louder. As she became more excited, she became increasingly verbal and expressive. The entire evening ended with an exclamation of "Don't stop, don't stop," and an erotic sigh of relief.

Before Trevor went to sleep, he thought about a comment his friend once made. His friend had commented that all women are the same. The idea he was trying to convey was that there was no need for a variety of women in a man's life.

Trevor had thought for a moment and replied to his friend, "Each woman has a unique quality that sets her apart from the rest." Lisa was smart and articulate. Not only did she have very large breasts, but they were also natural, perky, firm, and sensitive. They were perfect in every way.

Morning came and Laura was standing at the end of the bed whispering,

"What was his name?" She couldn't remember Jason's name. The ladies wanted to go out for breakfast. Jason mentioned that breakfast would already be prepared if everyone had stayed at his place. Trevor didn't know what Jason meant by the comment but thought it better to leave it alone.

Anyway, Jason and Trevor made their excuses for heading down the road and starting their busy day. This was the last time Trevor waited until this stage of the game to think of an excuse for an expedient exit. The standard excuse from that time forward was a ten o'clock tee time. He also made it standard issue to stay at the lady's house. It is much easier to leave than to ask someone else to leave. If you take someone to your place, they could want to stay until you get home from golf.

As Trevor and Jason were driving home, they began discussing yesterday's events. Jason looked at Trevor and said, "Man, you two were really noisy last night."

Trevor replied, "Yeah, she was singing and playing for quite a while."

Jason exclaimed, "It wasn't the singing and playing that was noisy."

Lisa had forgotten to close the bedroom door and the bedroom entrances were almost directly across from one another. Jason and Laura had been listening as Trevor and Lisa made love the night before. Yep, it must have been quite entertaining. Trevor laughed and mentioned that Jason could have closed the door.

Jason said, "There wasn't a chance. It may have been the best entertainment I ever had."

As if Trevor was defending himself, he said "I wasn't the one making noise."

When Trevor talked to Jason a few days later, Jason mentioned that Laura was blowing up his phone. When Trevor talked to Lisa, she mentioned that Jason was blowing up Laura's phone. Each was putting on an air about the other calling incessantly.

A few days later, Lisa and Trevor decided to go on a bicycle ride. Trevor rode to Lisa's place and they pedaled to a nice restaurant for drinks and dinner.

Since they could pedal all the way home, they had plenty of drinks. They were having a great dinner, kissing, flirting, and fooling around when the subject got around to Jason. Lisa asked Trevor if he had flown on Jason's jet.

Trevor laughed and explained that Jason does not have an airplane, that in fact, he doesn't own an automobile. He grew up in a large city and Ubers everywhere he goes. Trevor mentioned that Jason had told him about getting a DUI, so Trevor surmised that he had lost his driver's license.

The next question was "Have you ever been on his yacht?"

Trevor had to restrain himself to keep from busting out in laughter at this one. He said, "I would be totally shocked if Jason has a canoe, let alone a yacht." No, there is more to come.

"Do you know his housekeeper?" The light went on in Trevor's head as he put two and two together. The reason Jason had mentioned that breakfast would have already been prepared had everyone stayed at his place was because he had told Laura he had a housekeeper. Okay, he had told Laura that he had a private jet, yacht, and housekeeper who fixed his meals. Trevor explained that Jason did not have any of those things. Then he mentioned what he knew. He explained that Jason lived in a one-bedroom condo with an old cathode ray television and his condo had not been redecorated since his eighty-some-year-old mother lived there. Jason had lived in the condo for several years.

Trevor was totally embarrassed to think he had been associated with Jason. What kind of person could tell such whoppers? Okay, Jason had figured out that this is how he was going to get laid. He would lie to women about how rich and successful he was in order to get inside their pants. Trevor began thinking about the gold diggers who are suckered into Jason's line of bullshit. *Who is worse, the man who comes up with this kind of bullshit, or the woman who is impressed and taken in by it?*

After contemplating for a while, Trevor decided they deserved each other. The problem is that there are many, many innocent, gullible people who would never suspect total blatant lies. A person expects others to act like *they* act or be as truthful as *they* would be. Who could imagine such audacity?

Well, Lisa and Trevor had loosened up a little. They had a nice bicycle ride, good meal, and several drinks. Lisa said, "Laura mentioned something about us being a little noisy the other night."

Her face became flushed as she mentioned it, but she put it out there to see how Trevor would respond. Trevor concurred that Jason had also mentioned they had been a little noisy. Lisa was embarrassed and mortified by the thought of them listening in. She made up some excuse about the way the doors shut and this and that but nevertheless, it was what it was. Trevor and Lisa had shared the same embarrassing moment. Maybe it would be a bonding experience.

Nobody wants to be associated with someone who tells big whopping lies. Time passed and Trevor and Jason would see each other on the golf course from time to time.

One of the ladies who worked at the golf course was having a birthday party and she had invited Trevor. It was lady's night out with her and her friends; all women except for Trevor. This was Trevor's perfect setup because her friends were all gorgeous. He was very excited to get acquainted with them. When Jason found out that Trevor was going to her birthday party, he invited himself to go. Trevor asked the birthday girl if it was alright if Jason came. Jason was a personable guy and she thought it would be fun if he came also; after all, she probably still viewed Jason as Trevor's friend. Trevor explained to the birthday girl that he had lost respect for Jason because he seemed to lie a lot. She said she didn't care about that.

The birthday party consisted of the birthday girl, her five closest girlfriends, and Trevor. One of the birthday girl's friends was a mutual friend of Trevor's. They gathered at a country western bar. As the band played, everyone was talking and dancing. Soon Jason arrived. He had been drinking all day and was very intoxicated. Trevor didn't pay much attention to Jason. He was busy mingling with people and talking to the birthday girl's friends. Eventually two of the women in the birthday party took a liking to Jason. One of them asked Trevor if he thought she could tame him. At this point, it would look like sour grapes to say something negative about your supposed friend, so Trevor just said, "I doubt it."

Everyone went to another bar but Jason was so drunk they wouldn't let him in. Most of the party ended up going to a sandwich shop before going home. Jason was so drunk he could hardly walk, so Trevor bought him a sandwich and made sure he didn't pass out. After leaving the sandwich shop, Trevor, Jason, and three of the women took the same Uber home. One by one, the Uber dropped each person off. Trevor listened to everyone's conversation as they rode home. Jason's conversation didn't make sense but at least he didn't seem to be telling huge whoppers. Everyone had a wonderful time and Trevor was happy because Jason hadn't been a huge embarrassment.

A few days later, Trevor was talking to the mutual friend who had attended the birthday party. She was a cute petite blonde and a stay-at-home mom. Her husband was the bread winner in their family. She and her husband were Trevor's neighbors. She had worked at the golf course for a short time and that is how she became friends with the birthday girl. During her conversation with Trevor, she mentioned that she had been trying to get in touch with Jason. During the birthday party, Jason had promised her a job. She hadn't met Jason prior to the birthday party and he was not answering his phone.

Trevor told her the story about him and Jason picking up the ladies and later finding out that he had told them he had a jet, yacht, and housekeeper who fixed his meals, when in fact he didn't have any of those things.

After Trevor explained this to her, she exclaimed, "But what about my job?" He had been so convincing to her that she still did not understand that there wasn't a job and he did not have a job to give her.

So, Trevor further explained that he had lied about giving her a job. Trevor said, "He didn't have a job to give you unless you are going to be a flight attendant on his airplane that does not exist."

The neighbor chuckled and said, "I am so gullible."

Needless to say, Trevor distanced himself from Jason the best he could without causing hard feelings.

Trevor had been visiting with two ladies at a local hangout. One of the ladies had just made a comment about how she wished she could find someone who was honest. Jason called. Jason asked Trevor where he was and Trevor told him. Within minutes, Jason arrived. He had been drinking all day and was sloppy drunk.

Since Jason had the appearance of a beach bum or rock star, the lady who had just commented about finding someone honest asked him if he played in a band. Jason leaned back in his chair and told her he used to have a band and was a guitar player. He hadn't been touring recently but was thinking about getting his bus back on the road. The lady was impressed! That was just what she was looking for; a rock star.

Trevor knew for a fact that Jason had never played any type of musical instrument, let alone playing in a band or being on tour.

Trevor whispered in the other gal's ear, "None of it is true. I am telling you none of this is true."

She replied, "He seems very nice."

Trevor excused himself, paid his tab, and left the restaurant.

The next time Trevor saw Jason, he explained that it was totally embarrassing listening to him lie to the ladies at the restaurant.

Jason thought for a moment and replied, "I would never lie to you." That may be the most obvious lie Jason ever told! The odd thing about Jason is he knew that Trevor knew he was telling lies but continued to spin the tallest of tales. From that day forward, Trevor would pass pleasantries with Jason but cut any contact other than the passing of pleasantries.

Trevor knew a person's reputation had to be guarded and protected because success is mostly determined by a person's character. *If a person tells a lie and another person repeats the lie without knowing it is a lie, it still makes the person that repeats the lie a liar.*

From time to time, Jason would call and want Trevor to play golf with him and his clients from out of town. Trevor surmised his clients may have reservations about doing business with him. They may be wondering if he is an honest person and ask Trevor what his opinion was. He knew he couldn't vouch for Jason's honesty or integrity so he refused any offer to play.

Trevor realized that Jason was trying to use him and his reputation as an honest, well-respected person to portray himself as being honest and respectable. He had used Trevor and his relationship to him to portray himself to women as being honest and respectable. Now he wanted to use him to portray the same to his clients.

Trevor realized meeting a person's friends will tell you more about someone you just met than anything else. Liars, con-men, and criminals will exploit, to their benefit, any association they have with someone who has established a reputation of honesty, integrity, and character.

By the way, public records confirm that Jason doesn't own a condo and that the condo he lives in is owned by his mother.

Chapter 16

Rationalizing the Irrational

Tracy had finished her gig and loaded all of her equipment except her guitar. As she was organizing her load, Trevor walked up behind her with her guitar in hand. When she turned around, she was face to face with Trevor after a six-month gap in their relationship. Trevor handed her the guitar.

He had wondered how she would react. She could have a boyfriend. She could be angry and fly off the handle or she may act indifferent. Her reaction was that of a person in shock. As color fled from her face, she looked as if she had been jolted by a thousand volts of electricity. She placed her guitar in position and continued to look dismayed.

Trevor smiled and said, "It is good to see you."

Tracy looked aghast. She didn't speak or respond in any way. Trevor asked her if she would like to get a bite to eat.

They didn't dine right away. Hand in hand, they went for a walk, visited, and smiled. They felt as if they had never parted. Both of them could feel the undeniable feeling of love they shared. There was telepathy between their hearts. Tracy didn't want to go to her house or Trevor's house. They made love at an all-night restaurant, in the back of a pickup, in a parking lot, at three o'clock in the morning. It wasn't conventional sex; it was what you could do discreetly under a blanket, considering the circumstances. There they slept until the morning restaurant crowd drifted in.

Trevor fell back into the same old pattern. Almost every day he would help Tracy with her house, yard, swimming pool, gigs, and musical endeavors. He tried to get Tracy to have sex at his place or her place, but for the next two weeks they remained like teenagers, having sex in an automobile. At night, Tracy would sing and play. Trevor would help her set up, load her equipment, and socialize with her followers.

From time to time, her followers would ask if Trevor would be at her next gig. They had become accustomed to Trevor entertaining them, as well as Tracy. At times, they would only attend Tracy's gigs if Trevor was going to be present, which he almost always was. Trevor and Tracy would stay up most of the night doing gigs, and in the daytime, they would hike or ride motorcycle. The gigs provided a variety of people to talk and joke with, plus Trevor loved listening to Tracy sing and play. This was the good life.

Tracy also fell back into the same old pattern. She would learn any song Trevor enjoyed hearing. She would sing and play for Trevor in the mornings, and in the evenings she would entertain the crowds. It seemed like the perfect life for Trevor and Tracy.

There is always the other side of the coin. Although Trevor helped Tracy with her gigs, house maintenance, and finances, she would sometimes complain that he didn't do enough or had loaded the music equipment incorrectly. The equipment had to be loaded so it didn't rattle when driving. Men hit on Tracy at almost every gig and no matter what was said, her only boundary was to say nothing.

Trevor asked her what the rules were in the relationship. Should either of them tell the other if someone hits on them? Tracy said they didn't have to tell the other unless it was important. Evidently it was never important to Tracy. She also had a key sentence she would pull out of the blue. She would look at Trevor and say, "You lied to me."

Trevor would be in shock because he had been straight and honest with her at all times. He hadn't given her any reason to be even slightly suspicious of him. Besides, he had been with her or in contact with her every day. Trevor would ask her what he had lied about and she would not reply. Trevor knew liars accuse you of lying and cheaters accuse you of cheating. They expect others to act as they do.

Halloween rolled around and Tracy secured a private gig in a very affluent upscale neighborhood. She got it cleared with the host for Trevor to attend also. Trevor didn't know anyone at the event but decided to go anyway. It would be a challenge to see if he could successfully mix and mingle with a close-knit group he didn't know.

Tracy and Trevor got dressed in costume, went to the party, and set up the equipment. Tracy and her band were playing and the evening was going well. Tracy had a lead guitarist sitting in on the gig and his girlfriend was in the same position as Trevor. She was at an event where she didn't know anyone and was trying to fit in. She asked Trevor to dance, which was nice because neither one of them knew anyone at the party. They visited and danced a couple of times before Trevor decided to go into the house and circulate.

Trevor was dressed as a monk. He was standing at the center bar in the kitchen, talking to a tall blonde woman in a tiger costume, when Tracy entered. She was headed for the restroom and the look on her face said it all. She was livid beyond belief as she passed through the kitchen without a word. It would be accurate to say there were daggers protruding from her eyes. Trevor knew instantly she was upset because he was talking to the tall blonde woman in the tiger costume.

Evidently, Tracy had needed to go to the restroom and the lead guitar player was filling in for her. When Tracy came back through the kitchen, Trevor followed her into the yard. He tried to talk to her but she would not speak. Her only response was the shooting daggers protruding from her eyes. No matter what he said, she remained silent. Tracy climbed back on stage and Trevor returned to the kitchen.

When the gig was over and Trevor tried to start Tracy's car, the battery was dead. What great timing! The gig was over, Tracy was so pissed she wouldn't speak, and it was two thirty in the morning and the car wouldn't start. Trevor borrowed jumper cables from the homeowner and got one of the band members to jump start the car.

It was a seventeen-mile trip to get back to Tracy's house. Tracy didn't speak for the first eight miles but when she did, she told Trevor he had to promise not to talk to pretty women. That was a promise Trevor could not make. It was not just a double standard it was at least a quadruple standard. Tracy talked to handsome men all the time, did recordings, played music, and sang with them on a regular basis.

Trevor could not help but be slightly amused by the absurdity of the statement. He told Tracy he could not make such a promise. By the time they reached Tracy's house, she was hysterical. She could go from zero to hysterical in one minute and the thirty-five minutes to her house was torture. Logic or reason did not enter the picture and it was totally unattainable. By the time they arrived at her house she had become hysterical enough to grab one of her wooden bar stools by the legs, turn it upside down, and smash it continuously against the floor until it shattered into fragments.

Trevor had ridden his motorcycle to Tracy's house but he had removed some parts and it wasn't operable. He certainly wasn't subjecting himself to hysterical tantrums and tirades. Once again, his drama bucket was completely full. He was thinking he had done well at supporting her and fitting in and mixing with a group of strangers. He could understand Tracy being a little jealous, but this was way beyond any form of rational. He certainly wasn't going to stay the night at her place.

As Trevor pulled his phone out of his pocket to call for a taxi, Tracy became enraged and demanded he stay. She emphatically informed him that if he left he would never see her again. It would be over if he left. She was inferring that she would commit suicide.

There was nothing Trevor could say or do to improve the situation. The options were to stay and take more abuse or taxi home. Even if the scolding stopped, the anger would remain.

As the taxi approached and Trevor exited the house, Tracy was standing at her doorway in her white, see-through nightgown yelling at Trevor. She was leaning forward like a little girl throwing a temper tantrum, yelling "If you leave me now, it is over! You will never see me again!" She was using the most colorful adjectives she could think of to drive her point home.

It must have been quite a sight for the taxi driver as Tracy was a very sexy woman in a sexy white night gown that revealed her ample breasts, curvaceous hips, and legs of perfection. She was still yelling as Trevor opened the taxi door and crawled into the back seat.

As the taxi driver pulled away, he had a most curious look on his face. Trevor told the taxi driver that she was pissed. He wasn't telling the taxi driver anything that he didn't already know. It was very evident that she was totally livid. The taxi driver asked what set her off. Trevor explained that she had caught him talking to a beautiful woman. The whole incident was so absurd, neither the taxi driver nor Trevor could hold a straight face. They both started cracking up in unison.

So, Trevor was home but his motorcycle was still at Tracy's house. The next day he took a taxi to retrieve his motorcycle, but Tracy wasn't home, so the motorcycle remained at her place for several days. Trevor was so taken aback by the events of the Halloween party he just couldn't get emotionally prepared for dealing with the situation. When a man leaves his motorcycle elsewhere for several days, he is avoiding something unpleasant. If it hadn't been for the motorcycle being at her place, Trevor probably wouldn't have seen Tracy again.

Several days later, Tracy called and she was extremely distraught. She wanted to know why Trevor hadn't called her. She explained that she needed help and was in a state of despair. It was evident by her voice and conversation that she was in a state of deep emotional distress.

When Trevor arrived at her house, he could tell she was totally distraught. She was in such a deep traumatic state that she was talking about not wanting to live. She was so distraught she actually seemed suicidal. Trevor knew people threatened suicide as a way of controlling others, pleading for attention or gaining sympathy, but when you look in the eyes of someone in her state of mind, you know they are truly in a state of distress and confusion.

Trevor thought about calling 911 but knew it would be a big fiasco for both him and Tracy. Trevor could not leave her alone and stayed the night. By morning it was as if the night before had been a bad dream. All was back to normal.

Well, this event started the love machine and things went back to how they were before the Halloween upset. The ups and downs of the roller coaster continued.

During the six-month break in the relationship, Tracy had lined up a short tour. She had various gigs lined up in different towns and was planning on being gone for two or three weeks. Tracy would explain to her followers that she was going on tour and would be gone for a while. Tracy didn't invite Trevor and avoided any discussion about him going. Since Trevor attended all of Tracy's gigs, people would ask him if he was going. Trevor would reply that he was not invited and Tracy offered no comment or discussion.

Some people assumed that Trevor would be going, but it was evident that Tracy wanted to go alone. The dichotomy was that if Trevor was gone for one day, Tracy would be suspicious of him. When he was gone on a three-day business trip, she was completely hysterical. Now Tracy was going to be gone for several weeks and even though Trevor had no other obligations, she didn't want to take him along. Yes, in all instances, Tracy had double standards or more appropriately quadruple standards. To Tracy, there was no rationale for quadruple standards. It was just the way it was, a set of standards for Trevor but none for her.

The couple stayed in close contact while Tracy was on her trip. Sometimes Trevor would locate distances, hotels, and other information for her. Trevor had been spending all of his time with Tracy and now she was gone. His relationship with Tracy had isolated him from most of his friends, so he had to find new ways of occupying his time. He didn't know what to do with himself, because he had been spending all of his time with her.

Trevor had recently made acquaintance with a couple in his neighborhood (Kevin and Amy.) He didn't know them well, but they were very nice and invited him to join their pool party.

Tracy had been gone for a couple of weeks and Trevor was pleased to have some social interaction. It wasn't that he was looking for another woman or girlfriend. Despite the turmoil and double standards in his relationship with

Tracy, he had been completely faithful to her and had no desire to get involved with anyone else. Trevor realized that Tracy had issues, but he was trying to figure out if the issues were caused by her upbringing (environment) or if they were caused by her genetic makeup. If they were caused by her environment or previous traumas, they could be fixed. If they were caused by her genetic makeup, they could not be changed. If they were caused by her environment and could be changed, it would certainly be worth the effort. The chemistry between Tracy and Trevor was a once in a lifetime experience. It was a chemistry that most will not experience in their lifetime.

There were about twenty people at the pool party. It was not the typical get together where the people who invite you go out of their way to make sure you are comfortable and meet everyone. It was the kind of get together where many of the people know each other and you try to find someone to talk to. It was a slow start socially, but Trevor was a good listener and eventually became acquainted with everyone in the group.

The first thing that became evident was that Kevin, Amy, and all of their friends were professional drinkers. Trevor made it known that he had a girlfriend and some folks asked him for Tracy's Facebook information so they could check out her music and event calendar.

Towards the end of the get together, Kevin and Trevor got in a conversation about who they knew in the neighborhood. Kevin mentioned there was a beautiful blonde who lived close to Trevor and that he was surprised they didn't know each other.

Everyone had been drinking all afternoon. Trevor had been drinking his own concoction that consisted mostly of fruit juice, water, and a small amount of Vodka. When evening came, the party broke up and most of the folks walked over to the neighborhood bar.

Trevor didn't want to go, so he went home and changed into his athletic shorts and old black and silver striped polo shirt. He took out his garbage and threw it in the dumpster. As he turned to walk away, a good-looking blonde woman approached with her garbage. Trevor looked at her garbage and said,

"That looks like a lot of empty wine bottles."

That was all it took and the conversation was on. Come to find out, the woman with the garbage was the same woman Kevin had just told Trevor about. Now, this was a coincidence. Trevor had lived in his place for several years and had not met her. Kevin told him about her a couple of hours ago and now she and Trevor met for the first time. The conversation continued for a few minutes and Trevor asked her if she would like to go to the bar where Kevin and Amy were. She said she would love to go but had to walk back to her condo to tell her boyfriend she was leaving. Trevor asked her if her boyfriend would be upset, and she said she didn't like him that much anyway. Hum!

Kevin and Amy were shocked when Trevor and the blonde entered the bar. The four of them ordered drinks and sat at a table talking about what a coincidence it was that Trevor and the blonde had just met. As they were drinking and talking, a band was playing. People were dancing, visiting, and drinking. It was a busy hangout.

After they visited for a little while, the blonde leaned into Trevor as if she wanted a smooch. Trevor looked at her with a shit-eating grin and she asked him to dance. Things started getting fresh on the dance floor. Although Trevor was kidding the blonde about having a lot of wine bottles in her garbage bag, his insinuation was evidently quite accurate. It was obvious she had some drinks under her belt before coming to the bar. She was ready for action.

Men are boundary checkers. They like to see how far they can go and what they can get away with.

Trevor amused himself by checking the blonde's boundaries. The blonde was walking in front of Trevor as they left the dance floor and when he looked at her butt, he noticed she was wearing thong underwear under her yoga pants. He decided to see what she would do if he pulled up on her panties. Trevor tugged up on her thong. No reaction. She was enjoying the attention. He was trying to find her limits, so he pulled her panties up a little more. He was expecting her to protest but she didn't, she just kept walking. As they left the dance floor, Trevor was walking behind her, pulling her panties up as far as he could. The blonde did not react; her boundaries were yet to be determined.

When Trevor sat down, she looked at him with a *Come fuck me* look that told him she wanted to get nailed. She must have enjoyed getting her panties pulled up her crack.

It had been so noisy in the bar it would have been impossible to hear a phone ring. Trevor started contemplating the situation, reached into the pocket of his gym shorts, and pulled out his cell phone. It must have been intuition when he checked his phone. Instantly, a text from Tracy popped up. The text read, "I know where you are."

Trevor was thinking, "How could she possibly know where I am?" She was 1,200 miles away.

Another text popped up. "You are where we met."

Trevor was thinking, "This cannot possibly be."

Another text popped up. "You are wearing a black and silver shirt."

Holy shit! Trevor knew the jig was up and she had the inside scoop. Trevor also knew how jealous she gets and wondered what else she knew. Did she also know about him pulling up the blonde's panties? Maybe she knew about how fresh things got on the dance floor. Since Trevor had known Tracy, this was, without a doubt, the most inopportune time to be snitched on.

He had been solid gold and now he was getting caught pulling up the blonde's panties.

Trevor responded with, "I will text you in a moment." He made his apologies for having to leave in a hurry and said goodbye to all at his table. At least he got out of the situation with the blonde. Tracy had been so pissed about him talking to the gal at the Halloween party, now she probably knew he was pulling up the blonde's panties. She was going to be livid beyond belief. It wasn't so much that she would be upset, it was that it was a breach of trust. Trevor was glad she was 1,200 miles away.

It was about a half mile walk to get home. Trevor knew he would need to be home when he talked to Tracy. You cannot deny where you are these days because your phone has a camera and they could ask you to send a picture. The other thing is that if she knew what color of shirt he was wearing, there must have been someone watching him.

As soon as Trevor was home, he called Tracy to assess the damages. According to Tracy, the singer in the band had videoed the crowd leaving the dance floor. She then sent the video to Tracy. Tracy indicated that it was a random video her friend and fellow musician had sent her. She said it was entirely coincidental that he happened to be there. Whether she was covering for her friend or not, Trevor did not know, but the odds of the video being random was very slim.

The other thing that was amazing is that she recorded the video and sent it in the time it took Trevor to leave the dance floor and sit on a bar stool. Much to Trevor's surprise, Tracy did not go ballistic. She didn't fly off the handle, yell, or swear at him. The whole time Trevor had known Tracy, she had never believed him when he was telling the truth and he had never lied to her. There was no use in trying to lie now, he was on video. Trevor surmised that by the time the singer put down her microphone, grabbed her phone, and hit the record button, she may have missed the worst of the panty incident.

On the other hand, if Tracy mentioned Trevor pulling up the blonde's panties, it would be pretty hard to plead coincidence. The next night Trevor and Tracy had FaceTime sex for the first time. Trevor always wanted to watch the video of him leaving the dance floor but was afraid to mention it. Once that dog went to sleep, he wasn't about to wake it up.

Tracy would sing and play at old folks' homes and every so often Trevor would accompany her. The old ladies would talk to Trevor and explain that he should keep Tracy because there weren't many like her. They saw her as the sweet little pretty one with a beautiful voice and reserved personality. Little did they know, Tracy was always fighting her inner demons. Every once in a while, she would explain to Trevor that the only time she felt good was when she was playing music. The rest of the time she had confused thoughts and insecurities going around in her head.

Trevor eventually came to believe she validated herself as a worthy human being by singing and playing. Everywhere she went she took her guitar. Everywhere she went people would be in awe of her ability to sing and play. No one realized that a relationship with Tracy was a continual roller coaster filled with turmoil, double standards, and a lack of boundaries.

Trevor and Tracy rode the emotional roller coaster of ups and downs, and just when things seemed to be going well, a new challenge would appear.

Tracy wanted to get married and had a huge fear of abandonment. This fear was probably the biggest challenge to the relationship. Trevor mentioned that there were a lot of emotional challenges that needed to change if marriage was to occur. He had been in the relationship long enough to realize that Tracy's emotional issues were not a matter of environment. They were a matter of heredity. Her father had emotional issues, her cousin had emotional issues, and her sister, who had extraordinary musical abilities, had been married five times. Trevor loved Tracy dearly, but he had come to the conclusion that a life with her would always be one of continual turmoil and double standards.

From time-to-time, Tracy would have nightmares and wake up in a frightened state while vocalizing something from a terrifying dream. Trevor would sense the tension building and wake up as soon as Tracy started having the nightmare. He could sense her tension long before she woke.

With the same sense that allowed him to wake before Tracy awoke from a bad dream, he would sense when she didn't want to go to bed until very late at night. He would occupy himself until she indicated she was ready to retire to the bedroom.

It was very late one night and Trever could sense that Tracy didn't want to go to bed. Although Trevor sensed she didn't want to go to bed, he decided to ask her if she wanted to go. She told him she wasn't ready to go, so Trevor gave her a kiss and a hug before retiring. Soon Tracy entered the bedroom, stood at the foot of the bed in a trance-like state, and without rationale, rambled on about various subjects. This is what is termed as a quasi-psychotic episode. Quasi is defined as having some resemblance to. Psychosis is a condition that affects the way your brain processes information. It causes you to lose touch with reality. Tracy had definitely lost touch with reality. Trevor now understood what was going on in Tracy's head when she was being quiet.

Trevor was fixing coffee the next morning when Tracy looked at him, smiled, and said, "I was crazy last night." Trevor got the impression she remembered the episode but probably didn't remember the disjointed content of it.

When Trevor met Tracy, she had told him she was not normal. It isn't normal to have such extreme musical talent. It isn't normal to be able to listen to a song twice then sing and play it as if you had done it a thousand times. It isn't normal to wake up in the morning and write the music and lyrics to two wonderful songs, nor is it normal to have quasi-psychotic episodes.

Tracy was a tormented musician who could be included among the many talented musicians and artists with emotional issues. *It occurred to Trevor that a brain that is highly developed in one area is usually lacking development in another.*

Trevor had been helping Tracy every day for the last week. He spent the night at Tracy's house and had explained to her that he needed to get home and take care of things at his place. After breakfast, Tracy was in the bathroom getting ready for the day. Before saying goodbye and leaving for home, Trevor pulled his motorcycle out of her garage. As he was checking it over, Tracy came out of the house, thinking he was leaving without saying goodbye. In fact, he was just getting the motorcycle prepared for the trip home.

He had never left Tracy without a kiss and a long goodbye. It could be that she knew Trevor was not leaving without saying goodbye. It may have been that she was suspicious he was going to do something other than go home and catch up on things. Nevertheless, the results were that she was beyond angry as she exited the house and stormed across the garage floor and into the driveway. She was totally enraged as if Trevor had committed the most heinous of crimes. With anger emanating from every pore of her being and her body shaking with rage, she walked up to Trevor and stuck her face right up next to his. She gave him an angry sarcastic kiss with a force that pushed him backward.

Trevor told her he hadn't planned on leaving without saying goodbye. He realized he could not rationalize with Tracy when she was in a state of a rage. He felt bad thinking she may have thought he would leave without saying goodbye. He tried to put his arms around her to console her. He thought a hug might assure her his heart was in the right place. She pushed him away and her rage continued. Trevor backed the motorcycle out of the driveway and headed down the road.

This incident had been so bizarre and emotionally upsetting that Trevor didn't try to contact Tracy. Trevor was on the driving range the next day when Tracy called. Trevor didn't answer his phone but texted Tracy back. He told her he wouldn't talk to her until she apologized.

She texted him back saying she was sorry. Trevor called her back and she said she was sorry. Other than that, she acted as if nothing had happened. Trevor asked her if it was going to happen again and she said no. The odd thing about Tracy was that she may or may not say she was sorry after an incident like this. If she said she was sorry, that was as far as it went. If she was truly sorry and felt bad about what she had done, you couldn't tell it by her actions. She didn't try to make amends. If Trevor hadn't demanded an apology, she most likely would not have apologized. *An apology without amends is just a manipulation.*

The events of that morning had been so emotionally disturbing to Trevor that he didn't call or contact Tracy during the week. He knew it would take time for him to emotionally recover from the incident.

The following week Tracy had gigs in Trevor's neighborhood. They had stayed the night at Trevor's place because her gig the next morning was close to Trevor's house. That day, Tracy had a gig at a facility for people with disabilities and after that, she had another one at an assisted living facility. Trevor told Tracy he would go with her to the first gig and would take the rest of the day to catch up on things at his place.

The incident the week before did not enter the conversation. To Tracy, it was as if nothing had happened.

The people in the disability facility were all ages and it appeared most had mental disabilities. Tracy set up in the front of the room and began to sing and play as caregivers brought in the residents. When they arrived, the residents could sit anywhere they wanted. As Trevor looked around the room, he was having flashbacks from the movie *One Flew Over the Cuckoo's Nest*. Most of the residents were younger and dressed in street clothes. The group appeared to consist of people with cerebral palsy, autism, and various other afflictions.

As Trevor was sitting at a table in what appeared to be the art room, a young fellow came over and sat beside him. The young man was thirty-eight years old but looked much younger. Maybe he looked young because he spent his entire life in facilities such as this one. He was a nice-looking man and seemed to take a liking to Trevor. He had dark hair, dark eyes, and a handsome face. If you saw him outside of this setting, you wouldn't know by his physical appearance that he had issues. By his manner, Trevor was guessing he may have autism.

As they were sitting there, the young man mentioned his dad was taking him to a Neil Diamond concert. He also mentioned that his father was like Trevor. Kids usually love their father, so Trevor took it as a compliment. Maybe Trevor and his father were about the same age. Anyway, Trevor asked him when Neil Diamond was coming to town. He said he didn't know, so Trevor pulled out his iPhone and looked it up. Sure enough, Neil Diamond was coming to town the following month. The young man seemed slow at processing information but he may have been sharper than Trevor thought.

He looked at Trevor and asked him how to spell massage. Trevor spelled the word for him but he was not satisfied. He wanted Trevor to look it up on his phone, so he could see the word. Trevor typed the word massage into the Webster dictionary app so the young man could see it in print. That didn't satisfy him either, so he asked Trevor what a massage was. Trevor didn't know how to explain it to him. The young man wanted Trevor to look up massage on the phone, because he wanted to know how to do a massage. Trevor looked it up on Wikipedia and handed him the phone. Trevor began watching Tracy play and sing while the young man was looking at his phone.

When Trevor looked back at the young man, he was on YouTube playing a video of someone giving a massage. The woman getting the massage didn't have clothes on and the resident was engrossed in what he had found. Trevor had to chuckle as he thought about the young fellow being in the facility, the fact that he had probably never had sex, and how it must be for him to look at a naked woman getting a massage. He thought about asking for his phone, then looked at the young man watching the video and thought again about how he must be depraved of the sensuousness of seeing or touching a naked woman.

As Trevor looked at the young man, he couldn't help but be amused. He was smiling as the young man was engrossed in the video. Tracy noticed Trevor was laughing and a look of wonder and curiosity came across her face. She could tell Trevor was having a difficult time containing his laughter. When Trevor looked back at the resident, he noticed he had progressed to a site where both the masseuse and the person getting the massage were naked. There may have been more going on than just a massage. Trevor couldn't help but laugh. As she was singing on the stage, Tracy was watching Trevor and trying not to laugh. Trevor was having a difficult time containing himself. Everyone else in the facility looked like their medications had kicked in and they were complacent.

Well, all good things come to an end. A middle-aged black woman who was one of the orderlies came by and noticed the young man looking at porn on Trevor's phone. With a most curt and abrupt manner, she ordered the young man to give the phone back to Trevor. Trevor felt like a little kid in school thinking he was probably going to get scolded. The orderly disappeared and Trevor stuck his phone back in his pocket.

It was a beautiful day and Trevor offered to buy Tracy breakfast. On the way to the restaurant, Trevor told Tracy about the young man and how he had gotten Trevor to look up massage and that he ended up getting caught looking at porn. They shared a good laugh over the events of the morning.

The restaurant was very busy, so it was a thirty-minute wait for seating. Trevor and Tracy sat outside on the bench in front of the restaurant waiting for their name to be called. It was a beautiful day and Trevor said, "It is a nice day for a motorcycle ride."

In an instant, he realized that Tracy might take offense to the comment and think Trevor would go on a ride without her. Without hesitation, he added, "A bicycle ride or even a hike." It was too late. The comment had already set her off. By now Trevor had learned that Tracy would take offense to this type of comment. He knew she would assume he was going to do something without including her. Trevor had no intention of doing any of those things without her. He knew she had a gig that afternoon and he had work to do. It had only been a week since he had been chastised when leaving her place. She did apologize when Trevor told her he would not talk to her until she apologized. That was all she had said about the incident. If she was sorry, there was no way of knowing.

Now it was the same thing again. Trevor had things to do and she was not included. Trevor realized he couldn't continue to spend all of his time going to her gigs and doing things with her. He had neglected things and needed to take care of things that were fulfilling to him.

Trevor could tell she was instantly upset. There was no use in waiting to be seated and it would probably end up being a scene in the front of the restaurant. He asked Tracy if she wanted to leave and she said she did. As they drove back to Trevor's place, all rationale and logic faded from existence. Trevor knew the deep-seated fear of abandonment was at the root of this situation and the one the week before. The fear had not improved. With each incident, the fear had grown. Any form of independence on Trevor's part seemed impossible.

It is said that a woman gets married with the idea she will change a man. A man gets married with the idea that a woman will never change. Both are wrong.

It had taken Trevor this long to come to the conclusion that Tracy would never change and that her irrational behavior was caused by heredity, not environment. He had been putting himself in the position of a woman who wanted to change a man. He had been trying to help Tracy change her behavior. He now realized it is what it is and that is how it will remain. He needed to make a decision. Could he live with turmoil and double standards or more importantly, is it worth living with them?

By the time they reached Trevor's place, there was no resolution of issues. Tracy mentioned she was grieving over the death of their relationship. There was no rationale to the discussion and Tracy had to go to her gig at the old folk's home. The last thing Tracy said as she walked out the door was "I won't be calling you."

Although Trevor didn't say it, he knew he wouldn't be calling her either.

A few months later, Trevor was visiting with Justin and they were discussing life in general. Justin asked Trevor what happened to his relationship with Tracy. Trevor told Justin that Tracy was irrational. In confirmation, Justin said, "I know, I met her."

Trevor went on to explain that irrational means something doesn't make sense and that you cannot rationalize what is irrational. Furthermore, he explained that he had quit trying to rationalize what is irrational. Justin laughed because it was such an obvious observation. Sarcastically, Justin asked him how long it had taken him to figure that one out.

Trevor said he realized as a small boy that you cannot rationalize what is irrational but it had taken him until now to stop trying. Trevor told Justin he considered himself to be a quick learner. Almost everyone he knew was still trying to rationalize the irrational. Most people will continue do it for their entire life. If you don't think so, just take a look at the news or have a discussion with a friend. If you think about it, you will discover people trying to rationalize what is irrational everywhere you go. They are trying to figure out why criminals do what they do but there is no rationale.

A rational person cannot rationalize irrational thinking. It is irrational!

Chapter 17

Dinner Conversation

Amy

»

After a very hot day of golf, Trevor and his golf partner stopped by one of their favorite watering holes in a nearby hotel. It was happy hour and the lobby was chaotic. Shortly after they sat at the bar, a young lady asked Trevor if she could sit on the stool beside him.

Trevor replied, "Most certainly, I saved this seat just for you," as he patted the seat with his hand. It was his standard reply to a beautiful lady asking if she could sit beside him. Trevor ignored her for a while as he didn't want to appear desperate. Later he learned she was a yoga instructor from out of town and that she travelled to his area frequently.

Amy was about five feet one inch tall with auburn-reddish hair. Trevor estimated her weight to be no more than 110 pounds. She had practiced yoga for many years and was in top physical condition. For a young woman in top physical condition, she had ample breasts. Although she appeared to be of Irish descent, she had unusually deep, dark brown eyes. Her eyes, along with her freckled face, gave her a striking appearance.

Trevor and Amy went out to dinner, hiked, and got to know each other. When they were hiking, Trevor couldn't help but notice how flexible Amy was. She had a great sense of humor and a quick wit, although it would be fair to say she was a little quirky. When dining at a restaurant, she usually asked to be seated at a different table once or twice. The wine and food usually didn't meet her expectations either.

They had gone out a few times and the quirkiness began to wear on Trevor's nerves. He started wondering if it was worth putting up with all the quirkiness just to get in her pants.

The two planned a fun date, drinks, dinner, karaoke, and dancing. Trevor decided an Uber was in order since Amy's quirkiness seemed less irritating after a few drinks. The restaurant seating went smooth since Amy only had to change locations once. It was a small place so there weren't that many options. She researched the menu with scrutiny, then selected food and drink. The menu was similar to a Tapas menu in that you order a variety of food and mark the selections on paper.

The red wine turned out to be a perfect selection and the food was excellent. Trevor studied Amy as she took a bite of this and mixed it with a bite of that. They were sitting side by side as Trevor watched her reach across the table, grab an edamame (green soybeans boiled and steamed in their pods), open her mouth wide, insert an edamame pod, and in a most seductive fashion, strip the soft tender beans from their pod. A look of ecstasy came over her face as she turned and looked at Trevor sitting beside her. She moved in close and Trevor could feel the warmth of her breath when her lips caressed his ear, then she whispered, "Enter me slowly."

Her comment certainly set the mood for a fun evening! Amy turned out to be a better than average dancer, but to be honest, she wasn't much of a singer. That night, Trevor gained a strong appreciation for the art of yoga and what it can do for the human body, but more specifically, he gained an appreciation for what a yoga body can do!

Chapter 18

The Psychology of it All

Trevor had just ended his relationship with Tracy. He had been in the relationship for three years, including a six-month hiatus after the first year and a half. It was a nice sunny spring day as he carried his clubs to the golf course.

As he was walking across the well-manicured, freshly cut green grass, he contemplated the events of his former relationship. He knew that contemplating the relationship would be something he would do on a daily basis, for a long, long time. The relationship he and Tracy shared had been a very unique and passionate one. It had really been the only relationship in Trevor's life that had a profound effect upon his psyche. Maybe it had been a codependency. A codependency occurs when one person has problems and another person becomes dependent on helping them with their problems, therefore, they become dependent on one another.

Upon Trevor's arrival at the club house, he was informed that there was a frost delay and that his tee time would be delayed for two hours. It was a nice day so Trevor decided he would have plenty of time to hit a bucket of balls before his tee time. He downloaded a bucket of balls from the ball dispenser and headed for the patio to change from flip flops to golf shoes. As he approached the patio, he noticed two ladies sitting at the first table.

The patio was a concrete patio with tables and chairs. An umbrella extended from the center of each table making shade for people sitting around the tables. The two ladies looked amiable so Trevor asked them if he could share their shade. One of the ladies seemed to be about thirty-seven years old and the other in her mid-sixties. They were very receptive and talkative as he changed into his golf shoes.

The usual disclosure to determine Trevor's *currency* (attractiveness, charm, financial success, and status) began. Where do you live? Are you married? Do you have a girlfriend? What do you do? Yep, they were certainly curious about Trevor. Usually, if a strange guy approaches a couple of ladies, they are a bit reserved. The older of the two didn't say much but she contributed to the conversation when appropriate. It was easy to tell the gears were turning in her head as the conversation continued. Both of the ladies were totally at ease. It was refreshing for Trevor to have such ease of conversation. His girlfriend had been quite reserved and uncomfortable in these types of situations. To make it worse, she would have been totally jealous of Trevor visiting with the other ladies. Although Tracy was an entertainer, she was an introvert.

Andrea, the younger of the two ladies, was definitely an extrovert. Conversation flowed from her with ease. She was a very interesting conversationalist. She seemed very confident.

To continue comparing Andrea and Tracy, neither are very tall. At five feet two, Tracy may be two inches taller than Andrea. They are both petite with nice bodies. Andrea has shoulder-length brown hair. It is about one shade away from black. Her eyes are dark brown and shaped like Melania Trump's. In other words, they are not the type of big, bright eyes that Trevor prefers. They are shaped more like cat eyes.

In contrast, Tracy had long, natural, golden blonde hair that came down to the small of her back. She also had large blue eyes that usually had an adorable expression. Although Andrea was several years younger than Tracy, she did not appeal to Trevor in the same way. Most would likely agree that she was not as attractive as Tracy.

The older lady was Andrea's mother. She was from the Midwest and had come to visit and spend time with her daughter. Trevor and Andrea lived on the golf course and come to find out, they were also neighbors. They had not met each other before, but they knew many of the same people in the neighborhood. They talked about mutual acquaintances within the neighborhood and shared similar assessments of those they knew. It wasn't long until they asked if Trevor had a wife or girlfriend.

He explained that he didn't have either, which didn't satisfy their curiosity. They wanted to know if he had ever been married, had kids, and all of the usual questions that an interested female would inquire about. Although Trevor is usually reserved about talking of such things, he did mention he had recently broken up with his girlfriend. They wanted to know why he broke up with her, and he began fumbling for a way to explain. He didn't want to appear as if he was putting the ex-girlfriend down. He didn't want to seem like a guy who talks degradingly about their former partner. He had always admired the way his friend had handled questions about his divorce. People would ask him what happened and he would simply reply that he was an asshole. Since these people didn't know Trevor, he knew this would not be a good reply.

While Trevor was fumbling for a reply Andrea assessed the situation and replied to her own question. "She wanted to get married, didn't she?" She had hit the nail on the head.

Trevor told her that was the long and short of it. She had been very perceptive. That was not the end of questioning though. They had to know more. Andrea asked why Trevor didn't want to marry her. He was on the spot again. Sometimes it is best just to be honest, so he explained that probably the biggest reason was that from his point of view, Tracy had an abandonment disorder.

When he said this, Trevor noticed a flicker in Andrea's eye that indicated he had arrived at a satisfactory answer. Most people would have been bewildered and looked at him like he was from outer space. This reply must have spoken volumes to Andrea though. Later in the conversation, Trevor discovered she was a psychologist.

They asked him what he did for a living and Trevor gave them the short version, leaving out the most impressive parts of his resume. He didn't want people to like him for his accomplishments but for who he was as a person. Although he liked to create a little mystery, he did tell them he was an investor of primarily tangible assets. In reality, his background was highly diverse, and he didn't want to come across as the usual braggart or liar. He had lived a life out of the norm.

The ladies were so entertaining that Trevor ran out of time for practicing on the driving range. The two hours had passed and it was time to play golf. Trevor asked Andrea if she would like to be Facebook friends. She pulled him up online and the friendship began.

For the next few days whenever Trevor would play golf, go for a walk, or a bicycle ride, he would run into Andrea. She would usually be jogging along the bicycle path or getting her mail. She had told Trevor about an interesting movie and Trevor messaged her about the title of the movie. During the conversation they decided to go for drinks.

During drinks and dinner at a local hangout, Trevor learned that Andrea was not only a psychologist, but a relationship counselor. Yep, she made a living advising people how to have quality relationships. She would listen to people having trouble in their relationships or marriage and give them direction and advice on how to resolve their differences. She would teach them how to have happy, productive relationships.

Interestingly enough, Andrea was scheduled to be married in a few months. She looked around the patio and mentioned that her fiancé would be on edge in this environment. When Trevor asked why he would be on edge, she responded by saying that there was too much stimulation. Trevor could not imagine why it would be too stimulating. The patio was not overcrowded and there was soft music playing over the sound system. She went on to explain that he was a little quirky. He had a pattern of abnormal behavior characterized by a loss of external structure, unrealistic sense of self, feelings of worthlessness, and a fear of abandonment.

Trevor was all ears. The fiancé sounded just like Tracy. Although he was the opposite sex, they shared the same characteristics.

It was a great dinner with plenty of drinks complemented by intelligent conversation. When it came time to pay the bill, Trevor was pleased to pick up the tab. She was getting married soon. Was this really a date? Trevor always figured it was good relations to pick up the tab. Nobody likes a cheapskate. He concluded that whatever the situation was, it was well worth the cost of the meal and drinks because therapy is expensive and he had received free therapy.

As Trevor and Andrea were walking home, Andrea mentioned she would need to feed her kitty cat when she got home. She also mentioned that there was a very quaint, small town a couple hundred miles away and that she and Trevor should go there on his motorcycle the following day. They could stay for the weekend and it would be a blast.

Trevor asked her what her fiancé would think about them going on a motorcycle ride and staying for the weekend. She explained that he was staying with his mother and he would never know.

Later, Trevor was home in bed and just drifting off to sleep when his phone rang. It was Andrea; the drinks had evidently affected her and she wanted to talk. She mentioned there had been some activity on the street outside of her place. Trevor thought this may be a hint for him to go to her place under the guise of making sure she was safe. If this had been Tracy, he would have pulled on his clothes and been at her house in an instant. It was not Tracy though, and he was half asleep. Besides, she had a fiancé and was getting married soon. This could be a lot of trouble.

In the back of his mind, Trevor thought she may be looking for attention. Trevor didn't bite on the bait to rescue her. The conversation continued and Trevor agreed to take her on the motorcycle trip. Andrea had mentioned feeding her cat earlier so Trevor knew she had a cat. She had been talking for a long time and Trevor wanted to go to sleep, so he told her to pet her kitty and have a wonderful sleep. She picked up on the innuendo of petting her kitty (pussy) and having a wonderful sleep. Trevor knew, *insinuation is the art of seduction.* This insinuation served him well. She mentioned something about the trip and told Trevor she was offering him her kitty.

When Trevor talked to Andrea the next day, she was ecstatic. Her fiancé had bought her a new Mercedes. It was not just any Mercedes, it was a big, sporty looking car with all the amenities money could buy. It had a very attractive paint job, fashionable black wheels, and looked like an $80,000 automobile. Andrea said she loved her new car and her fiancé. There was no mention of a motorcycle trip to a small little town 200 miles away.

Trevor thought about the night before when Andrea was so excited and ready to go on a motorcycle trip. Now she was enthralled with her new car and her fiancé. Trevor enjoyed Andrea's company, but she didn't really ignite a spark within him. It was hard to believe Andrea's total turnaround and change of heart. It was not that Trevor cared about her doing a flip flop, it was that she seemed so shallow and easily swayed. Trevor contemplated the situation and concluded that there was only one satisfactory solution to this situation. He had to fuck Andrea in the back seat of her new Mercedes.

The following week Andrea called Trevor and wanted to go out for drinks. She wanted to pick Trevor up and give him a ride in her new car. During dinner, Trevor learned that Andrea's fiancé was a litigator. She talked more about his emotional issues and mentioned he had called her a few weeks ago claiming to be in Las Vegas when she later found out he was in New Jersey. She confronted him about why he would lie about where he was. His explanation was that he was going to commit suicide and thought it best to do it in New Jersey.

Trevor started putting two and two together. Her fiancé had a job that puts him out in front of the public, although he is very insecure. He is staying at his mother's place because he is depressed. He has an unrealistic sense of self and is impulsive. Although he made $170,000 last year, he was broke. He had also worked for three different companies in the last year. He drinks continuously and claimed he was going to commit suicide. Trevor had experienced someone with almost all of these characteristics.

Since Andrea was a psychologist, she would be able to label his illness. Trevor asked her if she thought he had some sort of mental illness. She explained that he had BPD (borderline personality disorder). All of the issues mentioned are classic characteristics of people with BPD. Although there are some characteristics, that male and female BPDs do not share, Trevor realized that Andrea's boyfriend and Tracy shared the same affliction.

On the ride home from the restaurant, Andrea was driving. Andrea's mother was in the passenger seat and Trevor was riding in the back seat. Trevor began commenting about how nice the car was and that the back seat was particularly nice. It had nice, smooth, soft leather and was big enough for a person to sleep on. He explained that a new car always needs to be initiated. He asked Andrea if they had initiated it yet. Andrea acted like she didn't understand.

Her mother spoke up and said, "You need to have sex in a new car to christen it." Yep, Andrea's mother knew what Trevor was talking about and she was right on cue.

Trevor had planted the idea of having sex in the car. It was the first step in the process. He knew he could work out the rest of the details if he took her out to dinner and loaded her with drinks. It was a matter of time until he completed his mission.

The following week, Andrea invited Trevor to the golf course for drinks. She had just received her wedding shoes and she wanted to show them off. She met Trevor in front of his place and they started walking towards the golf course. Soon into the conversation, Andrea mentioned that when she was in college, she used to have sex with women. She said she was going through a phase at that time but had since realized she was heterosexual and likes penises.

Trevor thought it was a little weird that she would mention this within a couple minutes of their walk. That seemed to be personal information. Why would she want him to know this?

When they got to the golf course, Andrea proceeded to show everyone her new wedding shoes. Before long, Trevor's friends Kevin and Amy appeared at the golf course. Andrea was excited to show them her shoes. There she was, sitting with Trevor, showing his friends her wedding shoes. Trevor knew his friends were wondering why she was there with Trevor if she was getting married. It was evident that Andrea could not care less what they thought.

Kevin was curious about Andrea's marriage plans and began asking her questions about her fiancé. He asked the usual. What does he do for a living? How old is he? How did you meet him? Was he ever married? Andrea explained that he was a few years older than her. That she had met him on a dating site, and he had never married. She went on to explain that he had a girlfriend for a couple of years, but they had broken up a couple years ago. Kevin asked a couple of questions about the girlfriend and Andrea was pleased to tell what she knew.

With a curious look on his face, Kevin asked Andrea a couple more questions about her fiancé. A look of surprise came over his face as he exclaimed, "I know his ex-girlfriend. Her boyfriend was a real freak."

Kevin owned a beauty salon, which explained why he would know Andrea's fiancé's ex-girlfriend. He had been doing her hair for years. Kevin began talking about the relationship between the ex-girlfriend and the fiancé. Evidently his client (the ex-girlfriend) had confided in him about her boyfriend (Andrea's fiancé) while she was getting her hair done. She had told him that her boyfriend would disappear without warning for days on end. When she asked him where he had been, he would not respond. She went on to explain that he had also committed parasuicide (attempted suicide without intending to be successful).

What Kevin was saying about the boyfriend was exactly what Andrea had been experiencing. It was obvious the fiancé and the boyfriend were the same person. To verify they were one and the same, Kevin got on his phone and called the ex-girlfriend. He asked the name of her ex-boyfriend and it was the same. He asked if she had heard from him lately and she said he had been leaving messages but she wouldn't respond. Furthermore, she explained that her relationship with him had thoroughly traumatized and scarred her for life.

Andrea paid for her half of the food and drinks. On the walk home, Trevor asked her what she thought about Kevin's enlightening conversation. Andrea said she already knew her fiancé had a borderline personality disorder. Trevor asked her if she still wanted to get married. Andrea said she didn't care about being married. She just wanted to have a ceremony and the hurrah that goes along with getting married. She was thirty-seven years old and hadn't been married. Trevor mentioned it might not be a good idea to get married knowing that the marriage would soon end in divorce.

Andrea insisted she wanted the attention and experience of getting married. She was determined to have that experience. She said she wanted to wear her fancy wedding shoes down the aisle. Trevor told her she might want to trade her wedding shoes for some good running shoes. For the price of the wedding shoes, she could buy the very best in running shoes.

All Trevor had invested in Andrea so far was a couple of meals and a lot of drinks. People pay her a boatload of money to help them with their relationships. Trevor thought it would be a good time to pick her brain. If he asked her the right questions, she may discover how absurd her marriage plans really were.

Trevor explained that he had been through marriage counseling several times. He mentioned that the counselor had advised him to date or know someone for at least two and a half years before he got serious or considered marriage. Andrea said that was too long and nonsense. How could you expect someone to wait that long?

Trevor explained that she may be in the initiation phase with her fiancé. People with BPD can act normal for a certain length of time and she had only known him for a little over a year. The longer you know someone with a mental illness, and the closer you become with them, the more pronounced their symptoms become.

Andrea agreed with Trevor's assessment. There is a seductive effect to dating someone with BPD. There are times that are very close and very intimate. For some irrational reason, the emotional roller coaster will instantly hit a low and the partner of the person with BPD will rack their brain to figure out what went wrong. If the partner eventually finds out what caused the sudden downturn, it will be something the partner considers irrational. Since they cannot rationalize what has happened, they begin to doubt themselves. They begin questioning if something isn't wrong with them. As time passes, the insanity of the incident fades and things get back to the passionate, intimate, euphoric stage of the relationship. As sure as the roller coaster goes up, it is going to come down and it comes down a lot faster than it goes up. The harsh reality of the last episode will be mostly faded from memory when the next one occurs. The cycle continues.

The longer a person is in the relationship and the more comfortable the person with BPD becomes, the closer together the incidents occur. In the beginning this is a very seductive cycle, but in the long term it is a living hell.

Andrea agreed with Trevor's assessment regarding the cycle of emotional abuse. She reiterated the fact that she didn't want to stay married. She was interested in the wedding ceremony and the hurrah that goes with it. Trevor mentioned that people like her fiancé realize they have issues and they want to get a ring on the finger before reality sets in. Andrea asked him if he really believed that and Trevor assured her he did.

The fiancé had romanced Andrea well. Supposedly, he had bought her a nice, top of the line Mercedes. He had taken her to Europe and dined her in the best of restaurants. When he ordered wine, it was not the cheap stuff. It was nothing but the best for him and Andrea. Andrea had come from old money and this was how she expected to be romanced. The wedding plans moved forward, flowers and caterers were arranged, and invitations were sent. Down payments were made and the balance was on contract. Andrea said her father had financed the entire extravagant affair to the tune of $80,000. Andrea also revealed to Trevor that in high school, she had been voted most likely to be a runaway bride.

A couple of months before the wedding, the fiancé went out of town on a fishing trip. He told Andrea he was going out of state and she would not be able to contact him while he was gone. This didn't sit well with Andrea. While he was gone, she did overnighters with her ex-boyfriend. Trevor asked her why she would do that.

Andrea replied, "He left me alone."

Trevor had heard women say that before. That is woman-ese for, *He hurt me by leaving me alone, and I paid him back by having revenge sex.* If you hear that phrase from a woman, it speaks volumes.

The fiancé liked to drink and take benzodiazepine (tranquilizers such as Librium and Valium). Andrea told Trevor she didn't think he went on a trip. She thought he stayed home and got high on his special concoction of pills and booze.

The fancy Mercedes started having problems and Andrea took it to the dealer for repairs. When the car was in the shop, they discovered it had been wrecked and that the frame was bent. Evidently it was a used car and the fiancé had not thoroughly checked it out before purchase. Basically, it would cost more to fix the car than it was worth. Come to find out, the fiancé had not paid anything down on the car. He had traded Andrea's car in as a down payment and Andrea was left paying a $900 a month car payment on a car that was neither drivable nor saleable.

About six weeks before the wedding, Trevor ran into Andrea. He asked Andrea if everything was coming together for the wedding. When he asked how things were going with the fiancé, she mentioned he was staying at his mother's. It seemed odd that he was staying with her when he had a nice big penthouse downtown.

Trevor asked why he was staying at his mother's. Trevor was thinking maybe his mother was sick or something. Andrea said he had lost the lease on his penthouse suite and that is why he was living with his mother. Trevor asked if the fiancé was having money problems and she said he lost his job. A little further into the conversation, Trevor found out that it was the fourth job he had lost during the previous year.

Mental illness has little to nothing to do with IQ. In fact, some of the most creative and brilliant people throughout history have had a mental illness. The fiancé was an interesting study. He must have been very intelligent to work as a courtroom litigator. Here he was, an extreme introvert who stood in front of groups of people and performed in a courtroom.

Trevor surmised that the fiancé validated his self-worth through his work and that the approval he received from others was his validation. The problem with this type of person is they are like a bucket with a hole in it. The validation is leaking out the bottom of the bucket as fast as it is poured in. They will put everything they have into keeping the bucket full. That is one of the reasons they become very good at what validates them. He and Tracy were both comfortable performing in front of large audiences, although they were introverts. Both validated themselves by their performances and were extremely good at what validated them.

The fiancé filed for bankruptcy a few weeks before the wedding. Andrea took a huge loss on the fancy Mercedes and traded it in on a crossover vehicle. The wedding was cancelled and the fiancé left for rehab. Andrea's father was left with an $80,000-tab for a wedding that never happened. There wouldn't be any trips to Europe, expensive dinners, or fancy cars. The bankruptcy was the death of the relationship between Andrea and her fiancé. Since the fiancé no longer had money, Andrea ended the relationship.

Well, the fancy Mercedes was gone, so Trevor was not going to be fucking Andrea in the back seat. Actually, his drive to complete that seduction had long since passed. There was no possible way he would ever have sex with Andrea.

There is no greater seduction than pulling away from someone who cares for you. Even though they hadn't slept together, Andrea had bonded with Trevor and he knew he was going to have a difficult time distancing himself from her. They were neighbors and they would obviously see each other from time to time. It wasn't that Trevor disliked Andrea, it was that he didn't want to have any part of her dramatic lifestyle.

Time passed and from time to time, Andrea and Trevor would go for a drink. Andrea said Trevor was too old for her and Trevor agreed. They were also neighbors. Both agreed their relationship should remain as friends. Even though two people agree on being friends doesn't necessarily mean they are being honest with themselves when they agree.

Andrea called Trevor early one morning and asked if he would like to go to breakfast at the golf course. Trevor said he would but wanted to finish sleeping first. He was thinking he would call her back when he woke up. A couple of hours passed and Andrea called again. She was hungry and wanted to eat. As it ended up, they made it to the golf course for brunch instead of breakfast. They sat on the patio where they had first met. They enjoyed cocktails, breakfast, and a gorgeous day. Breakfast went down quick and so did several cocktails. Andrea's phone needed charging so Trevor put it on a charger inside the club house.

A group of about thirty men began gathering in front of the clubhouse. They had just completed a golf tournament and one of them was standing behind a podium announcing winners and giving out prizes. Some of the men belonged to the men's club. The group of golfers looked like the type of men who hadn't had a real day of fun in their entire lives. The guy at the podium was acting like he had a stick up his ass as he was announcing the winners. He had the demeanor of a guy who had never accomplished anything of importance in his life, but now he was going to show everyone he was a champion golfer.

Trevor mentioned to Andrea that several of the men's club members had tried to get him to join the men's club. Meaning to be sarcastic, Trevor told Andrea it looked like a really fun group. Trevor laughed.

Andrea looked at the guy on the podium and announced to the crowd, "My dick is bigger than all of your dicks."

Trevor would have to give the counselor credit; she had made an accurate analysis. The guys were acting like they were in a contest to see who had the largest dick and the guy at the podium seemed to think he had the biggest one.

Now this was a very audacious statement for a woman to make in front of a large group of men. It was even bolder when you consider that Andrea stands about five feet tall and is the only woman on the patio. She had just addressed the group of golfers saying her dick was bigger than all of theirs, and the biggest asshole had the microphone in hand.

In one sense, Trevor had to admit to being a little amused at her audacity. But on the other hand, this was asking for World War 3. To publicly make fun of the size of a group of men's dicks is asking for trouble.

The golfers were seated in chairs facing the fellow at the podium. One of the golfers shouted across to Andrea, "What does yours look like"?

Andrea looked at Trevor and said, "I can handle these guys." It was as if she was looking forward to a little banter.

Another golfer said, "You have a dick?"

Andrea remained unaffected by the comments.

The guy at the podium must have had a little dick because he took the comment personal. He said, "How do you know how big it is?"

Andrea said she could tell from where she was sitting. She had one-upped the insecure guy behind the podium and humiliated him in front of the group. Trevor could see the anger on his face.

Another golfer exclaimed, "I like a woman who can say 'dick'". This guy began trying to win Andrea's favor. Trevor was totally embarrassed by the situation but knew if he said anything, it would create hostility and things would go from bad to worse. He would become the scapegoat.

The banter went on and eventually the hostility died down. Trevor and Andrea finished their drinks. They were ready to go, but Andrea's phone was on the charger inside the club house. Trevor asked Andrea if all would be cool if he went inside and retrieved her phone. He was the one who had put it on the charger, so it would be easier for him to retrieve it rather than explain where he left it.

While Trevor was inside retrieving the phone, World War 3 had erupted between Andrea and the golfer behind the podium. As Trevor stepped out the door, Andrea finished up a rebuttal to a comment from the golfer standing behind the podium. Andrea was cool, calm, and collected, and it was evident that Andrea's IQ was about forty points above the golfer's.

As Trevor sat down, the golfer behind the podium looked livid and said something about being the winner. Trevor could tell by the look on his face that Andrea had again put him in his place.

Addressing the crowd, the golfer behind the podium exclaimed, "Look at her old man, he isn't saying anything."

Well, Trevor had become the scapegoat without saying a word. Trevor was sitting in his chair beside Andrea and all was quiet. You could have heard a pin drop. Trevor looked at the golfer behind the podium and said, "It appears you have been looking for trouble. If trouble is what you want, I can most certainly help you out."

The golfer wouldn't look at Trevor and did not respond. For the first time, Andrea became angry. With fire in her eyes, she looked at Trevor and said, "He called you an old man."

Trevor assured her he didn't mean to say Trevor was old, he was using it in the context of Trevor being her husband or lover. In fact, Trevor was twenty-two years older than Andrea.

The presentation was over and the golfer from behind the podium gathered his paraphernalia. The fellow who was trying to win Andrea's favor came over to talk. He mentioned that the golfer from behind the podium was a real dick.

Trevor chuckled and said, "Evidently a small one." Trevor asked the fellow if the guy from behind the podium was a good golfer and the fellow said he was.

As the golfer from behind the podium left, he walked over and handed Andrea an eight and a half by eleven sheet of paper. He had scrawled across the paper the words *YOU ARE THE LOSER*.

Andrea looked at him and told him he could keep his award. "I don't want that," she exclaimed. Indignantly, the golfer threw the paper on the table and walked away. The golfer from behind the podium had deliberately avoided making eye contact with Trevor.

Trevor had been out with a woman who got in a brawl. He had been out with women who obviously had a mental illness. The relationship counselor had topped them all. She had put him in the most awkward, uncomfortable, and humiliating situation of them all.

It occurred to Trevor that chemical dependance counselors have been chemically dependent. Abuse counselors have been abused, and relationship counselors have had relationship problems. *A counselor almost always counsels people in the area in which they are, or have been, deficient.*

Chapter 19

The Hideout

Trevor had a special thirty-two-ounce insulated cup that sat in a drink holder attached to the handlebars of his motorcycle. The big, insulated cup had a lid that snapped on top and a thick plastic straw that ran through the center of the lid. The straw enabled him to suck drinks from the cup when he was going straight or sitting still. While moving, he could pick the cup out of the drink holder, tip it back with his left hand, and not have to stop. The only thing he could not do while drinking was use the clutch located on the left side of the handlebars. In hot weather, he always liked to keep the cup full. If something happened and he ended up stranded, he could at least stay hydrated.

Trevor hadn't ridden his motorcycle for a couple of weeks. He had been doing paperwork all day when he decided to do a little loop to charge the battery. Since it was a hot evening, he filled his insulated cup with ice and water.

It was a nice twenty-mile ride to some of his favorite watering holes. One of the watering holes had dollar bills stapled or taped all around the inside of it. There, Trevor had posted a dollar bill with his and his former girlfriend's initials. He had also drawn upon the bill a special intimate cartoon that only had meaning to the two of them. Except for one lone "T," the passage of time had little by little faded the markings upon the bill. Now, the only mark upon the bill is one solitary "T." Time had done something quite appropriate to the dollar bill. Since Trevor and his former girlfriend had the same first initial, the remaining T could represent either of them.

The appropriateness was that Trevor was now alone and so was his girlfriend. The lone T could represent either one of them as being alone. The cartoon had faded away the same as their relationship. Whenever he went through town, Trevor always stopped to check their dollar. The bill had become ripped and tattered over time. The last time he was there he had repaired it with Scotch tape.

The restaurant/bar wasn't very busy when Trevor arrived. That was fine, he just wanted to get in a short motorcycle ride. He checked his dollar bill and it hadn't changed. Since he was there, he thought he should have a drink because he felt funny about walking through and looking at his dollar without buying anything. He ordered a drink and got in a conversation with a lady about her friend's purse. She had a very pretty face and would have been attractive had she not been twenty pounds overweight. Trevor talked and socialized with her and her friends while finishing his drink. When he left, the overweight gal with a pretty face told him he was very cute. This probably boosted his confidence.

Trevor had one drink and was driving up the street when he noticed a band playing at one of the neighboring bars. He pulled his motorcycle into the parking lot where he left it parked facing straight out towards the street. To get on the road, he wouldn't have to back it up or make a turn. He would just drive straight ahead and be on the road. He wasn't planning on drinking alcohol but always liked to have his bike positioned so it was easy to get out of the parking lot. It just makes sense to position your bike so you can go straight out onto the street.

When Trevor entered the bar, he was startled by the fact that his friends and neighbors were sitting immediately to his left. One of them said that the other had just remarked, "Wouldn't it be cool if Trevor walked in?" What are the odds? Sometimes you just have to wonder. Trevor hadn't been to that bar for months and here are his neighbors sitting at the table. He was so glad to see them, he visited with them for some time before he became thirsty and thought about getting something to drink. Although he wasn't planning on drinking alcohol, it was a call for celebration, running into his friends and neighbors twenty miles from home on a Saturday night.

The group of friends and neighbors consisted of a couple, Kevin and Amy, who lived in the neighboring condo community. Amy's friend Emily and her son Kyle were also present. The gathering also included Amy and Kevin's son, Cody. Cody was eleven years old and Kyle was eight. They were good friends despite their age difference. Amy's friend Emily was going through a divorce, so divorce was her main topic of conversation. Trevor knew everyone in the group quite well. Emily, Amy, and Kevin were all professional drinkers.

Trevor stepped up to the bar to order drinks for him and his friends. It was the only polite thing to do. As Trevor was standing at the bar waiting for service, he looked to his left and said something to a man sitting on the stool. The man replied and said something about Stevie Nicks. Trevor looked to the right and the woman sitting to his right looked similar to a young version of Stevie Nicks. Trevor hadn't noticed the pretty woman because he had been so entertained visiting with his friends.

It was mostly the hairdo that made her resemble Stevie. Stevie usually wears black and this gal had on a low-cut black top and jeans. Other than that, there wasn't much of a resemblance, but she was prettier than Stevie Nicks. She had a similar face but she was perfectly built with natural looking breasts. She appeared to be about five feet two inches tall and perfectly proportioned. At forty-seven years old, she exuded sex appeal.

Trevor turned to his right, looked at Stevie Nicks (Cindy), and said, "He is right, you do look a little like Stevie Nicks, but you are prettier, though. Hopefully you don't sing like a goat."

Cindy replied in defense of Stevie, "She is one of my favorite singers."

Trevor had to recover a little now and said that she is a good singer but an even better song writer. Then he said, "Do you sing?"

Cindy explained that she was not a good singer. Trevor mentioned that he didn't mind his own singing, but others didn't seem to appreciate it. Cindy chuckled. Out of the corner of his eye Trevor could see the guy to his left wanting to enter the conversation. He was out of the picture at this point. Trevor was going to keep her all to himself.

Cindy was on a roll. Her verbal flood gates opened as she told Trevor about her kids, job, and soon to be ex-husband. Trevor knew that people love to talk. He also knew that if you are a good listener, they will bond with you. A man who tries to talk as much or more than the woman will miserably fail in this stage of the game.

Cindy began chattering and Trevor began thinking her speech resembled that of an automatic rifle spitting out bullets. She would need to reload eventually and Trevor would get in a word edgewise. She stopped to reload from time to time and Trevor would interject a phrase or comment. It wasn't that she wasn't interesting, she was. This was commonplace with Trevor. He gets women talking and adds tidbits from time to time. He used to wonder if women talked rapidly and continuously because they were nervous. After much thought, he eventually came to the conclusion that they were actually that comfortable with him. Women often mentioned how comfortable he made them feel. He was a good listener and knew how to get them talking.

Trevor reflected upon years ago. A little boy was having trouble getting along with others and Trevor's father was giving him advice. Trevor's father told him that he must first *become a good listener.* Secondly, he needed to *learn how to get others to talk* and third you must *never tell the biggest story.* What he meant by telling the biggest story is that you must not be a "one-upper." A one-upper is somebody who always tries to tell a story that is better than everyone else's. Everyone likes to feel they have something to offer. If you tell a bigger story, it makes them feel insignificant.

Trevor was probably twenty years old when he heard his father give the little boy this advice. He wondered why his father hadn't given him that advice. It may have been something like the parable of the Prodigal Son. Trevor surmised that he had always been a good listener but the other pieces of advice were also profound, as far as he was concerned. Trevor had incorporated this advice into his relations with others.

It often shows a fine command of language to say nothing. To say nothing takes control and finesse. Trevor was well known among his family members for his quote, *"You can't learn when you are talking."*

Cindy was talking away. Time was passing and Trevor ordered drinks. The conversation became more personal and Trevor ordered drinks again. Cindy told a story about playing pool and Trevor asked if she would like to play. She said she was too drunk to play pool. They had been sitting for a long time, so Trevor thought they should get up and do something. He mentioned playing pool again and she said she was too drunk. The conversation continued until all topics of conversation were on the table.

They talked about sex and how often they like to have it. They were compatible in that regard. Cindy explained that her husband was having sex with the babysitter and she asked him to leave. A tear rolled down her cheek as she started to cry. Trevor was really starting to like her. He instinctively took his hand and gently wiped the tear off her cheek. Cindy said she was sorry she was dumping on him and she didn't really want to go on about her problems.

Trevor could tell she had a lot bottled up inside and needed someone to talk to. His heart went out to her. She seemed so nice, vulnerable, and fragile, but at the same time intelligent.

Trevor looked at her hands and how petite they were. He had a few drinks under his belt and he was loosened up. Somehow, Trevor always seemed to do better with the ladies when he had a few drinks. He had come to the conclusion that it is because he was more reserved when he wasn't drinking. When he had a little buzz or a big buzz, he came right out with how he felt. He picked up Cindy's hand, looked at it, glanced up at her, and said, "Look at how petite your hand is, look at the difference between yours and mine, yours is so delicate and mine is hairy and big boned; I like that."

It wasn't that he was trying to seduce her, it is just what was on his mind and what was on his mind came out of his mouth. He was sincere. They looked at each other. Trevor looked at her lips and their lips met. Not only did their lips meet but their tongues. Some women like to extend their tongues as far into your mouth as they possibly can. Not Cindy. She had a petite, sensuous tongue and it was extremely erotic. It wasn't so much the way she moved it or anything she did with it. It was just the most pleasurable kiss. It was sexy, erotic, and most of all sensuous.

For the rest of the evening, Trevor would wonder what made her kiss special; he really could not figure it out. Maybe she was starting to like Trevor as much as he was starting to like her. Sometimes a kiss can be more personal than sex.

Cindy offered to buy Trevor a drink and Trevor accepted. He didn't fully understand why women liked to buy a man drinks. All he knew was sometimes women would buy him drinks and spoil him. He theorized that women sometimes like to feel as if they are in control of the seduction and want the excitement of seducing a man. Experience had taught him that he should let the lady be the seductress. In his younger days, he would have insisted on buying the drinks. Invariably the mojo would change and the seduction would take a turn for the worse.

He thought back to a time when he had met three women in a parking lot. They took him to a bar and took turns buying him drinks. He eventually ended up staying the night with them at one of their homes. The ladies had enjoyed feeling like they had the power in the seduction.

Trevor reflected upon another time when he was in his late twenties. He was hanging out in a bar and had hooked up with a lady named Patricia. She was about six years his senior. It was unusual for him to pick up someone older, but she was a good-looking woman and he made no bones about the fact that his interest was sex. Before long, Patricia's friend walked in and sat down at their table. She was the same age as Patricia but very hot. Her blouse was low cut and it appropriately displayed her exquisite cleavage. Trevor was more attracted to her than her friend. Her name was Robin. Shortly, a friend of Robins sat down at the table. He was a tall, lanky, nice looking fellow. By trade, he delivered milk, so Trevor referred to him as the Milk Man.

After many drinks and much conversation, the bar closed and Trevor invited Robin and Patricia for drinks at his place. The Milk Man tagged along. After drinks were served, Trevor and Robin went into another room and selected the perfect music to get the party started. They were only in the other room for a few minutes and Patricia accused them of having sex while they were gone. Trevor assured her he wasn't that fast. Robin and Trevor were sitting side by side as Robin explained that she had known the Milk Man for several years and she knew he had the hots for her. He had bought her a very expensive stereo for Christmas, fixed her car, and bought her various other gifts.

She laughed and said, "I feel sorry for him; there will never be anything romantic between us." Trevor understood that *if a man tries to buy a woman's affection, the only thing he will get is broke.*

Soon Trevor and the two ladies were in the middle of the living room dancing to upbeat dance tunes. Before things got too heated, one of the ladies invited the Milk Man to join in. He didn't join; he just leaned against the wall as if he was content drinking wine and enjoying the shit show. When the Milk Man didn't join the soiree, it signaled the green light for anything goes.

Soon Trevor and the ladies were topless and slow dancing while making out. The milk man made his exit and Trevor and the two ladies headed for the bedroom. Trevor discovered that romance was contrary to its portrayal in the movies. He learned that success with the ladies was not about buying expensive gifts, dinners, and exotic trips. It was about allowing the ladies to win your favor. He theorized that when either sex becomes the aggressor, the other one controls the seduction.

Cindy got up and headed for the restroom. This was the first time Trevor had gotten a good look at her body. He was surprised that she was not taller, probably because she had large, natural looking breasts. Her waist was small and her butt was proportionate. She had an excellent figure and a natural, down-to-earth look. She seemed like a wholesome person.

Since Trevor had been talking to Cindy for such a long time, he felt like he had neglected his friends. He got up and walked over to Kevin. He hadn't understood Cindy's name although he had her repeat it a couple of times. Since Trevor didn't know her name, he asked Kevin to ask her what her name was.

Kevin looked at Trevor with a shocked expression and said, "What, you don't know her? I thought you were old lovers or something."

Trevor said, "Nope first time I met her. She is very nice though." While she was gone, Kevin told Trevor he thought she was superb and he should hang on to her.

Emily and the two boys were in the corner of the room giving a punching bag their best shot. Emily actually had become friends with Trevor before she met Kevin and Amy. She had worked with Amy and they had become the best of friends. It seemed like another coincidental twist of fate that Trevor's friends had become each other's best friends. Trevor felt sorry for Emily because for the last four or five years, he knew she had a crush on him. The last time they were out together, he had run into an old girlfriend, and the time before, he ended up connecting with someone else. Each time he had felt sorry for her. Her disappointment was written all over her face. He felt even sorrier for her now because he really liked Cindy and was enjoying kissing her.

Cindy and Trevor had been sitting about ten feet away from Kevin and Amy. When Cindy came back from the restroom, she would pass between Kevin and Amy. Trevor was standing talking to Kevin and Amy when she returned. Before she got to her chair, Trevor introduced her to Kevin and Amy. Right on cue, Kevin asked her what her name was. Trevor got it this time. He brought up the fact that neither Cindy nor Amy knew who their parents were. Both had been adopted and Trevor knew this would bond them with a commonality. Sure enough, it opened up a conversation and developed a common bond. Cindy said she knew someone who looked just like Amy. She pulled up a picture on her phone and sure enough, the lady in the picture looked very similar to Amy.

Kevin started *the disclosure of currency and commodity* by asking Cindy how many kids she had. Cindy said she had four kids.

With a shocked look on his face, Trevor said "Four kids; you told me two."

Cindy said, "Two are gone and out of the house, so I didn't count them."

Trevor said, "Well if you would have been with me, you would have more than that." Trevor thought he should recover the situation so he looked at her flat stomach and with the back of his fingers touched her stomach lightly and said, "Your flat tummy doesn't look like you've had any kids."

Trevor pulled up a couple chairs for him and Cindy to sit on. She and

Kevin were having an extended conversation. Their conversation continued and Trevor was interjecting conversation every once and awhile.

As he was sitting there, he noticed how petite and perfectly shaped Cindy's feet were. He commented on her nail polish and asked her if he could see her foot. She put one foot upon his lap and he inspected her foot as he began massaging it. She was talking to Kevin as Trevor was massaging her foot, pulling on her toes, running his finger between them, applying pressure to the nerve centers, and softly caressing them. He was doing every sensuous activity he could possibly think of. He thought of other things he could do with her foot but didn't think it would be appropriate in this setting. He had already crossed the appropriate line a couple hours ago. Trevor mentioned that you should be able to tell a person's body type by their toes. If they are short and fat, you should have a short, fat body type. If they are long and skinny, you should have a long skinny body.

Cindy asked what her toes were saying.

Trevor looked up with a smile and said, "Perfection."

Trevor began feeling conspicuous as he was sitting in the bar giving Cindy a foot rub. Sometimes, Trevor liked to push the boundaries. He asked Kevin if he gives Amy foot rubs.

"No, I never give her a foot rub," Kevin explained.

"Well, you should start. It is like foreplay before foreplay," Trevor said. Trevor told Kevin he would get marathon sex later if he gave Amy a foot message.

Amy looked at Trevor while shaking her head from side to side in a *No, that's not going to happen* motion. Amy was shaking her head no as she placed her foot upon Kevin's leg. Kevin was giving Amy a foot massage while Trevor was giving Cindy a foot massage. Trevor insisted he was going to ask the barmaid if she had lotion behind the bar. Kevin and Cindy insisted that it would not be appropriate to ask. Trevor could tell the ladies were embarrassed at the thought of him asking the bartender for lotion, so he mentioned it a few times just to watch them squirm.

Kevin and Cindy were having a conversation that had to do with sex. Kevin made an innuendo and Cindy told him he had his own lover, right beside him. She seemed to like Kevin and Amy. Cindy had been offering her two bits to help spice up their love life. Kevin had taken it that she was hitting on him.

Every so often, Trevor would think about Cindy's kisses. Whenever he asked her for one, she would smile and tell him he could have one whenever he liked. It was not a peck on the cheek, it was always the same sweet French kiss. Trevor told her he was trying to figure out why he enjoyed her kisses so much. She surely thought it was a line of bullshit, but the fact was his thoughts were hitting his brain and running out his mouth.

The band had been playing all evening and Trevor and Cindy decided to dance. Dancing placed an intermission upon the conversation between Kevin and Cindy. Their conversation had run its course and a dance would alleviate the tension between the two. When they reached the dance floor, they began dancing apart. In a few seconds, they were dancing slow, then slow and sensuous, and before the dance was over, it had become a full blown make out session.

Trevor decided it would be a good time to ask Cindy if she would like to see his motorcycle. She said she would. They walked out to the motorcycle, which happened to be parked straight out from the entry of the bar. Trevor told Cindy she could sit on it if she liked.

She slid onto the driver's seat, then back onto the passenger seat. She said she liked it, mentioned how comfortable it was, then Trevor helped her off. When she stood up, they kissed again. Trevor moved her hair back over her shoulder and kissed her on the neck. She was very responsive, so Trevor kissed his way from her shoulder to her ear lobe and began kissing and biting her ear.

In response, she reached down with her hand and started massaging Trevor's privates. Trevor didn't want to appear selfish, so he moved his hand down and started massaging between Cindy's legs. He could feel her heat and sensuousness as she started writhing. The sweet spot between her legs was like her kiss. There was something extra sexy about it. Maybe it was the way her flat tummy curved down to the sweet spot between her legs or maybe it was that it was petite and sensual like the rest of her. Trevor could feel her heat. She was on fire. It wouldn't take much to make her cum. The motorcycle must have passed inspection!

They were standing alongside the motorcycle each with a hand down the other's pants. Trevor was moving his fingers back and forth, in and out, and around and around, thinking Cindy was going to cum. Cindy was standing there kissing Trevor, moving her hand up and down on his member, and every so often she would fondle his gonads.

Trevor heard some men laugh.

Cindy said, "Oh my god!"

When Trevor turned to see what her exclamation was about, he saw three men about ten feet away. All of them were laughing. Evidently, they had walked out of the bar and were headed to their automobile. They had come upon Trevor and Cindy with their hands down each other's pants. It must have been an amusing spectacle.

Trevor and Cindy pulled themselves apart as Cindy exclaimed, "I should go home."

Trevor said, "Yeah, I should too."

Cindy pulled out her phone and started looking at Lyft to see about getting them to pick her up. She was having trouble with her phone or the app. As she messed with the app and complained, she said something about what a pain it is to get a Lyft.

Trevor thought about giving her a ride on the motorcycle but he was smashed and so was she. Trevor was thinking he should get a Lyft or Uber, too. Trevor could tell she would like him to take her home on the motorcycle but didn't want to ask. Then he thought about leaving his motorcycle overnight and realized that he would need to ride it home. It would surely get vandalized if he left it there overnight.

Trevor had a lot to drink but started processing information. If Cindy took a Lyft home, he would not get laid. If he gave her a ride home, he would certainly get laid. He thought about Cindy's kiss, soft skin, and hot sensuousness.

He wondered what her face would look like when she was in the throes of ecstasy? Would she get goose bumps, tremble, and have aftershock orgasms? She was in such a mood she may end up crying in the afterglow. The other thing is; Trevor really liked her.

That is one thing about riding your motorcycle to a bar. If you get lucky, there is no privacy. The other thing is, if you leave it at the bar overnight, it may get vandalized. On top of that, it can be difficult to operate and balance a motorcycle when you are under the influence of alcohol.

Trevor weighed and balanced the information in his inebriated head until he reached a conclusion. He decided to do what any drunk, horny, infatuated, red-blooded man would do under the circumstances. He offered to give Cindy a ride home. Jail, death, what the hell, he was going to get laid by one of the hottest, coolest women he had ever met. He would die happy if he didn't get picked up by the police or run the motorcycle in the ditch. Maybe Cindy was not an experienced motorcycle rider. She could shift around on the curves and make it difficult to keep the motorcycle upright.

Trevor told Cindy he was going to go to the restroom and say goodbye to his friends before leaving. As he entered the restroom, he was wondering if she would still be waiting when he returned. When he exited the restroom, it looked as if Cindy had come back into the bar. It looked like she was standing and looking away from him.

Trevor came up behind her in his most seductive, sensuous fashion, put one arm around her waist, and pulled her in tight. As she turned, she was in prime position for another one of those splendid kisses. The problem was that it was not Cindy. It was someone who looked like her from behind.

There Trevor was, standing face to face with a lady he didn't know. She looked so much like Cindy it took him a few seconds to realize he had made a mistake and had gotten very fresh with a perfect stranger. There Trevor was, looking into the eyes of a woman who didn't even look surprised. She was probably so shocked she didn't know what to say or do.

Trevor said, "Oh, I am sorry."

He walked over and told Kevin he was going to take Cindy home.

Kevin said, "On the motorcycle?"

Trevor replied, "Yep, we are taking off." As Trevor turned to walk past the stranger he had accosted, he noticed a huge dude with his arm around her. He looked as if he was protecting her from the devil. When Trevor walked by her, he apologized, telling her he was sorry and that he thought she was someone else.

She smiled with a *Come fuck me* look, but the big gorilla with his arm around her looked as if he would enjoy tearing Trevor apart limb by limb.

The trouble with trouble is that it starts out as fun!

When Trevor returned to the motorcycle, Cindy was still standing beside it. On the pavement sat the two drinks they had carried out from the bar; Cindy's margarita and Trevor's vodka soda. Trevor picked up the thirty-two ounce cup and dumped out the water. He placed it back on the motorcycle and proceeded to dump the margarita and Vodka soda into the cup. The cup wasn't sitting level, so the drinks overflowed down the side of the gas tank.

"Oh well, it will clean off," Trevor remarked.

In a lot of states, there is a law requiring you to wear a helmet, but in this state, you are not required to wear one. However, you are required to wear eye protection. Anyway, it doesn't make sense to ride without eye protection. Trevor had a helmet and glasses in the motorcycle compartment but didn't use either. Most women are concerned about their hair blowing around and getting knotted up but not Cindy. Without helmets, eye protection, or her hair tied back, Trevor and Cindy headed out of the parking lot. Trevor was glad he didn't have to back up or turn; he just headed straight out to the road.

As they hit the road, Trevor swerved the motorcycle a bit. In his inebriated state, his reactions weren't as good as they could be. He corrected the swerve and Cindy reached around him with both hands and pinched both of his nipples. She laughed and Trevor exclaimed, "That feels really good."

Instantly Cindy pulled herself in close so her breasts were pressed up against his back. She then began shifting from side to side, stimulating her nipples against Trevor's back. She asked Trevor how he liked it.

So, Trevor was fully loaded with alcohol and trying to balance the motorcycle as they cruised down the road. Cindy's hair was blowing in the wind and neither of them were wearing helmets or eye protection. The thirty-two ounce cup was full of margarita and vodka soda and it had overflowed down the side of the motorcycle. Cindy was shifting from side to side, stimulating her nipples on his back and asking him if he liked it.

Trevor thought he should ask her to stop shifting around so it would be easier to manage the motorcycle, then he thought about the fact that she would quit stimulating her nipples across his back.

He replied, "Yep, I liiiike that!!" He became accustomed to compensating for the side-to-side motion. They developed a rhythm. From the time they left the bar until the time they reached Cindy's house; she was either squashing her breasts against Trevor's back or stimulating her nipples by moving from side to side.

They must have made quite a spectacle going down the road that night. A policeman or anyone else looking at them from a mile away would have suspicion of alcohol being involved.

When Cindy had described where she lived, Trevor had interpreted it as being much closer than it really was. In reality, her home was about fifteen miles out of his way. There were only three turns and they missed two out of the three. They would go past the turn and Cindy would say, "You were supposed to turn there." Trevor would pull a U-turn and they would be back on track.

When Trevor pulled into Cindy's driveway, he was thankful he had returned her safely home. Trevor stepped off the motorcycle and helped Cindy off. Cindy asked Trevor to retrieve her purse from the saddlebag. When Trevor handed her the purse, she explained that she had two teenage boys in the house; otherwise, she would invite him in. Trevor knew she was sincere and that she truly would like to invite him in.

He understood the circumstances since he had been in this position before. A young lady had two teenage daughters in her home when she invited Trevor in. She didn't want to take Trevor in her bedroom, so they made love in the living room. All the time they were making love she was trying to be quiet. In the end she lost control and probably woke the girls. It was just uncomfortable to think the boys might catch you in the act with their mother. It is not so much the act of being caught as it is the thought of kids seeing their mother in that way. Trevor had to respect Cindy for not inviting him in.

Cindy asked Trevor if she could give him her phone number. Trevor handed her his phone and she put her number in it. He rang her phone to make sure all was working and that she could also call him. Trevor asked her when he should call.

Cindy said, "Call me in the morning and we can do something tomorrow." She was very insistent on doing something the following day.

Trevor called her in the morning and sent text messages over the next couple of days but that was the last he heard from her.

Trevor surmised that Cindy's husband had cheated on her and she was getting even with him. She wanted to hurt her husband as bad as he hurt her.

If a spouse is unfaithful to their partner, it is common for them to feel they have a free pass to have sex with someone else.

Trevor and Cindy's escapade may have been the result of Cindy wanting revenge sex, or she may have been so embarrassed she didn't want to acknowledge the events of the evening. It is also likely that Cindy had been so inebriated, she didn't remember the last few hours of that evening.

Cindy and her husband probably made up and lived miserably ever after.

Trevor understood that the art of conversation is one of the most valuable skills a person can master and that one's character becomes transparent through conversation. Although it isn't possible to fully perfect the art of conversation, it can be honed and developed into a fine art. In order to develop this art, one must become conscious of practicing these skills during conversation. Anyone who develops enough self-control to *get others to talk*, *be a good listener*, and *never tell the bigger story* will be liked and people will enjoy their company.

Conclusion

It was a sunny spring day as Trevor and Andrea (the relationship counselor) were conversing in front of the club house. They were sitting under the umbrella on the patio where they first met. They were looking out over the well-manicured, fresh cut green grass and in the distance, there was a water fountain spraying at the center of a small manmade lake. They were each enjoying a Bloody Mary as they contemplated life.

A few years had passed since they first met and they had become friends. It was a unique friendship with a one-drink limit, but nevertheless, a valuable learning experience between a man and a woman.

Soon they were engrossed in a conversation about seduction. Andrea asked Trevor why some people seem accomplished at it and others are not. Trevor mentioned that "People who are accomplished in seduction understand, that *seduction is the art of insinuation.*"

By nature, women are experts in *The Art of Insinuation*. It is a learning process for men. Seduction is also *the process of getting someone to do what you want by making them think it was their idea.*

The conversation eventually got around to the differences between men and women. Trevor said, "No matter how adamantly society adheres to the principle of men and women being the same, they are not." In many endeavors, women are equal to or will surpass a man's ability to perform a specific task. *They are equal but they are not the same.* It is common to hear people talk about a double standard between sexes. This double standard is commonly applied to sex as if men and women are the same.

Andrea said, "Regarding sex, what is the real difference between men and women?"

Trevor explained that despite obvious physical differences and function, there is a difference in the basic nature of men and woman.

For example: Imagine there are one hundred men in a room and a beautiful woman enters the room. All of the men notice her when she enters the room. Trevor asked Andrea, "How many men out of the hundred will want to have sex with her later that evening?"

Andrea said, "All of them."

Trevor replied that he didn't think all of them would want to have sex with her because odds are there would be one gay guy in a group of one hundred men. The gay guy might not want to have sex with her, but more than likely, even he would like to investigate her breasts and get his picture taken with her.

Imagine there are one hundred women in a room and a handsome man enters the room. All of the women notice him when he enters the room. Trevor asked Andrea, "How many women will want to have sex with him later that evening?"

Andrea said, "None of them."

Trevor replied that he thought the odds would be more like two. He thought that out of that many women, there could be a hooker in the group. If another woman wants to have sex with him, she will most likely have a motive outside of sex. For the most part, a beautiful woman can have sex with almost any man she likes.

As Robin Williams once said, "Men and women are like automobiles when it comes to sex. Men are the gas pedal and women are the brakes."

Trevor went on to explain that nobody respects a man without gas or a woman without brakes. *Men and women may be equal; however, they are not the same.*

Andrea asked Trevor what he thought about the plethora of relationship books on the market. Trevor explained that "Women are the primary market for relationship books. Therefore, they are designed to appeal to that market." He indicated that there are four types of relationships a man can have with a woman. They are as follows:

The Gomer Bull—The gomer bull is procuring her to become his long-term nesting partner. He is probably buying her expensive presents, taking her to expensive dinners, and lavishing her with extravagant vacations.

The Bull—The bull keeps her satisfied while she is trying to convince a potential long-term partner to commit to a long-term relationship. For some reason, he doesn't have potential for a long-term relationship. Maybe he isn't interested in a long-term relationship or he doesn't provide enough security for one. She loves having sex with him, they have a great chemistry, and he knows how to please her. A lot of times, she is the one who buys meals and drinks. The bull generally does not wine and dine her. He will always be on her mind when her long-term relationship gets rocky.

The Stud—The stud may provide sex and excitement while a woman is in a committed relationship. He could be the one who provided sex and excitement while she was trying to get her partner to commit to a long-term relationship. He could be someone she became attracted to after she was in a committed relationship. He has slept with a lot of women and has developed a stable of women who call him when they get lonesome. He fills needs that her long-term partner doesn't. Some of these men provide an emotional connection that is not prevalent in her committed relationship. Women who spend time in close proximity with men easily form emotional connections. They may not have sex but often, but they become emotional cheaters. Although a woman may be in love with her husband or partner, it is common for her to fall in love with another man.

Romantic—The romantic is in a committed relationship in which both partners provide each other with sex, excitement, security, and contentment.

Nature has certainly ensured the propagation of the species not only by the physical and emotional attraction between men and women but also by the fact that the true nature of humans is to *not* be satisfied. When they aren't in a relationship, they long for companionship. When they are in a relationship, they long for freedom. "(I Can't Get No) Satisfaction" is not just a song by the Rolling Stones, it is the normal nature of humans. People who understand this can be truly happy whether they are in a relationship or not.

Andrea asked Trevor why so many talented people who have contributed so much to society don't appear to be normal. Trevor explained that "People use the word 'normal' to describe anyone who is average."

Andrea replied, "Alcoholics consider themselves to be abnormal because they can't have just one alcoholic beverage." Alcoholics can't have just one or two drinks; they always want more. They refer to folks who can drink just one or two alcoholic beverages as 'Normies.' "Normal" is always determined on a baseline from average, whether it is intelligence, looks, ability, or any other category. If a person has an IQ of 100, they have an average IQ. If it is somewhat above average, a person is considered smart. If it is somewhat below average, a person would be considered stupid or slow. So, a person's intelligence is based on the degrees above or below average. An average IQ would be considered normal. A person's attractiveness is also based on an average. If they are better looking than average, they are classified as good looking. If they are a lot better looking than the average person, they are considered gorgeous or very handsome. A person who is not as attractive as the average person is considered homely. If a person's attractiveness is way below average, they would be considered ugly. An average looking person is normal. To describe a person as being normal means he is average. It is the person who isn't normal who then creates and achieves extraordinary accomplishments. To lead a happy fulfilling life, one must venture out of the norm.

Trevor Sharp

Entrepreneur, author, golfer, motorcycle adventurist, investor and student of human nature.

Made in the USA
Las Vegas, NV
04 April 2025

c01bfb7b-48f2-47e4-b687-b08c69dcb8f6R01